Young People's Transitions from Care to Adulthood

Child Welfare Outcomes
Series Editor: Harriet Ward, Centre for Child and Family Research, Loughborough University, UK
This authoritative series draws from original research and current policy debates to help social work managers, policy makers and researchers to understand and improve the outcomes of services for children and young people in need. Taking an evidence-based approach, these books include children's experiences and analysis of costs and effectiveness in their assessment of interventions, and provide guidance on how to develop more effective policy, practice and training.

Young People's Transitions from Care to Adulthood

International Research and Practice

Edited by Mike Stein and Emily R. Munro

Jessica Kingsley Publishers
London and Philadelphia

First published in 2008
by Jessica Kingsley Publishers
116 Pentonville Road
London N1 9JB, UK
and
400 Market Street, Suite 400
Philadelphia, PA 19106, USA

www.jkp.com

Library of Congress Cataloging in Publication Data
Young people's transitions from care to adulthood : international research and practice / edited by Mike Stein and Emily R. Munro.
    p. cm.
    Includes bibliographical references.
    ISBN 978-1-84310-610-4 (pb : alk. paper) 1. Young adults--Services for. 2. Youth with social disabilities--Services for. 3. Youth--Institutional care. I. Stein, Mike. II. Munro, Emily, 1978-
    HV1421.Y683 2008
    362.7--dc22

                                            2007043511

British Library Cataloguing in Publication Data
A CIP catalogue record for this book is available from the British Library

ISBN 978 1 84310 610 4

Printed and bound in Great Britain by
Athenaeum Press, Gateshead, Tyne and Wear

Contents

List of Figures

List of Tables

Preface

This is the third in a series of books on Child Welfare Outcomes, commissioned by Jessica Kingsley Publishers and edited by Harriet Ward. The books are primarily written for academics, researchers, policy makers and professionals concerned with improving outcomes for vulnerable children and young people.

Research demonstrates that young people leaving care are at high risk of social exclusion, both in terms of material disadvantage and marginalisation. Findings also indicate that there are differences between groups of care leavers – some young people are very resilient. Cross-nationally there are differences in the policy and practice context, as well as in the way services are organised to assist young people. Yet, to date, there has been very little comparative work exploring these different dimensions. This book seeks to address this gap and presents an international perspective, drawing on material from 16 countries, on the transitions of young people leaving care to adulthood.

The ideas that motivated this work were those of Jackie Davis from the children's charity NCH. In collaboration with Harriet Ward, these ideas were taken forward. We are indebted to both for their contributions which inspired the development of this cross-national work.

The seminar series that facilitated the further advancement of ideas that led to the production of this book were part-funded by the Department of Health, Department for Education and Skills and the Department for Children, Schools and Families. We also acknowledge, with thanks, Queen's University, Belfast, the National Institute of Criminology, Budapest, and Trinity College, Dublin, for hosting these events.

The chapters in this book have been written by researchers from Europe, the Middle East, North America and Australia who specialise in a range of disciplines, including social policy, developmental psychology, social pedagogy and social work education and professional training. As editors we would like to thank the authors for their contributions and forbearance in revising draft chapters to make it as easy as possible for readers to compare the material presented in the country-specific chapters. We are also grateful to the following individuals who, in addition to the authors, contributed to the seminars and discussions that informed these chapters: Marie Anaut, Carolyn Davies, Jackie Davis, Tseventka Grudeva and Jane Scott.

We also greatly appreciate the administrative support of Sophie Astwood, Emma Batchelor and Suzanne Dexter. Our thanks must also go to Stephen Jones, our editor at Jessica Kingsley Publishers, for his help and support.

Editors' Note

Different chapters of this book have been written by authors from all over the world. The editors have made some changes to ensure that the information provided is as clear as possible. However, we have tried to avoid making substantive amendments, so as to prevent misinterpretations of what the authors originally wrote.

Chapter 1

Introduction

Comparative Exploration of Care Leavers' Transitions to Adulthood

Emily R. Munro and Mike Stein

The idea for writing this book, and the ideas that are contained within it, have evolved from three international seminars, held between 2003 and 2006, attended by researchers from up to 16 countries. Prior to the first seminar, held in Brussels in 2003, a growing body of international research findings had revealed the poor outcomes for looked after children, in comparison to children who had not been in care, especially in relation to their education, health and well-being. These findings had also shown the high risk of social exclusion of young people making the transition from care to adulthood. They were far more likely, than young people who had not been in care, to have poorer educational qualifications, be younger parents, be homeless, and have higher levels of unemployment, offending behaviour and mental health problems (Stein 2004).

The Brussels seminar brought together, for the first time, researchers from Europe, the Middle East and North America, to begin to explore in depth the issues underpinning these research findings. Prior to the meeting, participants completed a questionnaire which provided contextual information from each of their countries. This included: definitions of key terms, such as 'children in care', 'care leavers' and 'children in need';

official statistics, covering the total child population, children in care and care leavers; the legislation targeted at these groups of young people; the support available for young people leaving care moving to adulthood; the wider policy and agency context that may impact upon care leavers during transition; and research findings on children and young people living in and leaving care.

This detailed preparatory work furthered the two main aims of the seminar: first, to share research findings on the problems, challenges and outcomes for young people making the journey from care to adulthood; and second, to explore the social, political and legal structures that support or inhibit that transition.

The challenges of comparative work

The Brussels seminar opened up the complexities of work in this area, including the challenges arising from a comparative exploration of social problems, and learning lessons from the experiences, policies and practices in different jurisdictions (see, among others, Corden 2001; Hantrais and Mangen 1996; Hearn *et al.* 2004; Hetherington *et al.* 1997).

Consideration needs to be given to differences in the historical, social, cultural, political and economic context that influence social policy development. Interpretations and understandings of key terms and concepts are infused with social and cultural meanings that are unique to a given region or nation. For example, Hearn and colleagues (2004) identify how the Finnish term *lastensuojelu* tends to be translated into English as 'child protection' or 'child welfare'. However, *lastensuojelu* covers all children in society and its effects extend to health, education, housing services, the family and culture whereas the term 'child protection' is more narrowly construed in England. Ideologies and expectations behind terms therefore need to be acknowledged and discussed. Difficulties in developing shared understandings can also be exacerbated by the tendency to discuss and report on cross-national issues in English (Pinkerton, Chapter 18; see also Shardlow and Walliss 2003). In addition to conceptual and linguistic challenges, practical problems are not uncommon when undertaking cross-national work. These include variations in the availability, reliability and comparability of different data sets and the rationale behind their collection.

Despite these challenges, there is much to be gained from cross-national study, and the importance of developing global perspectives on social welfare issues is increasingly recognised (Anttonen and Spilia 1996; Hetherington *et al.* 1997; Pinkerton 2006). Cross-national exchanges and research provide an opportunity to learn from other countries' successes and failures. It is hoped that drawing on the experiences of other countries will maximise the likelihood of improving policy and practice and ultimately outcomes for vulnerable groups. Comparative material also encourages researchers, practitioners and policy makers to step outside their narrow and nationally specific frames of reference and facilitates consideration of alternative ways of perceiving and responding to social problems or issues.[1]

Recent contributions in the field of child welfare include a cross-national study on children in out-of-home care (Thoburn 2007) and an exploration of global perspectives on foster family care (Colton and Williams 2006a). The former contributes to an understanding of the similarities and differences between children in need of child welfare services in different countries and allows for reflection on how variations may impact on outcomes. For example, one might expect that early entrants to care in Norway (aged 0–4 years), children who remain in a stable foster placement, are likely to achieve well in their education and other aspects of young adult life, compared to countries such as Canada, where a higher proportion enter care when they are older and problems are already established (Thoburn 2007, pp.54–5).

Colton and Williams (2006b) explore cross-national variations in the philosophies, policies and practices of foster care systems. In doing so, they identify a number of emerging issues, including the stigma of welfare services in 'residualistic' welfare systems such as the US, compared to countries with a more institutional approach to welfare (for example, Sweden and France). They also identify the differential use and standards in relation to kinship care between countries (Colton and Williams 2006b, pp.99–119). Both of these contributions are valuable in developing our knowledge of, among other things, variations in thresholds for entry to care, reasons for entry and profiles of need, types of placement and the average length of time young people stay in care. Considering the experiences of children prior to entry to, and during their time in, care is important, as these factors are likely to have a bearing on the types of challenges young people face as they make the transition from childhood within a state system to adulthood in civil society. In addition, knowledge of these issues is important to aid understanding and interpretation of outcomes.

The challenges of comparative work on care leavers

International exchange of ideas and comparison of outcomes, concerning care leavers' transitions from state care, necessitates confronting the challenges of comparative work. Complexities are centred around definitions, language and terminology; legal and policy frameworks; and the quality and quantity of official data and research evidence (see also Courtney, Chapter 20; Munro, Stein and Ward 2005; Pinkerton, Chapter 18; Stein, Chapter 21; Ward, Chapter 19).

As identified above, the terms adopted in different countries, to describe similar populations, vary considerably. In the UK, academics and practitioners refer to 'looked after children', 'children in care or accommodation' and 'care leavers'. In the US the terminology is different, with children and young people in 'out-of-home care' going on to 'age out of the system' or to 'emancipation'. The subtle differences between terms are not always immediately apparent and subtle distinctions between terms and meanings may easily be missed.

In the UK the term 'care leaver' is narrowly focused on those making the transition to independence. In some other countries, the term has a wider meaning encompassing children and young people of all ages, who leave the care of the state for a range of reasons, including those who return home or who are adopted. In the US legal 'emancipation' to independent living usually occurs due to young people reaching the age of majority or upon graduation from high school.

Differences in language and terminology can reflect variations in legislative frameworks. For example, in England and Northern Ireland the classification of who is entitled to support is defined in legislation, under the

Children (Leaving Care) Act 2000 and Children (Leaving Care) Act 2002 (Northern Ireland). The Acts outline specific duties that local authorities have in respect of 'eligible', 'relevant' and 'former relevant' young people. These developments also need to be considered with reference to historical developments and the wider policy context.

In England, in recent years, there has been an increasing willingness to provide support and services to 'deserving' children and young people. The role of the corporate parent for children in public care and leaving care has also been strengthened. These changes are to be welcomed and targeted legislation serves to enhance protective and provisional rights for this group. While young people's rights may have been enhanced, arguably the United Nations Convention on the Rights of the Child (UNCRC) was not especially influential in these developments (Munro 2008). In contrast, in some other countries the UNCRC has had a greater impact on policy development.

In England, changes have been influenced by the prevailing philosophy and belief in the value of investing in children as citizen workers of the future. Supporting children and young people, especially those at risk of underachievement and adverse outcomes, is seen as desirable to address difficulties and therefore maximise their contribution to society and the economy in adulthood (Dobrowolsky 2002; Lister 2003, 2006; Williams 2004). Statistical returns allow the government to measure performance and progress in relation to key outcomes, including, for example, the number of care leavers who obtain GCSE qualifications.

Thoburn (2007) also identifies how countries with a culture of performance measurement, including the US and the four countries of the UK, tend to have well-developed data collection systems. In some other countries, including Sweden, systems data is used more for policy development and service planning purposes (Thoburn 2007) than for monitoring the performance of child welfare agencies. In Switzerland and Ireland virtually no data are collected. Different countries have different rationales for collecting information (or reasons for not doing so). There are also wide variations in, among other things, the type of information collected, who is included in the statistical returns and the frequency of collection and publication. All these issues complicate attempts to draw valid comparisons between countries.

These brief examples give a flavour of the debates, considerations and comparative issues that people need to be mindful of. Further exploration of comparative issues, drawing on the discussion at Brussels and the analysis of the questionnaire data, summarised above, gave a clear direction to the Belfast and Budapest seminars, and, subsequently, the content of this book (see also Munro *et al.* 2005).

The Belfast and Budapest seminars

By the time the Belfast seminar was held, in November 2005, the researcher representation had increased to 16 countries. This included researchers from Australia, Jordan and a wider European grouping, representing Scandinavian and former communist countries. The 16 countries included in this volume are: Australia; Canada; France; Germany; Hungary; Ireland; Israel; Jordan; The Netherlands; Norway; Romania; Spain; Sweden; Switzerland; United Kingdom; and United States.

In advance of the Belfast seminar, four briefing papers were prepared:

1. Welfare regimes – structuring the space for care leaving?

2. Transitions to adulthood of care leavers – legal frameworks and administrative structures.

3. Use of secondary data to understand the experience of care leavers.

4. Young people leaving care – a research summary.

Each of the papers identified key questions for participants to consider in light of their national experience, giving a shared focus for the exchange of views and experiences.

Again, as with the earlier Brussels seminar, the discussion opened up a wide range of issues and questions. Could a standardised 'welfare regimes framework', although allowing for international comparison, capture the range and diversity of individual countries' experiences? Was the absence of leaving care services in some countries due to inadequate state provision or strong community resources? What was the impact of global phenomena on national experiences, for example that of asylum seeking and unaccompanied children? How much impact does the UNCRC have on shaping law, policy and procedures in different countries? What is the impact of legal and administrative frameworks upon how groups of vulnerable young people with similar needs are defined? How could more use be made of secondary data, as a comparative tool, given the variations in the level of sophistication, availability and type of data collected? How do we get beyond a 'social exclusion' framework in our research agendas? What theoretical perspectives and concepts should guide our work?

It was evident from the Belfast seminar that participants wanted more time to engage with the issues raised by the thematic papers, and, specifically, to have an opportunity to explore further the implications in light of their national experiences. Also, to promote ongoing collaboration between seminars, it was agreed to set up a formal network, the Transitions to Adulthood for Young People Leaving Public Care International Research Group. The Budapest seminar, held in November 2006, provided the opportunity to revisit the issues arising from the thematic papers, and this led to the final agreement on the purpose and organisation of this book.

The purpose of this book

This book is the first in the field of young people leaving care to provide:

- a comprehensive description of young people's transitions from care to adulthood in 16 different countries
- an analysis of four cross-cutting themes: welfare regimes, legal and policy frameworks, the use of secondary data, and research findings
- summary messages for policy and practice
- the identification of the major sources of further reading for each country.

The organisation of the book

The book comprises two main parts and a conclusion. Part I contains the 16 international chapters. As regards the order of these chapters, following our discussions in Budapest, we have avoided the 'obvious groupings' of Scandinavian, Central and Southern European, Former Communist, Middle East and Former Commonwealth countries. Instead, we have adopted an agnostic stance. The chapters are presented in alphabetical order, and we will let the reader assess 'comparativeness', on the criteria adopted.

Each chapter provides a summary of key statistics, a brief outline of each of the countries' socio-political features, and two illustrative 'leaving care' case examples. This provides a backcloth for a more substantive exploration of the countries' welfare regimes, their legal and policy frameworks, the type and availability of secondary data, and a discussion of research findings on young people leaving care. Key messages for policy and practice are summarised at the end of each chapter.

Part II is made up of three thematic chapters. These three chapters draw upon the empirical and conceptual material discussed within the international chapters. Chapter 18, 'States of Care Leaving: Towards International Exchange as a Global Resource', discusses the challenges of international comparative work, including globalisation and the contribution of Esping-Andersen's (1990) comparative typology to an understanding of leaving care policies and practices. Chapter 19, 'Legal and Policy Frameworks', discusses some of the complexities in comparative work, arising from differences in definitions, language and terminology, and, drawing on material from the international chapters, identifies the implications of leaving care services. Chapter 20, 'Use of Secondary Data to Understand the Experiences of Care Leavers: Cross-National Comparisons', describes the different sources of secondary data on young people leaving care, including existing gaps and the potential for more comprehensive data sets.

The concluding chapter, 'Transitions from Care to Adulthood: Messages from Research for Policy and Practice', discusses the research findings from the international chapters, to review the evidence in relation to the social exclusion of care leavers, their transitions from care, the services they receive and the outcomes of leaving care services. Set in the context of the main themes emerging from earlier chapters, the key messages for policy and practice are summarised. Finally, the future challenges for comparative work in this field are identified.

Note

1. Caution is of course needed, as it cannot simply be assumed that interventions or policies can be effectively transferred to a different region or country, or that they will have the same effect.

References

Anttonen, A. and Spiliä, J. (1996) 'European social care services: Is it possible to identify models?' *Journal of European Social Policy 6*, 87–100.

Children (Leaving Care) Act (2000). London: The Stationery Office.

Children (Leaving Care) Act (Northern Ireland) (2002). London: The Stationery Office.

Colton, M. and Williams, M. (eds) (2006a) *Global Perspectives on Foster Family Care.* Dorset: Russell House Publishing.

Colton, M. and Williams, M. (2006b) 'Overview and Conclusions.' In M. Colton and M. Williams (eds) *Global Perspectives on Foster Family Care.* Dorset: Russell House Publishing.

Corden, A. (2001) 'Comparing child maintenance systems: Conceptual and methodological issues.' *International Journal of Social Research Methodology 4*, 4, 287–300.

Dobrowolsky, A. (2002) 'Rhetoric versus reality: The figure of the child and New Labour's strategic "social investment state".' *Studies in Political Economy 69*, 43–73.

Esping-Andersen, G. (1990) *The Three Worlds of Welfare Capitalism.* New Jersey: Princeton University Press.

Hantrais, L. and Mangen, S. (eds) (1996) *Cross-national Research Methods in Social Sciences.* London: Pinter and Cassell.

Hearn, J., Pösö, T., Smith, C., White, S. and Korpinen, J. (2004) 'What is child protection? Historical and methodological issues in comparative research on *lastensuojelu/*child protection.' *International Journal of Social Welfare 13*, 28–41.

Hetherington, R., Cooper, A., Smith, P. and Wilford, G. (1997) *Protecting Children: Messages from Europe.* Dorset: Russell House Publishing.

Lister, R. (2003) 'Investing in the citizen-workers of the future: Transformations in citizenship and the state under New Labour.' *Social Policy and Administration 37*, 5, 427–443.

Lister, R. (2006) 'Children (but not women) first: New Labour, child welfare and gender.' *Critical Social Policy 26*, 315–335.

Munro, E.R. (2008) 'Realising children's rights – progress, problems and prospects.' In M.S. Becker and J.N. Schneider (eds) *Human Rights Issues in the 21st Century.* New York: Nova Science Publishing.

Munro, E.R., Stein, M. and Ward, H. (2005) 'Comparing how different social, political and legal frameworks support or inhibit transitions from public care to independence in

Europe, Israel, Canada and the United States.' *International Journal of Child and Family Welfare 8*, 4, 191–202.

Pinkerton, J. (2006) 'Global approach to young people leaving state care.' *Child and Family Social Work 11*, 3, 191–198.

Shardlow, S.M. and Walliss, J. (2003) 'Mapping comparative empirical studies of European social work.' *British Journal of Social Work 33*, 921–941.

Stein, M. (2004) *What Works for Young People Leaving Care?* Barkingside: Barnardo's.

Thoburn, J. (2007) *Globalisation and Child Welfare: Some Lessons from a Cross-national Study of Out-of-home Care.* Social Work Monographs. Norwich: University of East Anglia. Accessed 1/10/07 at www.uea.ac.uk/swk/research/publications/monographs/welcome.htm.

Williams, F. (2004) 'What matters is what works: Why every child matters to New Labour. Commentary on the DfES Green Paper *Every Child Matters.' Critical Social Policy 24*, 3, 406–427.

Part I

International Chapters

Chapter 2

Australia

Judy Cashmore and Philip Mendes

Background and key statistics

- Australia is home to around 20.6 million people, approximately 23 per cent of whom are children aged 0–17 years.
- In 2005–2006, a total of 27,000 children were on care orders.
- A total of 25,454 children resided in out-of-home care.
- The most common placement type for children is home-based care – either foster care or kinship care – which accounts for around 94.4 per cent of placements.
- Care leavers tend to move to independent living at a much earlier age than other young people their age who increasingly live at home until their early–mid twenties.
- In 2005–2006, 1817 young people aged 15–17 years left care in Australia.

Key source

- Australian Institute of Health and Welfare (2007).

Introduction

Australia is a multi-party liberal democracy in which power is shared between the Commonwealth government based in Canberra and the eight state and territory governments. The centre-right Coalition of the Liberal Party and the rural-based National Party has ruled at national level for the last ten years, while paradoxically the centre-left Labor Party currently holds power in every state and territory.

In recent decades there has been increasing policy convergence between the major parties. Both the Coalition and the Labor Party are strongly influenced by neo-liberal ideology (called economic rationalism in Australia) which privileges small government and economic growth over social equity. Taxation rates are relatively low in Australia: it is the eighth-lowest taxing country in the Organisation for Economic Cooperation and Development (OECD) at 31.6 per cent of gross domestic product (GDP). The relatively low level of government revenue in turn influences a low level of social expenditure at 18 per cent of GDP, placing Australia at the eighth-lowest level among the 30 OECD countries (Raper 2006).

Australia has a population of 20.6 million, 23 per cent of whom (4.74 million) are children aged 0–17 years. Just over 27,000 children are on care orders, constituting 5.6 per 1000 children and including a disproportionate number of Indigenous children (29.9 per 1000 children). A total of 25,454 children live in out-of-home care. The vast majority (94.4%) live in home-based care – either foster care or kinship care – following a shift away from the use of residential care over the last few decades. The most recent figures indicate that over half (51.1%) had been in out-of-home care for less than a year; only 8 per cent had been in care for over five years. Nearly a third (32%) were aged 10–14 years, 29.7 per cent were aged 5–9 years, 24.7 per cent less than 5 years and 13.6 per cent were 15–17. A total of 1817 young people aged 15–17 years were discharged from care in 2005–2006 (Australian Institute of Health and Welfare 2007).

Young Australians are increasingly dependent on their families for longer periods. Nearly 60 per cent of 15–24-year-olds live with their parents, and the proportion of 20–24-year-olds living at home has increased from 37 per cent in 1996 to 40 per cent in 2001 (Fitzsimmons and Sandrejko 2004). The lack of guaranteed ongoing support for most Australian care leavers contrasts sharply with this general trend of longer financial dependence on families, encouraged by Commonwealth Government income support policies.

Case examples

James

James entered care on a court order when he was 13 following a break-down in his relationship with his elderly grandmother who had cared for him on a regular basis since he was five. He was placed in the care of his grandmother on a voluntary basis after various attempts to keep him at home safely failed. His mother's substance abuse had exacerbated her mental illness and his father was unavailable, having left the family when James was a pre-schooler. After several foster placements failed as a result of James' difficult behaviour, he was placed in residential care but he regularly absconded, and became involved in heroin use and street sex work. A court order was sought to place him in secure welfare for a number of months. James is now renting a bungalow in a friend's backyard, and has commenced an apprenticeship training scheme. While he seems more settled, he is spending a lot of time with his mother who is a daily marijuana user, and he is displaying disturbed behaviour at times.

Jim

Jim was brought up in a non-Aboriginal foster family and has had close ties with both his foster family and his Aboriginal kinship group. He left school before Year 12 because of bullying and racism, but qualified for entry to university at an external bridging course. He completed a computer course with departmental assistance with his fees. Four years after leaving care, he was half-way through a degree in journalism at the University of Darwin by correspondence. His foster parents have provided him with ongoing personal and financial assistance and welcomed him home between stays in college and independent accommodation. Jim has received some assistance from the State Department with his course fees and some establishment costs as well as a student living allowance from the Commonwealth Government and a one-off payment of $1000 (Transition to Independent Living Allowance) to help set him up in independent accommodation.

Australia's welfare regime

The Australian welfare state has always been based on a mixed economy of service provision. Voluntary agencies including church groups and other private charities have historically played a central role in the provision of health services and other social programmes. The Commonwealth Government takes responsibility for all income security, but the state and territory governments retain responsibility for Indigenous peoples, and for most forms of social welfare service delivery including education, health, and housing and community services (Bryson 2001). There is considerable regional variation in service provision, within and between states, and particular problems in relation to Indigenous communities.

Australia possesses one of the most selective income support systems in the Western industrialised world. Financial assistance is provided on a flat-rate basis, funded from general revenue rather than via insurance schemes. Welfare programmes are mostly means tested, targeted to the poor, and low in monetary value, at about 25 per cent of average weekly earnings (Mendes 2003). Consequently, international commentators such as the Swedish theorist Esping-Andersen (1990) have often described the Australian welfare state as a residual or liberal welfare state, typified by low levels of welfare spending and minimum interference with the free market or decommodification.

All welfare states contain a blending of social care or enabling aspects and more punitive or social control aspects. The application of these different approaches often seems to reflect the degree to which particular disadvantaged groups are considered deserving or undeserving of support. The current Australian government seems to be more punitive than supportive towards groups such as the unemployed, the disabled, and single parents. The federal government has progressively sought to reduce social expenditure, and to redirect responsibility for the disadvantaged from government to corporations, non-government organisations and charities, and families. For example, the Coalition government passed the Welfare to Work Bill in 2005 which tightened the eligibility criteria and significantly lowered the payment rates for new applicants for Parenting Payment and the Disability Support Pension.

Nevertheless, there is little evidence that the Australian welfare state is actually contracting. In fact social spending continues to grow and totalled 42.5 per cent of the federal government budget in 2005–2006. And while the government has been highly punitive towards some disadvantaged groups, they have been very generous with other groups such as the aged and low-income nuclear families with children. Total spending on assistance to families with children now amounts to $24.5 million per year, about 12 per cent of the federal budget. These divergent approaches to welfare recipients seem to reflect populist judgements about public political and electoral preferences rather than any objective judgements about the relative need of different groups.

In relation to care leavers, the federal government has recently established a Transition to Independent Living Allowance (TILA) as a one-off grant of $1000 to assist young people leaving care. It has also commissioned a study still unpublished to estimate the forward costs of disadvantaged young people. These 'intrusions' appear to be both pragmatic and ideologically underpinned. Once these young people are adults, the federal government has responsibility for income support and for some of the long-term costs of adverse outcomes. Hence, the government may be open to persuasion on narrow economic grounds that greater investment in leaving care and after care supports will promote the self-reliance of care leavers and save money in the longer term. However, given the neo-liberal bias of the current federal government, an emphasis on improved preparation for independent living (largely a state responsibility) is more likely than ongoing after care support.

Legal and policy framework

Child protection and out-of-home care are the responsibility of the community services or child welfare departments in each state and territory, each with their own legislation, policies and practices. The concept of 'corporate parenting' particularly with any ongoing responsibility is not strongly upheld and there are no uniform in-care or leaving care standards. The absence of effective national legislation or intervention means that separate campaigns have to take place in each state and territory to address legislative and programme responses.

Leaving care first came to public attention in 1989 when the National Inquiry into Homeless Children found that a large number of homeless young people came from state care backgrounds (Burdekin 1989). Further studies by a number of non-government charities confirmed these concerns (Hirst 1989; Taylor 1990). However, no action was taken by the Commonwealth Government to introduce national benchmarks for leaving care services, and significant policy and practice differences continue to exist.

Subsequent campaigns for leaving care services have been driven primarily by a coalition of peak child welfare provider groups, such as the Victorian Centre for Excellence in Child and Family Welfare and the New South Wales Association of Children's Welfare Agencies (ACWA), and consumer groups such as the Create Foundation, and the Care Leavers of Australia Network (Green and Jones 1999; Mendes 2002). Some semi-independent state and national government reports and inquiries have also been influential in provoking policy and political debate (Australian Law Reform Commission and Human Rights and Equal Opportunity Commission 1997; Public Accounts and Estimates Committee 2001). Yet currently, New South Wales remains the only state to have introduced uniform state-wide support services for care leavers, although Western Australia, Queensland and Victoria have made significant recent progress in this direction (Department of Human Services 2005; Mendes and Moslehuddin 2004a).

Secondary data

There are little reliable data in Australia on the number, characteristics and outcomes of young people leaving care. The best national estimate of the number of young people leaving care each year[1] is the number of 15- to 17-year-olds discharged from out-of-home care, based on the aggregated data from the states and territories, collected and published by the Australian Institute of Health and Welfare. Unit record data and administrative and case management records are separately maintained by each state and territory, and by government and non-government agencies that provide case management and services for children and young people in care. Basic demographic data on young people ageing out of care should be retrievable in each state and territory, and on a national basis, given consistent counting rules and the willingness of each state and territory department to do so. However, these data sets are not readily accessible or amenable to research purposes and the cost and difficulty of extracting consistent and reliable information from them on young people's families and their experiences before entering care, their functioning in care and their outcomes at discharge from care would be quite significant.

Although it should be a relatively simple task, matching data across Commonwealth and State databases, and even across departments and agencies within states, is also difficult because of bureaucratic and privacy constraints. It has only recently been undertaken for children and young people in care in relation to their educational outcomes, and only in a few states. There are as yet no large-scale or longitudinal studies of young people in Australia that have collected information that would identify those who have been in out-of-home care among their participants. Recent State and Commonwealth studies on the cost–benefit analyses of providing support for young people after leaving care have been conducted in the absence of such data, using estimates of the number of young people who have left care over the last decade or so, together with case studies to indicate the need for services and other forms of support (Raman, Inder and Forbes 2005).

The need for appropriate Australian data is clearly recognised by researchers, policy makers, practitioners and advocates for young people in care. In 1999, Maunders *et al.* bemoaned the 'woefully inadequate' data on young people leaving care in Australia. Little has changed since, and several national meetings have called for nationally consistent baseline data in relation to young people leaving care and research to identify the indicators and predictors of successful transition from care.

Leaving care research

Australian research on young people leaving care is still quite limited and falls into three main categories: primary research involving surveys and interviews with young people after they have left care; case file analysis; and analysis of the legislation, policy and practices of the various states and territories in relation to leaving care.

Several small-scale studies in the 1990s focused on the experiences and outcomes of care leavers, mostly in New South Wales and Victoria (Cashmore and Paxman 1996, 2006a, 2006b, 2006c; London 2004; Maunders *et al.* 1999; Moslehuddin and Mendes 2006; Owen *et al.* 2000). The first of these was a longitudinal study of young people leaving care in New South Wales which involved four waves of interviews with a cohort of 47 young people discharged from wardship over a 12-month period in the early 1990s (Cashmore and Paxman 1996, 2006a, 2006c). The four interviews were conducted three months before leaving care, three months and then 12 months after leaving care, and fout to five years later. Information was collected from the case files of all 91 young people who left care in that 12-month period. Two comparison groups of young people in refuges or living at home were also interviewed, as well as the case workers for the young people leaving care.

The experiences of young people leaving and after care, and their outcomes, were consistent with those reported in Stein and Carey's (1986) landmark study and other more recent studies in the UK, US and Canada (Biehal *et al.* 1995; Courtney *et al.* 2007; Kufeldt and McKenzie 2003; Pecora *et al.* 2005; Stein 2004). Their experiences and stability and felt security while in care, their circumstances as they were leaving care and the stability of their accommodation and the level of support available to them after leaving care were all significant predictors of how well young people were faring four to five years after leaving care (Cashmore and Paxman 2006a, 2006b).

Other studies, all conducted in Victoria, and based on different samples of young people leaving care at one point in time, have reported similar findings. In the only nationally focused study, Maunders *et al.* (1999) interviewed 43 young people across Australia aged 17–21 who had been discharged at least two years earlier after six months or more in care between the ages of 15 and 18. Nearly two-thirds were either unemployed or on sickness or supporting parent benefits and only one in five of these young people were completing or had completed their final year of secondary school. Like the earlier study (Cashmore and Paxman 1996), stability in care and a sense of belonging and connectedness, together with social support from a mentor, advocate and positive family contact, were reported as contributing to successful independent living. Lack of preparation, unresolved anger, unsuitable and unstable accommodation, and lack of adequate income support were found to have inhibited young people's transition from care. Other Australian studies have identified similar deficits in leaving care policy and practice (Bonnice 2002, 2005; Clare 2006; Green and Jones 1999; London 2004; Maunders *et al.* 1999; Mendes 2002, 2004, 2005b; Mendes and Goddard 2000; Mendes and Moslehuddin 2004a; Owen *et al.* 2000).

A recent collaborative study by social work researchers and economists estimated the costs of *not* supporting young people after they leave care (Raman *et al.* 2005). It was based on a purposive sample of 60 young people aged 18 to 25 years, again in Victoria: 30 young people in a 'positive outcome' group and 30 young people who were unemployed and disconnected and whose circumstances and outcomes were less positive. It provided estimates of the very significant economic costs to the state associated with service use by these young people (for example, for health and mental health services, police, criminal justice and housing) and lost earnings if young people are unproductive and unsupported.

Several other smaller qualitative studies came to similar conclusions based on interviews with a small number of young people or their workers from different agencies: for example, ten young people aged between 18 and 30 years in two non-government agencies in Victoria (Moslehuddin and Mendes 2006); ten young people who had left the care of MacKillop Family Services during the previous five years, together with 33 workers from the same agency (London 2004; London and Halfpenny 2006); eight young people from a larger study (Frederick and Goddard 2006); and six 17–21-year-olds as well as 28 workers at St Luke's Youth Services and the analysis of 50 case files (Bonnice 2002). In addition, a number of studies have compared Australian leaving care policies with those of over-seas jurisdictions (Mendes 2005a, 2005b; Mendes and Moslehuddin 2003, 2004b, 2006; Mendes, Moslehuddin and Yates 2003).

The most recent case file analysis study involved a sample of 138 case files randomly selected from the 989 young people aged 14–18 years dis-charged from custody or guardianship orders (of at least six months' dura-tion) during a three-year period in the mid-1990s in Victoria (Owen *et al.* 2000). More than half were discharged when they were 17 (34%) or 18 years old (23%). The results, using the seven 'Looking After Children' dimensions, were consistent with other studies in relation to the poor edu-cational attainment and difficulties at school associated with placement instability, and an over-representation of unemployment and involvement in some form of criminal activity.

Strikingly absent and clearly needed are systematic evaluation studies of the various programmes run by departmental and non-government agencies across Australia. These evaluations should focus on the accessibil-ity and effectiveness of the assistance provided by the specialist services and the statutory department as well as the operation of the relevant legis-lation and the different pathways taken by care leavers and their outcomes.

Conclusion

Australia possesses a relatively liberal welfare state with a preference for individualism and self-reliance rather than government assistance. The federal legislative framework and administrative structure is similar to that of the US in that it tends to mitigate against a consistent national provision of leaving care services. There are no uniform in-care or leaving care stan-dards. The key emphasis is on improved preparation for independent living rather than ongoing after care support. Apart from New South Wales, legislative and programme responses have tended to be ad-hoc and lacking a formalised role within the child welfare continuum. Victoria, Western Australia and South Australia now have legislation for after care support, and some specific after care services, but the other states and terri-tories continue to lack either legislation or specific services.

There are very limited secondary data available given the absence of large-scale or longitudinal studies that can be used to segregate the experiences of care leavers. We can utilise the Australian Institute of Health and Welfare figures to estimate the number of young people discharged from care each year, although these figures may not be entirely reliable due to different counting rules in different data sets. Much of the research has been small-scale and cross-sectional. However, it does show that the experience of young people in care, and their circumstances as they were leaving care, had a significant effect on their transition from care and their outcomes after leaving care. There is a particular absence of evaluation studies which explore the effectiveness of existing programmes and supports.

Key messages for policy and practice

- Compared with other young people their age, care leavers as a group face multiple disadvantages resulting from their pre-care, in-care and leaving care experiences. These include particular difficulties in accessing educational, employment, housing and other developmental and transitional opportunities.

- Successful outcomes for care leavers correlate with a level of stability and felt security in care, educational progress while in care, a planned transition from care, the provision of stable accommodation and ongoing social support from friends or family available after leaving care.

- There are significant social and economic costs to the state in terms of care leavers utilising health and mental health services, police, criminal justice and emergency housing if young people are not supported in their transition from care into adulthood.

Note

1. There is, however, some uncertainty about the figures because the definition refers to 'exit from care' where the child or young person left out-of-home care in 2004–2005 and did not return within two months. There are also discrepancies or different counting rules in different data sets.

References

Australian Institute of Health and Welfare (AIHW) (2007) *Child Protection Australia 2005–06. Child Welfare Series 40.* Canberra: AIHW.

Australian Law Reform Commission and Human Rights and Equal Opportunity Commission (1997) *Seen and Heard: Priority for Children in the Legal Process.* Sydney: Human Rights and Equal Opportunity Commission.

Biehal, N., Clayton, J., Stein, M. and Wade, J. (1995) *Moving On: Young People and Leaving Care Schemes.* London: HMSO.

Bonnice, J. (2002) *Young People Leaving Care and Housing Project.* Bendigo: St Luke's Youth Services.

Bonnice, J. (2005) *Final Report to the Colonial Foundation for the St Luke's Leaving Care and After Care Support Service.* Bendigo: St Luke's Youth Services.

Bryson, L. (2001) 'Australia: The Transformation of the Wage Earners Welfare State.' In P. Alcock and G. Craig (eds) *International Social Policy.* Houndmills: Palgrave.

Burdekin, B. (1989) *Our Homeless Children.* Canberra: Australian Government Printing Service.

Cashmore, J. and Paxman, M. (1996) *Longitudinal Study of Wards Leaving Care.* Sydney: Department of Community Services and Social Policy Research Centre. Accessed 25/04/07 at www.community.nsw.gov.au/DOCS/STANDARD/PC_100859.html

Cashmore, J. and Paxman, M. (2006a) 'Predicting outcomes for young people after leaving care: The importance of "felt" security.' *Child and Family Social Work 11*, 232–241.

Cashmore, J. and Paxman, M. (2006b) 'Wards leaving care: Follow up five years on.' *Children Australia 31*, 18–25.

Cashmore, J. and Paxman, M. (2006c) *Longitudinal Study of Wards Leaving Care: Four to Five Years On.* Sydney: New South Wales Centre for Parenting and Research.

Clare, M. (2006) 'Personal reflections on needs and services for young people leaving care.' *Children Australia 31*, 3, 11–17.

Courtney, M.E., Dworsky, A., Cusick, G.R., Havlicek, J., Perez, A. and Keller, T. (2007) *Mid-west Evaluation of the Adult Functioning of Former Foster Youth: Outcomes at Age 21.* Chicago: Chapin Hall Center for Children, University of Chicago. Accessed 20/2/08 at www.chapinhall.org/article_abstract.aspx?at=1355&L2=61&L3=130.

Department of Human Services (2005) *Protecting Children: The Next Steps.* Victoria: Department of Human Services.

Esping-Andersen, G. (1990) *The Three Worlds of Welfare Capitalism.* New Jersey: Princeton University Press.

Fitzsimmons, C. and Sandrejko, N. (2004) 'Smart, rich, but young staying at home.' *The Australian*, 6 February, p.3.

Frederick, J. and Goddard, C. (2006) 'Pathways to and from state care.' *Children Australia 31*, 3, 34–41.

Green, S. and Jones, A. (1999) *Standards and Practice to Support Young People Leaving Care in Victoria.* Melbourne: Children's Welfare Association of Victoria.

Hirst, C. (1989) *Forced Exit: A Profile of the Young and Homeless in Inner Urban Melbourne.* Melbourne: Salvation Army Youth Homelessness Policy Development Unit.

Kufeldt, K. and McKenzie, B. (eds) (2003) *Child Welfare: Connecting Research, Policy and Practice.* Waterloo, Ontario: Wilfrid Laurier University Press.

London, Z. (2004) *It's a Real Shock: Transitioning from Care to Independent Living.* Melbourne: MacKillop Family Services.

London, Z. and Halfpenny, N. (2006) 'Transitioning from (and with) care.' *Children Australia* *31*, 3, 42–46.

Maunders, D., Liddell, M., Liddell, M. and Green, S. (1999) *Young People Leaving Care and Protection: A Report to the National Youth Affairs Research Scheme.* Hobart: Australian Clearing House for Youth Studies.

Mendes, P. (2002) 'Leaving care services in Victoria: A case study of a policy debate.' *Developing Practice 3*, 51–58.

Mendes, P. (2003) *Australia's Welfare Wars.* Sydney: University of New South Wales Press.

Mendes, P. (2004) 'New leaving care initiatives in Victoria.' *Developing Practice 9*, 41–47.

Mendes, P. (2005a) 'From state care to independence: A comparison of the Australian and American leaving care debates.' *The Social Policy Journal 4*, 1, 51–63.

Mendes, P. (2005b) 'Graduating from the child welfare system: A case study of the leaving care debate in Victoria, Australia.' *Journal of Social Work 5*, 2, 155–171.

Mendes, P. and Goddard, C. (2000) 'Leaving care programs locally and internationally.' *Children Australia 25*, 11–16.

Mendes, P. and Moslehuddin, B. (2003) 'Graduating from the child welfare system: An overview of the UK leaving care debate.' *Youth Studies 22*, 4, 37–43.

Mendes, P. and Moslehuddin, B. (2004a) 'Moving out from the state parental home: A comparison of leaving care policies in Victoria and New South Wales.' *Children Australia 29*, 2, 20–29.

Mendes, P. and Moslehuddin, B. (2004b) 'Graduating from the child welfare system: A comparison of the UK and Australian leaving care debates.' *International Journal of Social Welfare 13*, 4, 332–339.

Mendes, P. and Moslehuddin, B. (2006) 'From dependence to interdependence: Towards better outcomes for young people leaving state care.' *Child Abuse Review 15*, 110–126.

Mendes, P., Moslehuddin, B. and Yates, D. (2003) 'Graduating from the state care system: Comparison of the Australian and New Zealand leaving care debates.' *New Zealand Social Work Review,* Autumn/Winter, 37–42.

Moslehuddin, B. and Mendes, P. (2006) 'Young people's journey to independence.' *Children Australia 31*, 3, 47–54.

Owen, L., Lunken, T., Davis, C., Cooper, B. *et al.* (2000) *Pathways to Interdependence and Independence: The Leaving Care Initiative.* Melbourne: La Trobe University.

Pecora, P.J., Kessler, R.C., Williams, J., O'Brien, K. *et al.* (2005) *Improving Family Foster Care: Findings from the Northwest Foster Care Alumni Study.* Seattle, WA: Casey Family Programs. Accessed 20/2/08 at www.casey.org/Resources/Publications/NorthwestAlumni Study.htm

Public Accounts and Estimates Committee (2001) *Report on the Review of the Auditor-General's Special Report No. 43 – Protecting Victoria's Children.* Melbourne: Parliament of Victoria.

Raman, S., Inder, B. and Forbes, C. (2005) *Investing for Success: The Economics of Supporting Young People Leaving Care.* Melbourne: Centre for Excellence in Child and Family Welfare.

Raper, M. (2006) 'Tax reform and its effects on services.' *ACOSS Impact,* Autumn, 14–15.

Stein, M. (2004) *What Works for Young People Leaving Care?* Ilford: Barnardo's.

Stein, M. and Carey, K. (1986) *Leaving Care.* Oxford: Blackwell.

Taylor, J. (1990) *Leaving Care and Homelessness.* Melbourne: Brotherhood of St Laurence.

Chapter 3

Canada

Robert J. Flynn and David Vincent

Background and key statistics

- In 2006, the population of Canada—a federal state made up of ten provinces and three northern territories—was 32.6 million people, 24 percent of whom were 19 years of age or younger.

- Each province and territory has its own child welfare legislation and delivers its own services; there is no national (federal) database on young people in out-of-home care.

- In 2003, 12.4 percent of Canadian children and adolescents aged 0–17 years (i.e., 843,000 young people) lived in low-income families.

- In 2003, an estimated 80,000 children and adolescents were living in out-of-home care, approximately 1 percent of the population aged 0–19 years.

- In 2000–2002, aboriginal children made up less than 5 percent of the child and adolescent population in Canada but comprised 30–40 percent of young people placed in out-of-home care during that period.

- Young people are eligible to receive child welfare services up to the age of 18 or 19; they may also receive extended services and financial support up to age 21 in seven provinces or territories and up to ages 19–23 in the six other jurisdictions.

Key sources

- Faris-Manning and Zandstra (2003).
- Gough *et al.* (2005).
- Statistics Canada (2006a, 2006b).
- Tweddle (2005).

Introduction

In this chapter, we use Breen and Buchmann's (2002) sociological theory of institutional variation to examine Canadian young people's transitions to early adulthood, both in the general population and from public care. The theory holds that cross-national differences in key societal institutions—welfare regimes, educational systems, and labour markets—have an important impact on young people's social positions and behaviour. Institutions are seen as influential in two ways: they provide opportunities and impose constraints on education, work, and relationships, and they shape norms about appropriate behaviour.

Canada's child welfare system

Founded in 1867 by the union of several British colonies in North America, Canada is a federal state composed of ten provinces and three northern territories, with Ottawa its capital. The legal system of the province of Quebec is based on civil law, whereas the legal systems of the other 12 provinces and territories are derived from common law. The provinces and territories fund and deliver their own health, educational, and social services, including child welfare services, with financial assistance from the federal government. There is thus not one but rather 13 child welfare systems in Canada, each governed by its own distinct legislation (Trocmé *et al.* 2005). In most jurisdictions, child welfare services are delivered by government employees. The main exception is the province of Ontario, where independent, not-for-profit Children's Aid Societies deliver services, with full government funding.

Children in need and in public care

In 2006, Canada's population was 32.6 million people, of whom 24.0 percent (7.8 million) were aged 0–19 years, 62.8 percent were aged 20–64, and 13.2 percent were aged 65 and over (Statistics Canada 2006a). Differing legal definitions from jurisdiction to jurisdiction of key terms such as "child in need" or "child in care" mean that we do not have precise national data on the number of such young people. Regarding children in need, we note that, in 2003, 12.4 percent of all Canadian children aged 0–17 (843,000) were living in low-income families. We also know that higher family income in Canada is consistently related to better physical, social-emotional, cognitive, and behavioural well-being among children, at all income levels (Statistics Canada 2006b). Concerning children in public care, we estimate that, in 2003, there were about 80,000 children and adolescents in out-of-home care, an estimate half-way between the 76,000 mentioned by Faris-Manning and Zandstra (2003) and the 85,000 referred to by Tweddle (2005). Thus, about 1 per cent of the Canadian population aged 0–19 is in public care. There are very large differences, however, between the rates of placement experienced by aboriginal and non-aboriginal children. Gough *et al.* (2005) stated that aboriginal children constituted 30–40 percent of those in public care, despite accounting for less than 5 percent of the total child population. A recent human rights complaint (Centre of Excellence for Child Welfare 2007) asserted that there were 27,000 First Nations children in the child welfare system, a figure that yields a similar estimate (i.e., 27,000 is equal to 34 percent of our earlier estimate of a total of 80,000 young people in public care).

The lack of national data sets means that we do not know how many young people leave public care each year in Canada. Recent Ontario data allow us to make a crude estimate. In 2005, there were about 19,000 children and adolescents in public care in Ontario (Ontario Association of Children's Aid Societies 2006), equal to roughly 25 percent of the total in Canada. Fifteen hundred (8%), aged 18–21, were making the transition from care, and another 7500 (40%), aged 13–17, had begun or were about to begin the process. Thus, of the approximately 80,000 young people currently in care in Canada, we estimate that, in a given year, about 6500

(8%) young people are actively engaged in the transition from public care, and another 32,000 (40%) have begun or will soon begin the process.

Case examples

Joe

Joe, aged 12, currently lives in a residential treatment facility. He attends a special school on the campus of the facility, which is located in a residential area of a medium-sized city. Joe was born addicted to cocaine. He lived with his mother, a single parent, until the age of two, when he was placed in out-of-home care because of severe neglect and physical, emotional, and sexual abuse from his mother and her male partners. Joe's mother is herself a graduate of the child welfare system and has a history of alcohol and drug addiction. It is not known which of her male partners is Joe's father. A diagnostic assessment described Joe as having severe emotional and behavioural problems and an attachment disorder. It also mentioned that he has a strong interest in music.

Jennifer

Jennifer, a young aboriginal woman, is 18. She lives with her ten-month-old daughter in a publicly subsidized apartment in a large city and receives social assistance. She entered care at the age of 12 as a result of sexual abuse in her birth family. Because of her rebelliousness and binge-drinking, she experienced a series of foster homes during middle adolescence and was ultimately placed in a group home. Upon turning 16, she left the child welfare system to live with her boyfriend in an apartment. He abandoned her upon learning that she was pregnant. Her former child welfare worker helped her to secure social assistance and gain access to her subsidized apartment. When her daughter is enrolled in day care two years from now, Jennifer plans to obtain her high school diploma at the local adult high school and find a suitable job. After that, she would like to attend the local community college and train as a restaurant chef.

Canada's welfare regime

Breen and Buchmann's (2002) theory of institutional variation seeks to explain cross-national differences in youth transitions in Western European and non-European English-speaking countries. It is based upon a typology of national welfare regimes, and their correlated national educational and labour-market systems, derived from earlier research by Esping-Andersen (1990) and others. The fourfold typology includes the conservative, family-oriented, high-benefit regimes of German and French-speaking countries of continental Europe, the liberal, market-oriented regimes of Anglo-Saxon countries, the social-democratic, universalistic regimes of Scandinavia, and the conservative, family-oriented, low-benefit regimes of southern European countries, especially Spain and Italy.

With its strong British demographic and parliamentary roots, Canada has a mainly liberal, market-oriented welfare regime. Like other English-speaking countries, Canada has traditionally emphasized individual and family self-reliance, especially where non-universal services (i.e., those other than health or primary and secondary education) are concerned. Thus, in the provision of non-universal child development services, for example, Canada has lagged behind many Organization for Economic Cooperation and Development (OECD) countries (see d'Ercole and Salvini 2003, Table 1, p.46). It has had below-average proportions of three–six-year-old children in day care facilities, below-average private and public expenditures on pre-primary education (d'Ercole and Salvini 2003, Figure 21, p.51), and above-average levels of relative child poverty.

Like those in other liberal, English-speaking countries, Canada's education system has always been relatively non-vocational in emphasis, only loosely aligned with specific jobs. Compared to those in other OECD countries, Canada's schools have been found to perform well, with above-average literacy (reading) performance and below-average inequality in literacy attributable to parental socio-economic inequality (d'Ercole and Salvini 2003, Figure 22, Panel B, p.56). Also, the percentage of Canadian young people not completing compulsory schooling or without upper secondary education is below the OECD average, while the proportion completing post-secondary (tertiary) education is much above average (d'Ercole and Salvini 2003, Table 2, p.55).

In keeping with its liberal welfare regime, Canada provides only weak employment protection legislation (Organisation for Economic Cooperation and Development 1999) and spends much less on youth labour market programs than the OECD average (Quintini and Martin 2006). Its labour market has been flexible, however, with above-average rates of youth employment, below-average rates of youth unemployment (especially long-term unemployment), and below-average proportions of young people who leave school without basic skills or who are neither in education nor in employment (Quintini and Martin 2006).

Transition in the general youth population

The school to work transition includes two periods: completing post-compulsory education and settling into the work force. OECD data suggest that the school to work transition is comparatively easy for young people in two types of welfare regimes (d'Ercole and Salvini 2003): the liberal regimes of the English-speaking countries, with their flexible labour markets and ease of combining study and work, and the social-democratic regimes of the Nordic countries, with their specific programs that assist young people at risk. At the other extreme, youths in southern European regimes often experience difficult school to work transitions because of high employment protection for people already in the labour market and problems in settling into jobs. In Canada, in 1996, young people took an average of seven years (i.e., between the ages of 16 and 23) to make the school to work transition. This was an increase of almost two years between 1990 and 1996, close to the OECD average and due mainly to greater time needed to settle into the labour market. The duration of the school to work transition in 1996 varied substantially among OECD countries, from a low of five years in the liberal regimes of the US and the UK to a high of more than 11 years in the southern European regime of Italy (d'Ercole and Salvini 2003).

Despite their relatively easy school to work transitions, young people in English-speaking countries have also been found to exhibit comparatively high rates of anti-social and aggressive behaviour (Eisner 2002; Heuveline 2002). Breen and Buchmann (2002) hypothesize that the highly competitive, laissez-faire, individualistic cultures of the liberal English-speaking countries exert strong pressure on young people to engage in relatively high rates of violence, property crime, or drug use. In contrast, young people in the social-democratic welfare regimes of the Nordic countries are influenced by a cultural emphasis on universalistic principles and responsible citizenship, such that they exhibit generally low levels of problem behaviour and high levels of life satisfaction.

As products of a liberal welfare regime, Canadian young people have comparatively high rates of behaviour problems, as Breen and Buchmann's (2002) theory of institutional variation would predict. Heuveline (2002), for example, found that Canada ranked poorly (20th among 26 countries) in terms of its overall mortality rate from three causes—suicide, homicide, and motor vehicle injury—among young people aged 15–35, during the 40-year period of 1955–1994. On each of the three mortality indicators, Canada also ranked poorly: 17th on suicide, 21st on homicide, and 21st on motor vehicle injury. Other liberal-regime, English-speaking coun-tries—New Zealand, Australia, and the US—ranked even lower than Canada in terms of their overall mortality rates. Similarly, Eisner (2002), in a cross-national study of 37 countries, found that the liberal-regime English-speaking countries (Australia, Canada, England and Wales, New Zealand, Scotland, and the US) formed a distinct cluster marked by high rates of four youth behaviour problems: violent crime, property crime, drug use, and alcohol abuse. Among the 37 countries, Canada had the 14th highest violent-crime rate, the 8th highest property-crime rate, the 7th highest drug-use rate, and the 10th highest alcohol-abuse rate.

The recent UNICEF (2007) report on children's well-being in rich countries provides further evidence in favour of Breen and Buchmann's (2002) contention that the institutions and cultures of liberal English-speaking countries such as Canada are likely to facilitate the school to work transition but also exert pressure in the direction of youth behaviour problems. Among 21 industrialized countries, Canada ranked 12th overall, based on the average of its ranks on six specific dimensions of chil-dren's well-being. The Netherlands and Sweden ranked highest, while the

US and the UK ranked lowest. On the six individual dimensions, Canada's performance was highly variable: good on objective factors likely to facilitate the school to work transition (2nd on educational well-being and 6th on material well-being), middling (13th) on health and safety, but poor on personal, family, and behavioural factors that play an important role in transitions (Canada was only 15th on subjective well-being, 17th on behaviour and risks, and 18th on family and peer relationships).

Legal and policy framework

The foregoing description of the broad context within which transition takes place in the general youth population in Canada suggests that young people leaving public care are likely to have both advantages and disadvantages. On the one hand, the transition from school to work may be somewhat easier in Canada than in countries with conservative welfare regimes and less flexible labour-market systems, and the country's high-performance education system may be an asset, especially for good students. On the other hand, the very demands of the education system may be a formidable obstacle for the many young people in care whose success in school is quite limited (Flynn *et al.* 2004). Also, even though Canada's labour market may provide ready access to jobs, its low minimum wages may trap unskilled young people in relative poverty.

Depending on the province or territory, the young person's eligibility to receive child welfare services ends at his or her 18th or 19th birthday. To facilitate transitions, however, services may be extended to age 21 in most jurisdictions—the maximum varies between 19 and 23 in the others. Depending on the jurisdiction, transition supports may include residential services (i.e., continued foster care or independent living), a basic living allowance, counseling, dental care, tuition support, or assistance with vocational training (Serge *et al.* 2002). Consistent with Canada's liberal welfare regime and our later review of Canadian research on transitions, however, the current level of supports and the age limits on eligibility for them are widely seen as inadequate, with policy changes needed in relation to human and financial resources. Moreover, the level of social-assistance, housing, or employment support available to young people from generic agencies beyond the child welfare system is only modest.

Secondary data

Currently, publicly accessible provincial or territorial administrative data sets linking young people's in-care experiences with their post-care educational, labour-market, and personal outcomes do not appear to exist in Canada. Also, few young people in care are participants in two longitudinal national surveys being conducted by Statistics Canada and Human Resources and Social Development Canada. In the National Longitudinal Survey of Children and Youth (NLSCY), only 35 young people in foster care were included in Cycle 1 (1994–1995), and all were dropped from subsequent biennial cycles. In the Youth in Transition Survey (YITS), only 106 young people in foster care were included in Cycle 1 (2000). With an overall retention rate of about 85 percent in its three subsequent biennial cycles, however, the YITS may offer some limited potential for research on Canadian care-leavers.

Leaving care research

To date, no large-scale, prospective investigations of transitions from public care in Canada have been conducted, and thus we have little precise information on care-leavers' trajectories. A few small-sample studies have been completed, however, and we summarize these below. On the whole, they suggest that care-leavers' experiences in Canada are more akin to the compressed and accelerated transitions described by Stein (2006) than to the extended period of role experimentation and identity exploration discussed in Arnett's (2000) portrait of emerging adulthood.

Kufeldt (2003) followed up 87 graduates of guardianship care (i.e., permanent wardship) via mailed questionnaires and interviewed 14 of them. The graduates had a lower level of education than the general population, 46 percent were unemployed, and those employed had mainly lower-level, low-income jobs. Overall, the graduates lagged behind the general population in attaining the usual developmental tasks of young adulthood. Mann-Feder and White (2003) conducted focus groups with

21 care-leavers in Quebec, concluding that child welfare staff needed to continue to support the young people after the latter had left care, given the lack of such support from the young people's birth families. Rutman *et al.* (2003) interviewed 20 care-leavers and 15 caregivers or service providers in British Columbia. The young people said they were most in need of an adequate income that would enable them to avoid social assistance, continue their studies, and facilitate residential stability and ongoing healthy relationships. Leslie and Hare (2003) conducted focus groups with 28 young people who had experienced child welfare services. The youths indicated that life in care had been stigmatizing, that they had had limited influence on the way services were delivered, and that current time limits on care provision needed to be extended. Of 16 care-leavers who had completed self-report questionnaires, only a third felt they had been prepared for transition to independent living, a quarter were still involved with child welfare workers because of protection concerns regarding their own children, many struggled to achieve a sense of belonging and personal identity, and a good number emphasized the importance of preparing for employment and experiencing transition as a gradual rather than abrupt process.

Callahan *et al.* (2003) studied 11 young mothers, aged 16–24, who were either still in or had recently left public care. The young mothers took pride in having survived very difficult childhoods and in coping with an often unpredictable child welfare system. They expressed sadness at losing relationships, especially with social workers, but pride in forging new ones: many experienced pregnancy as a positive event and a gateway to a better future, but felt anxiety at being constantly scrutinized regarding their care of their children and at the need to 'jump through hoops' to secure resources for themselves and their children. Finally, the Ontario Association of Children's Aid Societies (2006) and 23 local Children's Aid Societies (CASs) conducted focus groups with over 300 former Crown wards, aged 18–21, who were currently receiving extended-care services, and with more than 300 child welfare staff members from the 23 CASs. The young people emphasized the importance of having at least one supportive adult upon whom they could rely during transition and adequate financial support, particularly to finish high school and pursue post-secondary education.

Conclusion

Canada, a predominantly English-speaking country with a liberal welfare regime, provides a general context for transitions that presents advantages and disadvantages. On the one hand, Canada has an educational system that performs well and a flexible labour market. On the other hand, it has relatively high levels of child poverty and youth crime, drug use, and alcohol abuse. Current provincial and territorial levels of financial, educational, and social supports for transition, and the age limits on eligibility for them, are widely seen as insufficient. Little research has been conducted to date on transitions from care. Especially needed are prospective studies, based on relatively large and representative samples, and high-quality evaluations of the effects of specific evidence-based transition interventions.

Key messages for policy and practice

- Large-sample prospective studies are needed to compare the transition trajectories of care-leavers with those of their peers in the general population, to place policy and practice on a firm empirical footing.

- Care-leavers identify as their single greatest need the emotional support and guidance during transition of at least one caring adult.

- Provinces and territories should provide financial assistance that is above the poverty level and covers key transition costs, such as moving expenses, renting an apartment, clothing, and transportation.

- Care-leavers' educational costs should be covered, with the goal of increasing their rate of post-secondary participation to that of youths in the general population.

- Extended-care funding, regular contacts with child welfare staff, and free dental and mental health services should be made available up to age 25.

- The provinces and territories should monitor young people's outcomes for five years after they leave care, to improve the effectiveness of transition interventions on a continuous basis.

References

Arnett, J.J. (2000) "Emerging adulthood: A theory of development from the late teens through the twenties." *American Psychologist 55*, 469–480.

Breen, R. and Buchmann, M. (2002) "Institutional Variation and the Position of Young People: A Comparative Perspective." In F.F. Furstenberg Jr. (ed.) *Early Adulthood in Cross-National Perspective. Annals of the American Academy of Political and Social Science 550*, 1, 288–305.

Callahan, M., Dominelli, L., Rutman, D. and Strega, S. (2003) "Underdeserving Mothers: Lived Experiences of Young Mothers in or from Government Care." In K. Kufeldt and B. McKenzie (eds) *Child Welfare: Connecting Research, Policy, and Practice.* Waterloo, ON: Wilfrid Laurier University Press.

Centre of Excellence for Child Welfare (2007) *Canadian Human Rights Complaint on First Nations Child Welfare Filed Today by Assembly of First Nations and First Nations Child and Family Caring Society of Canada.* News release, 23 February. Ottawa: Centre of Excellence for Child Welfare.

d'Ercole, M.M. and Salvini, A. (2003) "Towards Sustainable Development: The Role of Social Protection." *OECD Social, Employment and Migration Working Papers 12.* Paris: Organisation for Economic Cooperation and Development.

Eisner, M. (2002) "Crime, Problem Drinking, And Drug Use: Patterns of Problem Behavior in Cross-National Perspective." In F.F. Furstenberg Jr. (ed.) *Early Adulthood in Cross-National Perspective. Annals of the American Academy of Political and Social Science 550*, 1, 201–225.

Esping-Andersen, G. (1990) *The Three Worlds of Welfare Capitalism.* New Jersey: Princeton University Press.

Faris-Manning, C. and Zandstra, M. (2003) *Children in Care in Canada: A Summary of Current Issues and Trends with Recommendations for Future Research.* Accessed on 05/06/05 at www.nationalchildrensalliance.com/nca/pubs/2003/Children_in_Care_March_2003.pdf

Flynn, R.J., Ghazal, H., Legault, L., Vandermeulen, G. and Petrick, S. (2004) "Using general-population measures and norms to identify resilient outcomes among young people in care." *Child and Family Social Work 9*, 65–79.

Gough, P., Trocmé, N., Brown, I., Knocke, D. and Blackstock, C. (2005) *Pathways to the Overrepresentation of Aboriginal Children in Care. CECW Information Sheet 23E.* Toronto, ON: University of Toronto. Accessed on 28/02/07 at www.cecw-cepb.ca/files/file/en/AboriginalChildren23E.pdf

Heuveline, P. (2002) "An International Comparison of Adolescent and Young Adult Mortality." In F.F. Furstenberg Jr. (ed.) *Early Adulthood in Cross-National Perspective. Annals of the American Academy of Political and Social Science 550*, 1, 172–200.

Kufeldt, K. (2003) "Graduates of Guardianship Care: Outcomes in Early Adulthood." In K. Kufeldt and B. McKenzie (eds) *Child Welfare: Connecting Research, Policy, and Practice.* Waterloo, ON: Wilfrid Laurier University Press.

Leslie, B. and Hare, F. (2003) "At Care's End: Child Welfare Grads and Street Youth Services." In K. Kufeldt and B. McKenzie (eds) *Child Welfare: Connecting Research, Policy, and Practice.* Waterloo, ON: Wilfrid Laurier University Press.

Mann-Feder, V. and White, T. (2003) "The Transition to Independent Living: Preliminary Findings from the Experiences of Youth in Care." In K. Kufeldt and B. McKenzie (eds) *Child Welfare: Connecting Research, Policy, and Practice.* Waterloo, ON: Wilfrid Laurier University Press.

Ontario Association of Children's Aid Societies (2006) *Youth Leaving Care: An OACAS Survey of Youth and CAS Staff.* Toronto, ON: Ontario Association of Children's Aid Societies.

Organisation for Economic Cooperation and Development (1999) *Employment Outlook 1999.* Paris: Organisation for Economic Cooperation and Development.

Quintini, G. and Martin, S. (2006) *Starting Well or Losing Their Way? The Position of Youth in the Labour Market in OECD Countries.* OECD Social, Employment and Migration Working Paper 39. Paris: Organisation for Economic Cooperation and Development.

Rutman, D., Barlow, A., Alusik, D., Hubberstey, C. and Brown, E. (2003) "Supporting Young People's Transitions from Government Care.' In K. Kufeldt and B. McKenzie (eds) *Child Welfare: Connecting Research, Policy, and Practice.* Waterloo, ON: Wilfrid Laurier University Press.

Serge, L., Eberle, M., Goldberg, M., Sullivan, S. and Dudding, P. (2002) *Pilot Study: The Child Welfare System and Homelessness among Canadian Youth.* Ottawa, ON: National Secretariat on Homelessness, Government of Canada. Accessed on 25/10/06 at www.cecw-cepb.ca/files/file/en/HomelessnessAndCW.pdf

Statistics Canada (2006a) "Canada's population by age and sex, as of July 1, 2006." *The Daily,* October 26.

Statistics Canada (2006b) "Family income and the well-being of children." *The Daily,* May 11.

Stein, M. (2006) "Resilience and Young People Leaving Care: Implications for Child Welfare Policy and Practice in the UK." In R.J. Flynn, P.M. Dudding, and J.G. Barber (eds) *Promoting Resilience in Child Welfare.* Ottawa, ON: University of Ottawa Press.

Trocmé, N., Fallon, B., MacLaurin, B., Daciuk, J. *et al.* (2005) *Canadian Incidence Study of Reported Child Abuse and Neglect—2003: Major Findings.* Ottawa, ON: Minister of Public Works and Government Services.

Tweddle, A. (2005) *Youth Leaving Care: How Do They Fare? Briefing Paper.* Prepared for the Modernizing Income Security for Working Age Adults (MISWAA) Project. Toronto, ON: Laidlaw Foundation.

UNICEF (2007) *Child Poverty in Perspective: An Overview of Child Well-Being in Rich Countries.* Innocenti Report Card 7. Florence, Italy: UNICEF Innocenti Research Centre.

Chapter 4

France

Annick-Camille Dumaret

Background and key statistics

- In 2006, France had a population of 61.5 million people, with 13.6 million youths aged 0–18 and 2.4 million aged 18–20. Those aged 0–20 still represent 25 per cent of the French population.

- In 2005, a total of 138,300 were in out-of-home care under the *Aide sociale à l'enfance* (ASE), including 116,800 entrusted to the services and 21,500 placed directly by judges. Furthermore, 133,400 benefit from educational measures.

- 18 out of every 10,000 young people aged 0–18 benefit from child protection measures.

- In 2005, 16,000 young adults aged 18–21 benefited from administrative measures of the ASE and around 3000 were looked after through Judicial Juvenile Protection. They represented 0.9 per cent of young people in their age group.

- The statutory sector provides 80–85 per cent of placements; the others are provided by non-profit and government-approved organisations. Foster family care is the most common type of placement (55%). Thirty-seven per cent of looked after children live in institutions, 4 per cent are adolescents housed independently, and 4 per cent live in other types of accommodation.

- Returning home is often problematic for adolescents in the absence of family support.

Key sources

- *Direction de la recherche, des études, de l'évaluation et des statistiques* (DRESS 2006).

- *Institut national de la statistique et des études économiques* (INSEE 2005, 2007).

- *Observatoire national de l'enfance en danger* (ONED 2005, 2006).

Introduction

Every year, national data on looked-after children are collected from the local authorities and centralised by the *Direction de la recherche, des études, de l'évaluation et des statistiques* (DRESS) and the *Direction de la Protection judiciaire de la jeunesse* (DPJJ). It is difficult to compile exact figures on the number of children 'in danger', as definitions vary between institutions. Based on data from children who are in danger and who are looked after by the child welfare services or judicial authorities (Table 4.1) (which does not rule out double-counting), more than 271,000 children are supported by child welfare services. The number of children receiving educational assistance in their families (133,400) is slightly lower than that of children in out-of-home care (138,300). The most common reasons for admitting children into care are neglect (30%), abuse (15–20%), and parental mental illness (40%). Other problems include parent–child relationship troubles, alcohol or drug abuse, and social pathology (Dumaret and Ruffin 1999; Naves and Cathala 2000). The average (mean) age of children is 12–13 years. One in every six are under six years of age and one in seven are young adults. Children admitted by court order stay in care two to three years longer than those admitted through administrative measures. Of particular concern is the situation of young immigrants, especially illegal ones. Their numbers are unknown (1500 to 3000), but more than half of them are in care, including a large number in the Paris ASE and Parisian suburbs.

Table 4.1: Children placed under the ASE in 2005

Children 'at risk': administrative measures (25%)	
Wards	2674
Temporary care (<18)	10,858
Temporary care (18–21)	16,035
Total	**29,567**
Children 'in danger': judicial measures (75%)	
Guardianship by ASE	3322
Placements by ASE	80,667
Parental rights delegated to ASE	3192
Parents who have lost their rights	26
Total	**87,207**
Total children entrusted to the ASE	**116,774**
*Children 'in danger' – direct placement by judge**	*21,500*
Total children in care of the ASE	**138,274**

Source: DRESS 2006

* Placed with members of the extended family, trusted persons, with public or non-profit organisations.

Case examples

Kevin

Kevin, aged 12, has been brought up by his mother who has mental health problems and an unstable marital situation. He is very neglected by his mother's new boyfriend who is violent. His birth father has disappeared. After a short-term placement, following the birth of his sister, a new placement was decided upon by the judge because of the troubled relationships in the family: the baby is placed in a nursery and Kevin is placed with a foster family. He has behaviour problems but is supervised by a psychologist in a specialised centre. Regular contact with his mother is organised by the foster care agency.

John

John and his brother lived with a foster family for four years. During this time they had contact with their grandmother and received irregular visits from their mother. Their father was in prison. John is 17 years old, has no self-confidence and always asks for help to do things. As he has minimal qualifications, he has been enrolled in a vocational training programme. Currently, John is sharing a flat with an adolescent placed by the same foster agency. Both have to do housekeeping and prepare meals. John's social worker notes his investment in the project, and the ongoing difficulties he has with family relationships. When John comes of age, he signs a contract with the child welfare services and receives allowances to support him while he finishes the vocational programme and his diploma. John rents a small flat not far from the technical college. He is still monitored by his social worker. He also maintains contact with his brother, the foster family and some friends with whom he was raised.

The French child welfare system: a dual youth protection system

The first charitable organisation for the care of orphans and illegitimate children was created in the 17th century. Since the French Revolution brought about the concept of the primacy of paternal power, parents' obligations have been written into the Civil Code. During the 19th century, the state became responsible for protecting abandoned children and for punishing juvenile delinquents, and a series of labour and mandatory schooling reforms saw the introduction of legal rights for children. As the separation between the responsibilities of church and state began to appear, so too did the notion of the interests of the child. Created in 1904, the *Assistance Publique* looked after children up until the age of 16: wards of the state, children placed in temporary care, children whose parental rights were delegated to the state and those placed through court orders.

In 1956, this organisation became the *Aide sociale à l'enfance* (ASE; child welfare service). It was not until the eve of World War I that the first courts for children and adolescents were created, and not until the end of World War II that childhood delinquency reforms were put in place by the 1945

Edict (Penal Code) and juvenile court judge positions were created. As punitive principles gave way to education and treatment, children up to the age of 18 were protected by the *Protection judiciaire de la jeunesse* (PJJ; Judicial Juvenile Protection).

For the past 50 years, the French child welfare system has been divided into two distinct sectors. The first is administrative: social protection through child welfare services, which are under the responsibility of the local authorities. The second is judicial: Judicial Juvenile Protection, which falls under the responsibility of the state, and which was created to deal with instances of failure in paternal authority (transformed into parental authority in 1970). Two foundational codes have set the standard for France's child welfare system, and both deal with young adults aged 18 to 20. First, the Edict Order of 1958 (Civil Code) deals with the protection of vulnerable youth and expands the judicial protection of children and adolescents. Children's judges have the power to limit parental responsibilities, and in the event of threats to the child's well-being, the judge may order mandatory measures. Second, the Statutory Order of 1959 (Family and Social Welfare Code) deals with the social protection of vulnerable children, and defines the preventative measures child welfare agencies may take on behalf of 'families whose living conditions risk imperilling the health, safety, morals or education of their children'. Judicial and administrative protection are independent but complementary. When administrative measures providing support on a voluntary basis, in partnership with parents, prove difficult to implement, court orders take precedence over them. Children's judges are the guarantors of the child's right to an education.

After an economic boom starting in 1955 that lasted for nearly 30 years, a socialist government held the reins of power in France for two decades. It launched de-centralisation (1983–89), transferring power in many areas from the central government to the *Conseils Généraux* (local authorities). Each one is made up of three departments:

1. The social services department and social welfare agencies provide services for people who cannot take care of themselves due to old age, handicap, or social difficulties.

2.   The *Protection Maternelle Infantile* (Department for the Protection of Maternal and Children's Health) for children aged 0–6.

3.   The child welfare services responsible for administrative protection.

In the struggle to balance children's welfare with respect for parents' rights, the best interests of the child must take precedence in all decisions concerning them, in full accordance with the United Nations Convention on the Rights of the Child (UNCRC). Growing awareness of child maltreatment led to the 1989 law (with a free phone hotline) and to the creation of the *Observatoire de l'action sociale* (ODAS) in 1994, and the *Observatoire national de l'enfance en danger* (ONED) in 2004. The ONED was created to collect more detailed data and figures, evaluate caretaking practices, better coordinate the regional and local authorities and the non-profit organisations and develop survey research.

France's welfare regime

Based on Esping-Andersen's (1990) typology and the clustering of countries according to conservative, liberal and socialist regime attributes, France scores strongly on conservative attributes. It has a medium score with regards to the degree of liberalism and a low score on socialist regime attributes (p.74). Overall, it joins Germany and other continental European countries in the conservative cluster and like others in this group can be seen as corporatist and 'etatist' and fairly modestly de-commodifying (Esping-Andersen 1990, p.77). It can also be seen as family-oriented and committed to citizenship and social rights – arguably, indicative of more liberal social welfare regimes.

Social policy in France adheres to a republican model, in which a predominant role is given to government. As indicated above, the place of children is considered to be within their family, even when they are at risk. Within the French cultural heritage, and the secular tradition in education, social workers privilege the recognition of citizenship.

Legal and policy framework

The French child welfare system traditionally favours the birth family. The law of 1984 reaffirms the family's rights. Keeping a child in his/her family is a priority, but it does not exclude placement options. Each child or family measure must be reviewed annually. When children are placed, their return to the family unit must be prepared. If such a reunification is impossible (due to parental mental illness or serious social pathology, for example), long-term placement is a solution, but parents still keep their parental responsibilities except for the right to keep the child at home. Placement officially stops when the children's judge decides this (the child returns home, generally with an educational measure to support the family) or when a young person reaches the age of majority.

With societal changes (single-parent families, socio-cultural integration difficulties, increasing economic precariousness) important critiques on the child welfare system have emerged (Grevot 2001; Naves and Cathala 2000). The child protection system has been evolving to reinforce preventive measures and improve family and professional relationships. New methods of helping youths are gradually allowing more diversified and better adapted responses to family needs (sequential or alternate hosting, home placement, daytime hosting). The law reforming child protection was voted in, in March 2007. As for ex-care youths who leave 'home' much earlier than their peers, the question of reinforcing their support networks is raised.

Young people leaving care

For three decades, the child welfare system has been offering support when young people in care come of age at 18 (*Jeunes Majeurs*) and to every young adult without adequate family support networks. Requests are filed with local authorities, private agencies or with a children's judge. Young adults receive a personal budget to help with educational or job training projects (grants to finish their studies, driver's licences or other means of transportation, supplies for job training, personal loans). They may stay with their foster families, in residential or specialised institutions, or have independent accommodation. These allowances and financial benefits stop at 21 years of age. After this, the *Jeunes Majeurs* have to face a four-year gap in provision, since welfare allowances are only available from the age of 25 (unless the young adult is head of a household). Some local authorities with special funds and charitable organisations may exceptionally help them until they reach the age of 23.

Transition to adulthood for youths and vulnerable populations

Significant gaps remain in the educational experiences of youths from low-income environments (including most children in care) compared to those from middle- and upper-class environments. Each year, 150,000 youths leave the educational system without any real skills or without academic or technical diplomas, and spend half of the first three years of their economically active lives unemployed (Caille 1999; Trémintin 2002). The importance of obtaining a diploma in order to enter the labour market has been highlighted (Caille 2003).

Between 1982 and 1989, support services and emergency allowances for 16–25-year-olds were created by national, regional and local authorities: informational and guidance structures; social support through contact people tasked with helping youths develop self-confidence; motivational drive; searching for employment; and providing career guidance and group support. In the fields of education, special programmes were created: one against exclusion for 16–18-year-olds without diplomas, providing continuity in training for 18 months with emergency allowances; another for 18–25-year-old French and resident alien youths unable to benefit from other forms of state aid. The 'Youth Aid Funds' gave an average €240 (varying by local authority) to each of the 100,000 young recipients (specific financial aid for food, housing, training, transport and social integration). Other measures were developed in the manufacturing and service sectors, for housing (rent subsidies for workers and students) and health (since 2001, Social Security has made free medical care available to all). Public expenditure increased threefold between 1985 and 1997 for young adults, particularly deprived youths. However, worsening impoverishment of 16–25-year-olds has been observed: one-third live in social reinsertion centres while two-thirds are unemployed and receive no benefits (Trémintin 2002).

Secondary data

Reliable administrative data on the experiences of care leavers do not exist. Furthermore, some data are not retained for longer than five to ten years (judicial data and administrative measures). It is impossible to link administrative data and other data banks. National and regional statistics do not allow care leavers to be singled out. Nevertheless, some large surveys allow us to identify groups who have been in care, allowing comparison with peers and providing a better understanding of some of their experiences. For example, statistics from the Ministry of Education showed that, at entry to the secondary school cycle, 57 per cent of wards of the state, 32 per cent of children with unemployed parents and 16 per cent of those from the lower-income families were already two years behind their peers, or were in classes for slow learners (national average: 13% in 1994).

A study of the National Institute of Demographic Studies comparing 461 vulnerable homeless youths aged 16–24 in the Paris area with their peers found that the former come from lower-income backgrounds, are often born abroad, have suffered maltreatment (35–45%), and that over a third had been placed formerly (Marpsat and Firdion 2001). They are also more likely to have attempted suicide or to have run away, and one-fifth of the males have served jail time. Eight out of ten are housed in emergency or long-term shelters, or in hostels paid for by organisations. Only a third work full time; most are helped out by friends or make do with odd jobs and black market work. They complain of difficulties finding work, lodging, establishing meaningful relationships or of their isolation from family and a lack of affection.

Leaving care research

Studies are difficult to conduct and require deontological (ethical) safeguards: personal consent must be obtained, and most research protocols are submitted to the Freedom and Information Ethics Committee. Some studies were conducted with ASE and/or PJJ populations, others with non-governmental organisations and private institutions. Most of the studies are heterogeneous as to their objectives, their results, and attrition in the samples (Frechon and Dumaret forthcoming). Comparative analysis is difficult as 'the children's legal status (wards of state, temporary or substitute care), the type of foster care provided, the length of separation from the family, and the time spent in care all vary from study to study' (Dumaret and Coppel-Batsch 1998, p.32).

Leaving care – which paths lead to independence?

A few studies on short- and medium-term outcomes analyse needs, material problems and integration strategies. They show that youths are confronted with difficulties in managing lodging, jobs and relationships; most mention feelings of abandonment and a lack of preparation for reaching autonomy. They mention unskilled jobs and the weakness of social support and feelings of guilt that prevent family reunification (Corbillon, Dulery and Mackiewicz 1997). At 24–27 years of age, about 10–25 per cent are still not living autonomously, but live with friends, in residences, or in poor lodgings (Bauer, Dubechot and Legros 1993; Corbillon *et al.* 1997; Frechon 2003). A biographical approach was used by Frechon to study the situation of 68 young women aged 19–32 years, who at 15–17 years old had lived in an educational residence. Analysis of their conjugal, residential and professional evolution show a more rapid progression towards autonomy than in the general population, as determined by employment or marital profile (Frechon 2003, 2005).

Other results indicate transitional situations: subjects generally moved within the first few years and psychiatric hospitalisations ended within two years of them leaving their placements (Frechon 2005; Hubert *et al.* 2006). Only one study of 50 young men aged 24–29 collected data on criminal records (Sawras 1981). Thirty per cent of these care leavers (from institutions) committed misdemeanours, and some of them were imprisoned. Two studies on long-term placements – the CREDOC study of 500 adults 21–24 years old (Bauer *et al.* 1993) and the Grancher Foundation study of 45 adults 23–39 years old – noted that psychosocial difficulties occurred most frequently in the early years after leaving care: alcohol and drug abuse for 13–33 per cent of them; run-ins with police and the courts for 10–15 per cent (Coppel and Dumaret 1995; Dumaret and Coppel-Batsch 1998). Lack of autonomy may explain these difficulties, as findings from several studies indicate that approximately 25 per cent of ex-care adults were still receiving support from social work teams.

Long-term outcomes by placement type, stability, duration of care and age

Better outcomes are observed for those raised in foster families or in family units than those in residential care. Lengthy placements most often lead to higher levels of education, and therefore to better professional qualifications. Ex-care adults possess fewer diplomas than the general population; the opposite is true with technical diplomas. Fewer than 10 per cent obtained a diploma equivalent to or better than the baccalaureate (12 years in school). Unemployment figures vary from 26 per cent to 53 per cent. For young adults who had been raised in children's villages (family units for siblings), unemployment was higher for the 18–25-year-olds than for those aged 30 or above (Dumaret 1982). In samples of older ex-care adults, approximately one-third were home owners (Coppel and Dumaret 1995; Corbillon and Auscher 1990; Corbillon, Assailly and Duyme 1990). Research generally highlights their weak relationship networks and a sense of isolation, related to discontinuity in placement (Gheorghui *et al.* 2002). The importance of choosing a partner or spouse as a means of support has been shown (Dumaret and Coppel-Batsch 1998; Frechon 2003), and psychologists have described the identification models, the pre-eminence of attachment towards a family (foster carers or birth parents) and slow psychological evolution of ex-care patients, which may explain better adaptation among the oldest groups (Dumaret, Coppel-Batsch and Couraud 1997; Mouhot 2001).

In comparison with other types of studies, retrospective studies have found higher proportions of ex-care adults having illegitimate pregnancies or their own children entering care placements (Anaut 1997). However, other studies have shown that inter-generational continuity of care placements is low (rates between 7–11%). Similar results were found in a study in Algeria of 287 children abandoned at birth and assessed at a mean age of 28 (Moutassem-Mimouni 1999). However, studies show that 'social reproduction' remains high: over half of the care leavers later worked in jobs in the same professional category as their parents. A healthy adulthood is generally within reach, even though psychosomatic problems are mentioned 15–20 per cent of the time, but a lack of standardised questionnaires prevents a clear definition of such mental health problems from emerging (Bauer *et al.* 1993; Coppel and Dumaret 1995). Institutional support and therapeutic care during placement has certainly familiarised ex-care adults with this type of help and made them more aware of resources providing help and guidance (Coppel and Dumaret 1995; Frechon 2003). A large number of ex-care adults have been able to mentally integrate their traumatic experiences, particularly when helped by psychologists, psychiatrists and social workers during and after placement.

The negative consequences of severe neglect and abuse have a greater impact on adult integration than the placement itself (Corbillon *et al.* 1990). Cumulative risk factors (family adversity, maltreatment, multiple placements) have a direct effect on adult integration (Dumaret *et al.* 1997). Recently, a study on adults of 23–50 years of age, who had been raised (long term) in children's villages, highlighted severe behaviour and mental health problems during childhood and before leaving care, and their impact on educational outcomes and integration not only at the point of leaving care but also years later (Dumaret, Constantin-Kuntz and Crost 2006, 2007).

Conclusion

Centred on child protection and rehabilitation during the care period, the child welfare services have largely been transformed to adapt to societal changes. Since the end of the welfare state era, a new notion influences the social policy sphere – 'quality process'. The need for evaluation, introduced by law in 2002, will allow the development of research on care practices not only on young adults but also on children leaving care. Research has shown that, compared with people of the same age and social backgrounds, outcomes are less negative than one might think, particularly for those who had stable placements. On the whole, numerous adults recognise that placements offered them a window on the world as well as material improvements to their birth family situation (pocket money, education, stability). However, care leavers' perceptions of having been tossed aside by institutions, with few abilities to cope with the new challenges in their daily life, raise the issue of the need for specific preparation towards autonomy and more active support for all.

Key messages for policy and practice

- Screening for mental health problems in order to meet individual care needs during placement and the transition period.

- Reinforcing support for education and professional training and developing socialisation and communication skills with adults to prevent violence, future isolation and exclusion.

- There is a huge need for specific support for adolescents who return home, particularly in 'at risk' families. Partnership and coordination of all social services should be enhanced.

- The lack of support after 21 years of age must be addressed in order to compensate for deficiencies in family solidarity.

- Private and public institutions should cooperate to develop adequate standards and research tools for evaluation when designing research on outcome of care leavers.

References

Anaut, M. (1997) *Entre Détresse et Abandon, la Répétition Transgénérationnelle Chez les Enfants Placés.* Paris: CTNERHI.

Bauer, D., Dubechot, P. and Legros, M. (1993) *Le Temps de L'établissement: Des Difficultés de L'adolescence aux Insertions du Jeune Adulte.* Paris: CREDOC.

Caille, J.P. (1999) 'Qui sort sans qualification du système éducatif?' *Note d'Information du Ministère de l'Education 30*, 1–6.

Caille, J.P. (2003) 'L'école réduit-elle les inégalités sociales?' *Education et Formations 66*, 177–185.

Coppel, M. and Dumaret, A.C. (1995) *Que Sont-ils Devenus? Les Enfants Placés à l'Œuvre Grancher. Analyse d'un Placement Spécialisé.* Ramonville Saint-Agne: Erès.

Corbillon, M. and Auscher, T. (1990) *Le devenir des enfants placés dans la Nièvre. Convention d'étude. Rapport au Conseil Général de la Nièvre.* Olivet: GERIS.

Corbillon, M., Assailly, J.P. and Duyme, M. (1990) *L'enfant Placé: De l'Assistance Publique à l'Aide Sociale à L'enfance.* Paris: Documents affaires sociales, Ministère de la solidarité, de la santé et de la protection sociale.

Corbillon, M., Duléry, A. and Mackiewicz, M.P. (1997) *Après les Cèdres Bleus... Quel Devenir à l'issue d'un Placement dans une Maison d'Enfants?* Olivet: GERIS. Accessed 01/09/07 at http://oned.gouv.fr

DRESS, Ministère des Affaires Sociales, du Travail et de la Solidarité (2006). 'Les bénéficiaires de l'aide sociale départementale en 2005.' *Etudes et Résultats 514.*

Dumaret, A.C. (1982) *Enquête Sur les Aînés de 18 ans et plus Ayant été Placés en Village d'enfants. Rapports de recherche à l'Association des Villages SOS d'enfants de France.* Paris: Convention d'Etude.

Dumaret, A.C. and Coppel-Batsch, M. (1998) 'Effects in adulthood of separation and long term foster care: A French research study.' *Adoption and Fostering 22,* 1, 31–39.

Dumaret, A.C. and Ruffin, D. (1999) *Bilan Socio-scolaire et Prises en Charge des Jeunes Accueillis en Placement Familial. Analyse des Comportements et Perceptions des Adultes. Rapport de Recherche à la SLEA.* Lyon. Accessed 01/09/07 at http://oned.gouv.fr

Dumaret, A.C., Constantin-Kuntz, M. and Crost, M. (2006) *Devenir adulte des jeunes placés avec leur fratrie au Village d'enfants de Marseille. Rapport final de recherche à l'Association des Villages d'enfants SOS de France.* Villejuif: Inserme-U750, CERMES

Dumaret, A.C., Coppel-Batsch, M. and Couraud, S. (1997) 'Adult outcome of children reared for long term period in foster families.' *Child Abuse and Neglect 21,* 911–927.

Esping-Andersen, G. (1990) *The Three Worlds of Welfare Capitalism.* New Jersey: Princeton University Press.

Frechon, I. (2003) *Insertion Sociale et Familiale de Jeunes Femmes Anciennement Placées en Foyer Socio-éducatif.* Thèse de Doctorat. Paris: Université de Paris X.

Frechon, I. (2005) 'Stratégies féminines d'entrée dans la vie adulte après un placement à l'adolescence.' In E. Callu, J.P. Jurmand and A. Vulbeau (eds) *La Place des Jeunes dans la Cité 2.* Paris: L'Harmattan.

Frechon, I. and Dumaret, A.C. (forthcoming) 'Bilan critique de cinquante ans d'études sur le devenir adulte des enfants placés.' *Neuropsychiatrie de l'Enfrance et de l'Adolescence.*

Gheorghui, M., Labache, L., Legrand C. and Quaglia, M. (2002) *Rapport Final de la Recherche Longitudinale sur le Devenir des Personnes Sorties de l'ase en Seine Saint Denis Entre 1980 Et 2000.* Bobigny. Accessed 01/09/07 at http://oned.gouv.fr

Grevot, A. (2001) *Voyage en Protection de l'enfance. Une Comparaison Européenne.* Vaucresson: CNFE-PJJ.

Hubert, T., Tournyol du Clos, R., Cosio, M. and Fréchon, I. (2006) *Le Devenir des Jeunes Pris en Charge par les Services de la PJJ.* Paris: Centre de Recherche Populations et Sociétés (CERPOS), Université de Paris X, CNFE-PJJ.

INSEE Institut National de la Statistique et des Etudes Economiques (2005, 2007). 'Bilan démographique, enquêtes annuelles de recensement, 2005, 2007.' Accessed 20/02/08 at www.insee.fr/fr/ffc

Marpsat, M. and Firdion, J.M. (2001) 'Les ressources des jeunes sans domicile et en situation précaire.' *Recherches et Prévisions 65,* 91–112.

Mouhot, F. (2001) 'Le devenir des enfants de l'Aide sociale à l'enfance.' *Devenir 13,* 1, 31–66.

Moutassem-Mimouni, B. (1999) 'Devenir adulte des enfants abandonnés à la naissance en Algérie. Etude comparative du devenir des adultes élevés en famille d'accueil et en institution.' *La Psychiatrie de l'Enfant 2,* 623–645.

Naves, P. and Cathala, B. (2000) *Rapport sur les Accueils Provisoires et les Placements d'enfants et d'adolescents.* Paris: La Documentation Française, tomes I et II.

Observatoire National de l'enfance en danger (ONED) (2005, 2006) *Rapports Annuels au Parlement et au Gouvernement.* Accessed 01/09/07 at http://oned.gouv.fr

Sawras, J. (1981) *Le passé, le Séjour, le Devenir des Garçons cas 'Sociaux' Ayant été Placés dans un Foyer de Semi-liberté (Étude Portant sur 108 Adolescents).* Thèse de Doctorat. Paris: Université de Paris VIII.

Trémintin, J. (2002) 'Le problème de l'accompagnement dans l'entrée de la société adulte.' *Journal du Droit des Jeunes 212*, 26–29.

Chapter 5

Germany

Stefan Köngeter, Wolfgang Schröer and Maren Zeller

Background and key statistics

- Germany is home to around 82.4 million people, approximately one in seven of whom are children under the age of 15.

- In 2005, a total of 112,170 young people received care, representing 64 children per 10,000 of the population.

- Children in care are most commonly placed in residential care homes (living units or assisted living for young people); less than half are placed with a foster family (50,364 placements in 2005).

- 20,930 young people left care in 2005, more than half of whom were aged 15 to 18 years, less than 40 per cent were aged 18–21 years, and about 5 per cent were 21 years old or above.

- More than half of these young people leave care before the age of 18.

Key sources

- *Arbeitsstelle Kinder- und Jugendhilfestatistik* – Research Centre for Child and Youth Service Statistics, Dortmund University, Germany.

- *Statistisches Bundesamt Deutschland* – Federal Statistics Office Germany.

Introduction

In Germany research on children and young people growing up in care has a socio-pedagogical tradition, dating back more than a hundred years, in which the transition to adulthood is considered successful if care leavers do not become delinquent in future years, pass through the educational system, find employment, and are able to live independently. The focus on these institutionally defined normative categories of the life course – and consequently on the disciplinary measures towards young people in residential care – was seriously challenged by socio-political criticism during the 1960s and 1970s. Against this background, the introduction of the Social Security Code VIII (SGB VIII) in 1990 emphasised support and services through a significant increase in the provision of easily accessible assistance for families and young people, to increase their capacity to cope with everyday life. However, these laws were still oriented along the lines of a standard life course, in respect of young people's transitions to adulthood. Only recently have the shortcomings of this approach concerning work and education been noticed (Schröer 2004). In current research on residential child care and education, the biographical dimension is increasingly reflected in so far as the social status of care leavers and their chances of participation are analysed by means of subject-oriented and biographical methods.

Case examples[1]

Ina

After Ina's parents separated when she was seven years old, she lived alternately with her father and her mother. Disputes continued to arise and then escalated when her mother moved in with a new partner. After visiting a child guidance centre Ina, now aged 14, moved into a residential home. There she started taking drugs and dropped out of school. She was almost 16 when the Youth Welfare Office gave her a last chance. Ina seized this chance and moved into a small living unit for girls in a different city. Here she gave up drug abuse with the help of a therapist and prepared for her final school examinations. She also moved into an apartment that became available in the house and, thus, moved to assisted living for young people. The service expired as soon as she started training as a salesperson when she was 19 years old.

Marion

Having had a difficult family background herself, Marion had a baby when she was 17 years of age. She was not able to cope with this situation and for the first three months her child was placed with a foster family. She was required by the Youth Welfare Office to have a fixed abode as a condition for her child's return, a condition which she fulfilled. Shortly afterwards, Marion's current partner moved in. In order to supplement the family's income, Marion decided against obtaining her qualifications and instead took up a job. Another pregnancy brought another crisis. After hesitating for a long time she appealed to the Youth Welfare Office for support. Subsequent to the birth of her second child Marion received family support and child guidance. In twice-annual care planning reviews the objectives and the intensity of care assistance are agreed and possible employment opportunities are discussed with Marion.

Germany's welfare regime

Conservative welfare regime within a socio-pedagogical tradition

Germany can be considered as the ideal type of the conservative welfare state regime (Esping-Andersen 1990). Its main characteristics are a medium degree of de-commodification, the determination of benefits and entitlements by occupation and social status, traditional parenthood and traditional gender roles, and intermediate social bodies, such as churches and non-profit welfare organisations. However, despite all these factors, this classification of the welfare state system does not fully explain the thinking behind the provision of child and youth services in the German welfare system. There is also a socio-pedagogical tradition that stresses the education and upbringing of children and young people as well as the counselling of their parents. This practice, which moreover is affected by the strong position of the welfare organisations, made it possible to provide parents and their children with flexible forms of assistance at an early stage. In the last 30 years non-residential forms of assistance, such as educational counselling, family assistance, social group work, and so forth, have supplemented residential care and have been made a part of the welfare system.

Legal and policy framework
Child and Youth Care Act – SGB VIII

In Germany, the basic legal framework for child rearing support (*Erziehungshilfen*) is the SGB VIII. Hence, Germany as a federal state with its 16 *Bundesländer* and more than 320 urban and rural authority districts (town councils) has on the one hand a coherent piece of social legislation at the federal level and on the other the municipalities, which are seen as responsible for the implementation of the welfare services at the local level: thereby, the principle of subsidiarity[2] is of central relevance to German social legislation – particularly for the care and education of children and young people.

As a federal legal framework, the SGB VIII determines the requirements and the conditions for the realisation of care and education of children and youths in Germany. The central point of this framework, pertaining to all young people until the age of 27,[3] is the child's right to assistance in its upbringing and education.[4] This right of the child is closely related to the natural right of the parents to provide this care and education.[5] Therefore, the family, as a site for the assistance and education of the child, is assigned a major role, whereas the state in terms of the principle of subsidiarity oversees this obligation, and in particular supports the parents to claim their legal entitlement. Accordingly, the range of social services in the domain of care and education has been expanded, a legal entitlement to child rearing support has been implemented (cf. SGB VIII, §27), and numerous opportunities to participate in the arrangement of care have been offered to the family.

The implementation of the state's policy is carried out by the statutory local services for child and youth care and education, and this is usually put into practice by the communal Child and Youth Welfare Office. However, the SGB VIII explicitly draws attention to the 'variety of bodies' that may provide services and to the option that services can be provided by private bodies as well,[6] so that the majority of child rearing support is performed by such institutions. Nevertheless, the Child and Youth Welfare Office has a major role, as it is responsible for the whole process of care management. This complex connection (Schwabe 1996) between parents, young people and statutory and private bodies determines the legal situation for children receiving care.

The two main types of placements in Germany are full-time fostering (§33) and residential care (§34), which usually occurs in decentralised group homes. For young people aged 16 and over the situation is more complex, since as under-aged persons they depend on their parents to apply for care assistance – even though there may be conflicting interests. For young people there are two possible forms of assistance. First, the youth welfare system continues supporting them (SGB VIII, §41) either in the form of (single or group) accommodation with social worker support (assisted living) or with non-residential assistance (for example, counselling). Second, as part of becoming independent, during the transition to adulthood, their entry into vocational training and employment, among other things, is of vital importance. In this regard, the SGB II (basic security for job-seekers) and the SGB III (employment promotion) become relevant for socially disadvantaged young people leaving care. In particular, a number of new divisions have emerged in practice between the SGB II and the SGB VIII since the implementation of the SGB II in early 2005. As part of these new legal guidelines, employable young people receive basic social services and a partly pedagogically oriented assistance. Although the SGB VIII has a clear legal priority when the interests of the child are concerned, in practice it can be observed that the municipalities administer the provision of services for youths aged between 16 and 18 considerably more stringently. Thus, more and more young people leave care early, and the legal scope of the SGB II is applied to them, which stresses the principles of demand and support.

Secondary data

In Germany, information on benefits claims for care and education is held on an extensive and complex database.[7] Some information, however, is missing, including: information on the situation of former care recipients, after they have left care; whether care leavers seek state services again; whether they have become integrated into the job market; how they manage their family lives, and so forth. Nevertheless, from the existing data an initial impression of the number of claims for care and education in Germany can be drawn, and some hypotheses on the problem of transition can be developed. In 2000 the number of people in residential and foster care (SGB VIII, §33, §34) was 152,932[8] and in 2005 it was 145,397. In relation to the total population of the relevant age, these numbers indicate a ratio of 64 per 10,000 young people under the age of 21 receiving child rearing support (Fendrich and Pothmann 2006). While the number receiving non-residential assistance has increased over the years (ibid), a decline in foster and residential care has recently been detected. A breakdown of the data shows that this decrease only applies to residential care (§34) and other forms of assisted living (-11.4%), while there has been a moderate rise (+2.8%) in (full-time) foster care (§33). The importance of this phenomenon for our purposes becomes clear when we look at the figures for current care according to §34 by the relevant age groups (see Table 5.1).

Table 5.1: Current provision of residential care (according to §34) by age group

Age group (years)	Current residential care (according to §34)		
	2000	*2005*	*% change*
15–18	25,843	25,200	-2
18–21	12,312	9,032	-27
>21	987	919	-7
Total	**39,142**	**35,151**	**-10**

Residential care for young people has generally declined, the biggest drop occurring in the 18 and over age group. It can thus be assumed that these statistical findings result from 'regulative strategies and activities of the Child and Youth Welfare Offices' (Pothmann 2005, p.2) – as there is no evidence of demographic changes or a decreasing burden in the socio-economic situation of the young people and their families (BMAS 2005). The data, therefore, show a trend that has been recognised for a long time in professional practice, resulting from cuts made by many authority districts (Schilling 2006): in general care provision has become increasingly restrictive, particularly for the group of young people who have reached the age of majority. Furthermore, data focusing on the termination of assistance (see Table 5.2) are of interest in exploring transitions to adulthood.

Table 5.2: Terminated assistance by age group

Terminated assistance of full-time foster care and residential care (according to §§33 and 34) by age group (years)	2000	2005	% change
15–18	10,919	11,263	+3
18–21	9,101	8,597	-6
>21	1,206	1,070	-11
Total	**21,226**	**20,930**	**-1**

In 2005, 20,930 young people aged 15 to 21 (or above) 'terminated assistance'. In 2005, a third of assistance (under §34) ended once the stated objectives had been achieved. A fifth dropped out at their own instigation, or at that of the person with custody, and a further fifth made the transition to alternative (mostly non-residential) provisions and assistance. Approximately two-thirds of young people aged 18 or above (according to §34) moved to independent living after leaving residential care. Of those in the youngest age group (aged 15 to 18) more than half (55%) return to their parents.[9] The category 'without fixed abode' accounts for 8 per cent of young people and is mostly made up of those aged between 18 and 21. More than half of the young people were aged between 15 and 18 years old when receipt of assistance ended. For most of these young people the transition into adulthood and vocational life begins at the point of leaving care. For this group the risky 'transition' period is at a younger age and is much more rapid than for others (but similar to socially underprivileged young people under 18). The precarious situation facing care leavers is illustrated in Table 5.3. It indicates that almost a third of these young adults were neither attending school nor undertaking vocational training when their assistance ended.

Table 5.3: School / training at the time of the completion of assistance (residential care / §34, 2005)

Age group (years)	School	Professional training	Neither
15–18	61%	19%	20%
18–21	25%	43%	32%
>21	10%	46%	44%

Leaving care research

Criminal behaviour and school and vocational success

Three major studies have been carried out into the criminal behaviour, as well as into the educational and the vocational success, of young care leavers in Germany. First, an early study by Pongratz and Hübner (1959) examined, by means of a standardised survey ($n = 960$) undertaken five to seven years after the young people had left care, whether they had proved themselves in the areas of responsibility, work and social life. The study itself qualifies its results, as it could not control for environmental factors in relation to the indicators. However, it introduced the term '*Lebensbe-währung*' (proving oneself in life) to the research on residential care in Germany and furthermore called attention to the 'fate' of care leavers in the 1950s.

The second study (Bieback-Diel 1978) was carried out around the time the age of majority was reduced to 18 (during 1975). It questioned whether young people in residential care were prepared for the transition to adulthood at the age of 18, as they would require appropriate educational qualifications. The study was based on a written survey of 29 statu-

tory bodies in seven federal states in which the co-workers gave information on the situation of 453 care leavers. Findings revealed the limited
school success of young care leavers. This study was significant as it was
the first to highlight 'school success' as an indicator.

The third study examined school or vocational qualifications and
'criminal behaviour in the sense of the avoidance of social exclusion as a
result of judicial sanctions', on the basis of a complete survey of two age
groups ($n = 222$) released from residential care (Bürger 1990, p.42). On
the basis of the findings it was suggested that 'the claim that residential
care is a breeding ground for delinquency which disturbs social participation, is wrong' (Bürger 1990, p.193).

Studies on the effect of residential care

In the broad spectrum of studies into the effects of residential care, two
directions of research, each having different criteria and disciplinary backgrounds, can be distinguished: (1) studies on personality development and
psychologically defined challenging behaviour and (2) studies using
socio-pedagogical criteria (e.g. coping with life's challenges).

In addition to the comprehensive study of Hansen (1994), which is
representative of a whole range of studies on personality development, a
study into the effects of assistance on young people (Jugendhilfe Effekte
Studie 2002) can be singled out. It is a representative longitudinal section
study in which 233 cases were examined. In particular psychological
means of measurement were used for the evaluation of the effect of the different forms of care. In addition to the young person's overall challenging
behaviour (according to ICD-10), functional level (the age-appropriate
perception of development tasks) and distressing factors in their environment were measured. At the termination of the assistance the research
group calculated an average reduction of 34.4 per cent in the child's overall
challenging behaviour. These effects proved to be stable a year later (at
follow-up).

The research group Jugendhilfeleistungen Studie (JULE) (1998) chose
a broader socio-pedagogical approach. By means of a representative file
analysis, 284 cases were examined. Seven categories were used to evaluate

the course and the success of the assistance: school and vocational training situation, criminal behaviour, social relations, life management, personality development, family background, and central constellation of problems. According to that research, the individual development of the young person is the central frame of reference, but needs to be considered in the context of different living situations. The level achieved also needs to be considered with reference to young people's circumstances and functioning at the outset (starting point) (Jugendhilfeleistungen Studie 1998, p.20). The findings of the study show that assistance was successful in 57 per cent of all cases, and that in 16 per cent positive aspects could be drawn. So in about three-quarters of the cases the situation was at least improved. Of particular relevance for research on transition is the second part of the study, in which by means of qualitative interviews the benefit of the assistance four to five years after its termination was balanced. Even though no statistical representation is certain, the positive balances and the retrospective high satisfaction with the assistance and the current living situation showed that the achievements of residential care were maintained (Jugendhilfeleistungen Studie 1998, p.517).

Subject-oriented and biographical analysis research

Subject-oriented research, which mostly uses biographical research methods, has been used, particularly in academic theses in the domain of care and education, since the beginning of the 1990s. Yet, in only three of these studies (Finkel 2004; Normann 2003; Wieland et al. 1992) were interviews with young adults conducted after assistance ended. These studies focused mainly on recipients' subjective coping performance and on learning and development processes. Finkel's study (2004) is based on 15 biographical narrative interviews, in which young women were questioned retrospectively about their lives approximately three years after leaving care. The results show that the ability to connect biographically developed patterns of actions, and coping with institutional benefits, plays a central role. Young women's capacity to obtain an adequate lifestyle significantly depended upon the support they received as they strove to become independent.

Normann's research (2003) was based on eight guided interviews with young adults who had left care between six months and seven years earlier. Findings revealed that early independence for young adults was difficult and constituted an 'excessive demand' upon them. Normann critically observed that independence was prescribed when certain criteria were fulfilled from the perspective of the Youth Welfare Office, and not when the time was right from the young person's perspective (Normann 2003, p.158). In this context, a qualitative study that accompanied a federal pilot scheme called INTEGRA (2004), and which focused on the integrated organisation of education and care (for instance by means of youth welfare stations), proved that knowledge of the option of a further possible period of support in a youth welfare station after the termination of assistance was of relevance for the recipients (Peters and Koch 2004; Zeller 2006). Beyond such pilot schemes the option for further support is usually only given through 'private' contact between single co-workers and former recipients.

Transition

By and large, the studies reported so far take transition into account only implicitly. Systematic research using the term 'transition', in a theoretically established manner, has yet to be developed in the context of care and education. However, some first attempts at such an approach have emerged in the last few years. These were initiated by research on youth careers and the transition of young people into employment, but they remain attached to an institutionally oriented point of view on the job market and educational system. For instance, secondary analysis of statistical data on vocational and social integration of young people who received residential care (Pies and Schrapper 2001) examined whether these young people had 'specific problems' in the transition into employment, and whether appropriate support for young people of legal age – although the law permits it (as laid out in §41 of KJHG) – was lacking. Unsatisfactory performance in school, as well as subsequent difficulties in finding adequate vocational training, were identified again. These interpretations were the starting point for an EU Equal Development Partnership in three federal states of East Germany.

It can be assumed that young care leavers bear a 'double disadvantage', since their life chances are limited by the regional job market situation as well as by their respective life situations. According to this, these young people have to overcome biographical challenges that additionally hamper their access to the job market. Moreover, their supportive network does not usually provide any appropriate economic, social, or cultural capital which could ensure equal opportunities for them (Köngeter, Schröer and Zeller 2006). The projects of the Equal Development Partnership attempt to establish a network between care bodies, employment promotions, and local employment offices.

Perspective: transition research – domains of the individual ability to act

In the future, research into the transition of young care leavers in Germany will need to broaden its scope from the more institutional perspective including: indicators of educational and employment success; normative development requirements; and occasionally on crime statistics. A wider approach would include the recipient-oriented perspective, which, starting from 'criticism of the bureaucracy of expertise and institutions' (Bitzan, Bolay and Thiersch 2006), has influenced the reform of residential care in the past 30 years and finally made subject-oriented research possible. Following this approach, the term 'transition' provides – in our opinion – further understanding, for the reason that the 'institutional perspective' is not set in opposition to the biographical subject-oriented one. In fact, according to this term, residential care is considered as an area within the social domain, in which development processes of the individual ability to act can be analysed. Therefore, future research into the transition of young care leavers into adulthood would need to devise indicators to measure the development of the subjective ability to act in terms of social factors and thus also provide room for institutional manoeuvre.

Conclusion

Germany can be considered as the 'ideal type' of the conservative welfare state system. Nevertheless, there is a strong socio-pedagogical tradition that stresses different forms of social services for young people and their parents. For young care leavers there are two possible forms of assistance. First, the youth welfare system continues supporting them either in the form of accommodation with social worker support or with non-residential assistance. Second, the social codes of 'basic security for job-seekers' and 'employment promotion' provide basic social services and a partly pedagogically oriented assistance. There is an extensive database of claims or benefits for care and education. The data show a growing gap in the socio-educational support for care leavers. However, some information is missing on the situation of care leavers. A systematic body of research using a theoretically established concept of transition has not yet been developed. However, catamnestic[10] research has shown that the positive effects of residential care prove to be stable after leaving care. In the future it will be necessary to improve the social services provided to young care leavers, especially by establishing participation-oriented cooperation in the different parts of the welfare system. The basis for this is research which concentrates systematically on pedagogical attitudes that take the subjective perspective of transition into account.

Key messages for policy and practice

- Social services and support for young care leavers should be provided at least up to the age of 25.

- The deeper involvement of the children in their residential and foster care placements and in the process of their transition into adulthood is necessary.

- Cooperation between the different social services providing residential care, school and job centre case management should be established.

- The transition to adulthood is the key point to improve sustainability in residential and foster care.

- The database of young care leavers and children in residential and foster care has to be improved and structured in a systematic way.

- Further research should concentrate on pedagogical attitudes from the perspective of those in transition and not just on evidence-based criteria.

Notes

1. Both examples are quoted from biographical interviews conducted with young women that have received care (Zeller 2008).

2. Subsidiarity is interpreted in different ways. In the domain of child and youth care its meaning refers to welfare; in the domain of basic social security for job-seekers it has a liberal market meaning ('demanding and supporting').

3. This right also pertains for young people without a German passport, though only as long as they hold a residence permit.

4. 'Every young person has a right to assistance in his or her development and to an appropriate upbringing so that he or she can be a responsible member of society' (SGB VIII, §1, para. 1).

5. 'Care, upbringing, and education of children are the natural right of parents and their primary duty. The public community watches over the fulfilment of that duty' (SGB VIII, §1, para. 2).

6. With the introduction of the Child and Youth Care Act (KJHG) individuals and private bodies can function as providers of social services as well.

7. The Child and Youth Act specifies which data are collected, and in which time-frame, for the nationwide child and youth care statistics (SGB VIII §98–§103).

8. Summation of care cases that were continuing on the 31st of December and terminating in the upcoming new year (Fendrich and Pothmann 2006).

9. The category 'parents' involves 'single parent with step-parent/partner' or 'single parent' as well.

10. The medical history of a patient following an illness; the follow-up history.

References

Arbeitsstelle Kinder- und Jugendhilfestatistik (Research Centre for Child and Youth Service Statistics) Germany: Dortmund University. Accessed 07/08/07 at www.akjstat.uni-dortmund.de

Bieback-Diel, L. (1978) *Heimerziehung- und was dann? Zur Problematik Heimentlassener Jugendlicher und Junger Erwachsener.* Frankfurt: Institut für Sozialarbeit und Sozialpädagogik (Schriftenreihe).

Bitzan, M., Bolay, E. and Thiersch, H. (2006) *Die Stimme der Adressaten. Empirische Forschung über Erfahrungen von Mädchen und Jungen mit der Jugendhilfe.* Weinheim/München: Juventa.

BMAS (ed.) (2005) *Lebenslagen in Deutschland. Der 2. Armuts- und Reichtumsbericht.* Berlin: Schriftenreihe des BMAS.

Bürger, U. (1990) *Heimerziehung und Soziale Teilnahmechancen.* Pfaffenweiler: Centaurus.

Esping-Andersen, G. (1990) *The Three Worlds of Welfare Capitalism.* New Jersey: Princeton University Press.

Fendrich, S. and Pothmann, J. (2006) 'Umsteuerung bei den Hilfen zur Erziehung setzt sich weiter fort. Zahl der familienersetzenden Hilfen rückläufig.' *KOM^{DAT} Jugendhilfe 9,* 3, 2.

Finkel, M. (2004) *Selbständigkeit und etwas Glück. Einflüsse öffentlicher Erziehung auf die Perspektive Junger Frauen.* Weinheim/München: Juventa.

Hansen, G. (1994) *Die Persönlichkeitsentwicklung von Kindern in Erziehungsheimen. Ein empirischer Beitrag zur Sozialisation durch Institutionen der öffentlichen Erziehungshilfe.* Weinheim: Deutscher Studienverlag.

Jugendhilfe Effekte Studie (JES) (2002) *Effekte erzieherischer Hilfen und ihre Hintergründe.* Stuttgart: Kohlhammer.

Jugendhilfeleistungen Studie (JULE) (1998) *Leistungen und Grenzen von Heimerziehung. Ergebnisse einer Evaluationsstudie stationärer und teilstationärer Erziehungshilfen.* Stuttgart: Kohlhammer.

Köngeter, S., Schröer, W. and Zeller, M. (2006) *PAKT – Neue Übergänge in Beschäftigung. Kooperation von Kinder- und Jugendhilfe und Beschäftigungshilfen.* Accessed 05/08/07 at http://equal-pakt.de/downloads/Evaluationsmodul_1_Zielfindung.pdf

Normann, E. (2003) *Erziehungshilfen in biografischen Reflexionen. Heimkinder erinnern sich.* Weinheim: BeltzVotum.

Peters, F. and Koch, J. (2004) *Integrierte erzieherische Hilfen. Flexibilität, Integration und Sozialraumbezug inder Jugendhilfe.* Weinheim/München: Juventa.

Pies, S. and Schrapper, C. (2001) *Studie zur Beruflichen und Sozialen Integration Junger Menschen aus Einrichtungen Stationärer Erziehungshilfe in Rheinland-Pfalz.* Accessed 10/05/07 at www.uni-koblenz.de/sempaed/soz_pae

Pongratz, L. and Hübner, H.O. (1959) *Lebensbewährung nach öffentlicher Erziehung. Eine Hamburger Untersuchung über das Schicksal aus der Fürsorge-Erziehung und der Freiwilligen Erziehungshilfe entlassener Jugendlicher.* Darmstadt u.a.: Luchterhand.

Pothmann, J. (2005) 'Rolle rückwärts in der Heimerziehung?' *KOM^{DAT} Jugendhilfe 8,* 2, 2.

Schilling, M. (2006) 'Konsolidierungskurs für die Kinder- und Jugendhilfe – Ausgabenentwicklung stagniert.' *KOM^{DAT} Jugendhilfe 9,* 3, 1–2.

Schröer, W. (2004) 'Befreiung aus dem Moratorium? Zur Entgrenzung von Jugend.' In K. Lenz, W. Schefold and W. Schröer (eds) *Entgrenzte Lebensbewältigung.* Weinheim/München: Juventa.

Schwabe, M. (1996) 'Wer sind unsere Kunden? Wie definieren sich unsere Aufträge? Worin bestehen unsere Leistungen? Wie die Dienstleistungs-Metapher der Jugendhilfe zu neuen Einsichten verhelfen kann!' *Widersprüche 16,* 59, 11–29.

Statistisches Bundesamt Deutschland (Federal Statistics Office Germany). Accessed 07/08/07 at www.destatis.de/jetspeed/portal/cms

Wieland, N., Marquard, U., Panhorst, H. and Schlotmann, H.O. (1992) *Ein Zuhause – Kein Zuhause. Lebenserfahrungen und Entwürfe Heimentlassener Junger Erwachsener.* Freiburg im Breisgau: Lambertus.

Zeller, M. (2006) 'Die Perspektiven von AdressatInnen als Ausgangspunkt für die Weiterentwicklung flexibler, integrierter und sozialraumorientierte Erziehungshilfen.' In M. Bitzan, E. Bolay and H. Thiersch (eds) *Die Stimme der Adressaten.* Weinheim/München: Juventa.

Zeller, M. (2008) 'Forschungsnotiz – Lern- und Bildungsprozesse von Mädchen in belasteten Lebenslagen.' *Forum Erziehungshilfen.*

Chapter 6

Hungary

Mária Herczog

Background and key statistics

- Hungary has a population of about ten million inhabitants, including 2,180,666 children under the age of 18 (2006).

- 225,365 children and young people are at risk (10.3%), 18,813 (0.86%) are registered as in need of special protection and 21,216 (0.97%) are in public care (December 2005).

- 9981 (47%) of children in care were placed in residential care – among them 4249 in group homes – others in traditional children's homes and 11,235 (53%) in foster care (among them 2061 in 400 professional foster families).

- 4240 young persons (24.3% of all children in the care system) are provided with after care services, 2189 in residential homes, 1930 in foster care (most of them living in their former placements) and 1631 living independently.

- In 2005–2006 young adults receiving after care were aged between 18 and 24. Those studying or who cannot take care of themselves (unemployed, lack of accommodation opportunities) can stay in care until they are 24 years of age.

- Among those receiving after care services, 705 young persons spent more than 17 years in care, and 615 between 10 and 16 years.

- 1144 persons left the care system at the age of 18, and 1178 as their after care ended by 31 December 2005.

Key sources

- Central Statistical Office, Budapest (2007).
- Department of Child and Youth Protection, Budapest (2006).

Introduction

Hungary's current legislation on child welfare and child protection was introduced in 1997. It is based on the principles of the UN Convention on the Rights of the Child (UNCRC) which Hungary ratified in 1991. The preparation of the 1997 law took a long time, as the previous legislation dated back to 1901. The 1901 Act was a progressive and comprehensive piece of legislation, at that time, declaring the State's responsibility for the well-being of children under 15. In 1948 the age limit was changed and young people in public care could stay until the age of 18.

The state agencies responsible for children and young people in care have changed over time: from the Ministry of Education (up until 1986), to the Ministry of Social Affairs, which changed its name to Health and Social Policy, then to Family, Youth, Equal Opportunities and Social Affairs, and from 2006, to the Ministry of Social Affairs and Labour. These changes reflected changes in ideological and theoretical approaches. The area of child protection and welfare was seen as an educational problem concerning both children and their parents – based on the Soviet model of telling and teaching people what is good for them. Not until the late 1980s was it recognised as a social issue, resulting from changes in the political situation that allowed acceptance of the existence of poverty and social deprivation. Prior to this it had been considered as a private mistake or 'bad habit', not as a social phenomenon. The introduction of social work as a profession in the late 1980s had a dramatic effect on the way child welfare was thought about, but its impact on practice has just started to be visible in the last couple of years.

From 1993 the operation of services was decentralised, leading to a very fragmented system. The administrative organisation included Budapest, the 19 counties and 3177 local authorities. As the daily operation of services, and resource problems such as variable service provision, became a growing and visible issue, regulations were introduced to encourage closer, sub-regional cooperation. This has led to many joint institutions, schools, social and medical services, and smaller settlements providing joint services. This in principle should guarantee higher professional standards and more opportunities. However, because of the lack of resources, transportation problems, and political and financial conflicts of interest, many smaller communities lack regular basic child welfare services, as well as health visitors and GPs. There has been an ongoing shortage of professionals – social workers, psychologists, psychiatrists – in the least privileged part of the country, often leading to either placement of the child outside the family or lack of any attention to their needs.

The local service providers are registering 'children in need', but there is no universally accepted definition or measurement of this category. Those at risk can voluntarily ask for, or accept, services provided by local organisations. In the case of more severe problems, children can be put on a special register, placing the parents and children under an obligation to follow professional advice. In cases where there is no local service provision, children are often placed outside the family. These actions may be taken on the basis of social work and agency beliefs, rather than based on evaluation and assessment of prior activities and interventions (even though documentation is obligatory). The most probable causes are poverty related, but there may be many additional risk factors, following the root cause. Once children are placed out of home the chances of family reunification decrease, parallel with the amount of time spent in the care system.

The political-economic transition period has had a two-sided effect. First, the economic crisis led to the collapse of the former economic structure, and while unemployment was growing rapidly, state revenues and family incomes did not increase. Second, Hungary had a strong social welfare system – called an 'early-born' one (Kornai 1992) – meaning it was too expensive and too widespread and universal compared to the development stage and opportunities of the economy.

The ideological, professional and structural changes in the Hungarian child welfare and child protection system have been influenced by a mixture of components, including 'imported' ideas and experiences from different parts of the world. The American and British influence can be seen, but without the traditions and conditions for their adaptation. The Austrian and German influence, although culturally closer, has not been in favour, as the introduction of social work and its educational background was seen as being derived from the 'old ways' of thinking. The Nordic examples have always been mentioned as an 'ideal social democratic' way of managing social welfare and child protection programmes, but the main argument against this was lack of wealth and availability of resources, as well as the different social climate.

The current Hungarian child protection system, influenced strongly by the English Children Act 1989, is based on the preventative approach. In principle, children and families should be provided with all possible forms of help and support locally, as close as possible to the family. In practice most of those in need are not well informed, lack basic information on the eligibility criteria and do not have access to many services or help. Placing children out of the family cannot be based on exclusively financial reasons, though according to research data one-third of the cases are in this category, despite the prohibition of this in the legislation (Herczog 2007).

The decision-making procedure on placement is based on an assessment and placement meeting, to which all professionals involved should be invited, together with the family and children (depending on their maturity and age). In practice the lack of proper placements – not enough foster families and suitable therapeutic placements – means that children are directed to vacant places. Despite the compulsory planning and reviewing procedure, based on the Hungarian adaptation of the Looking After Children Assessment and Documentation system, most of the children do not have proper assessments, personalised care plans or services. Often, only a formal review is carried out and children are trapped into the care system with very poor outcomes in terms of their educational level, health and opportunities for a successful, independent life.

In practice, the 'rescue model' is still dominant but without evaluation of the effects of out-of-home placement. The number of foster families has been increasing since the mid-1980s, but in the last couple of years only those counties where the unemployment rate is very high can recruit enough carers. Older, troubled and Roma children, or those with special needs – disability, behavioural problems and a history of abuse – are hard to place, as are those who have an intense relationship with their biological family.

The proportion of older and multi-problem young people coming into care is growing fast, showing both the weakness of local services and the growing awareness of the disadvantages of institutionalisation. The basic problem is that knowledge of the negative impact of out-of-home care is not accompanied with more careful local service provision nor with evaluation or outcome measurement of the different interventions, or the responsibility and accountability of those making decisions and providing services.

Case examples

Anna

Anna requested a placement in a residential home at the age of 13 with her two younger siblings – aged seven and ten – after their father died and their mother started drinking and cohabiting with an abusive alcoholic man. She got pregnant at the age of 15, and her 16-year-old partner ended up in a detention centre after committing criminal offences. She wanted to keep the baby. She continued her studies at a secondary grammar school and aimed to be placed together with her siblings and the baby in a foster home. After her 18th birthday, she was offered after care and was able to stay with the mother of her partner, where he joined them later. As the relationship with her partner broke down, she moved into a rented room with further financial help. At the age of 20 she was still studying and taking good care of her daughter and the other two siblings. She was eligible for the 'life starting' allowance which was enough to pay the rent for two years, but not sufficient for buying an apartment or house. As her income is low and the minimum amount for a bank loan is 50 per cent of the price of the real estate, she does not have any hope of owning her own property.

John

John, a Roma child, spent his entire childhood, from birth, in the care system. He lived in different residential homes, partly due to the reorganisation of the system, and partly because of the obligation (at the time) to place children according to their age in different institutions. He was separated from his four siblings and had very limited contact with them. As a Roma child with learning and behavioural difficulties it was not possible to place him in foster care. He did not finish special needs schooling, or get any job or training. He left the care system at the age of 18. His biological family took all the 'life starting' money that he received from the state. Subsequently he ended up homeless, a substance user, unemployed and having different partners, mostly young women, who were also brought up in the care system. The social worker responsible for his after care could not help him because of the lack of services and because John disappeared from time to time and could not be found. He was offered different vocational courses but because of his learning difficulties he could not finish any of them. He was looking for unskilled work. His family were not interested in him once they had spent his money and his siblings were in similar situations.

Hungary's welfare regime

According to Esping-Andersen's (1990) typology Hungary is hard to place, based on the country's changing social–economic situation since the transition from Communism. There is a new category used for the countries in the region: post-socialist welfare models, as one of the leading Hungarian social policy experts, Julia Szalai, describes in her new book (Szalai 2007). The mixture of a liberal–social democratic model is most probable for the future, and the features of the current system seem to be closer to this than any other type. The leading Socialist Party is committed to a social democratic vision of the welfare model, but not agreeing on the basics, namely the fundamental nature of the health and social welfare model, with their liberal coalition partner. There is pressure to make fast decisions and steps because of the declining socio-economic situation.

The former and existing model is a mixed conservative–liberal model taking into consideration the fact that for 50 years Hungary had a system which originated from a semi-feudal and not very well-developed capitalistic heritage. After the Second World War, it was transformed into a Soviet-type centralised authoritarian welfare model, and since the 1980s has an ongoing overspend caused by the deep structural and social tensions which originated from this. The underdevelopment and weakness of independent civil society is leading to a struggle for power, resulting in political and state control over resources once again, instead of a decrease in state power. As Zsuzsa Ferge (2000), the well-known theorist, says, there is a liberal rhetoric with a voluntaristic practice present. The financial support and service provided is not coherent, often based on local decision making, opportunities and personal devotion. It has not been accompanied by any planning, coaching, evaluation or assessment of outcomes, despite the requirements of the legislation.

Legal and policy framework

The legal framework for care leavers is part of the Child Protection Law (1997/XXXI). This states that everyone spending at least three years continuously in the care system, ending with his/her adulthood, is entitled to support setting up a home. It is not automatic; young people have to apply for it and the County Custodian Office makes a decision based on their circumstances.

The sum is given if the young person's own wealth is not greater than an amount equal to 60 times the minimum old age pension. The former sum of the family allowance, allowance for orphaned children and his/her own income from work cannot be taken into consideration. The money can be used for buying any kind of property or renovation. In exceptional cases it can be used to pay for a placement in a special needs home for the disabled. The young person must cooperate with the after care social worker as a condition of eligibility. The participation in after care, in case of financial aid, is compulsory, lasting until the settlement of accounts, but for a maximum of one year. The amount given to young people depends on the length of stay in the system: the longer they spend in care the more they get. For four years spent in care, 40 times the minimum old age pension is given; after five years, it goes up to 60 times. In cases where property is bought, the State has the right to ensure that it will not be sold for up to five years.

Children under the age of 18 living in out-of-family placements, depending on their status, are eligible for different allowances and financial support. For those in the care system the monthly family allowance is put in a special bank account they can access after leaving the care system, at the age of 18 (with a few exceptions such as marrying earlier and legally becoming an adult). This sum can be used during their care with the permission of the custodian office. Health care and education is free for everyone under the age of 18 regardless of their legal status or placement. Over the age of 18, one is insured, if studying full time, registered unemployed for a certain amount of time, or a retired, invalid pensioner.

New legislation (introduced in April 2007) and stricter supervision may leave some young people leaving care without any kind of health insurance. On leaving care everybody is entitled to one year's after care service, ordered by the county custodian office, apart from those staying in residential care or with foster parents, or in special after care homes, or, in the case of students, those in dormitories or rented accommodation. In exceptional cases the young person can be placed together with his/her child as well. They get full lodging and after care. In these cases the County Child Protection Service decides on the responsible person to act as the after carer; in most instances this is a staff member or foster parent. It includes life management advice and help to integrate. At the latest, after care lasts until the young person is 24 years old.

Secondary data

There is no data collection or systematic research of any kind, other than basic administrative data on the number and age of care leavers, and their type of placement. In addition, it is also known how many of those over 18 are in after care placement and receiving after care services. We do not have any data or comparison on their education, health, employment and involvement with the youth justice system or about family reintegration. Their care histories are also unknown. The only reliable secondary data source concerning young people leaving care is the administrative collection of basic numbers based on county reports to the Ministry of Labour and Social Affairs and the central statistical office.

Leaving care research

Research data are not available and nothing has been gathered based on research or service provision. The only available information is on some projects dealing with after care services. Based on research in 16 counties out of 20, 442 young persons' data and 114 interviews in six counties are available mainly on general lessons (known already). A pilot programme financed by the National Occupational Fund looked at the opportunities for social inclusion through employment and training programmes provided for care leavers. Fifteen young people were involved in the complex pilot project in 2004, providing some data and a readiness to extend the programme to some other places as well, based on the outcomes. The *Diótörés Alapítvány* (Nutcracking Foundation) offers training, support and shelter for those leaving care and for those who are already trapped in difficult situations. Their figures record their activities, the available placements and staff members, together with the data on those young people who approached them for help.

Conclusion

In Hungary social policy and child protection are based on different systems. A seemingly generous system of helping the needy – free health care and education for children – is unfortunately accompanied by a growing segregation and unequal access to services, non-professional assessment, service provision and lack of evaluation and outcome measurement. This is because the services and financial support provided for them are based on a statutory legal and policy framework. Young care leavers are getting financial and 'in kind' help, but are not prepared for living an independent life, having had hardly any chance to integrate and learn not to repeat their parents' lives. The after care is a paternalistic way of continuing the direct intervention and dependency-based care, both by providing care until age 24 in the former institutional settings or providing assistance for a year after leaving care. According to the limited research and knowledge on young people leaving care, it is clear that the care system is not preparing them for adulthood despite the lengthy periods many spend in care. Their level of education and social skill is very low, their family ties weak if any. The secondary data available are not helpful in providing any reliable information about this.

Key messages for policy and practice

- Young people leaving care are often not ready for independent living despite the long time they have spent in the care system.

- Young adults over 18 would rather remain in the care system in after care than leave it, because they are institutionalised.

- After care is considered as part of the child welfare system and not as preparation for employment, education, training or as a social issue.

- Those growing up in the care system are not prepared for adulthood and independent living.

- In most instances the families of those in care do not get proper support to reconnect with their children.

- Care leavers have low levels of education and are mostly unskilled, so it is hard for them to find work.

- The money provided for those spending more than three years in the care system is not enough to buy a place to live, especially in the cities where they want to live and work.

- It is estimated that approximately 40 per cent of care leavers end up as homeless, many are unemployed, substance abusing and experience family breakdowns, and their children often become institutionalised as well.

References

Central Statistical Office (2007) *Statistical Yearbook*. Budapest: Central Statistical Office.

Department of Child and Youth Protection (2006) *Statistics on Child and Youth Protection*. Budapest: Ministry of Social and Labour Affairs.

Esping-Andersen, G. (1990) *The Three Worlds of Welfare Capitalism*. New Jersey: Princeton University Press.

Ferge, Z. (2000) *Elszabaduló Egyelötlenségek (Inequalities Out of Control)*. Budapest: TWINS.

Herczog, M. (2007) *Child Abuse*. Budapest: Complex Kiadó.

Kornai, J. (1992) 'The postsocialist transition and the state: Reflections in the light of Hungarian fiscal problems.' *American Economic Review 82*, 2, 1–21.

Szalai, J. (2007) *Nincs Két ország...? Társadalmi Küzdelmek az állami (túl)elosztásért a renszerváltás utáni Magyaronrszágon [Isn't It Two Countries? Social Struggle for the (Over)redistribution in the After-transition in Hungary]*. Budapest: Osiris.

Chapter 7

Ireland

Robbie Gilligan

Background and key statistics

- Population: 4,239,848 (2006); 1,013,031 aged under 18.
- Children in care – 4984 (2003).
- Rates – 4.91 in care per 1000 population under 18 (calculated by using 2003 in-care figure and Census data for 2006).
- Forms of placement – family placement 80 per cent (55% foster care; 25% placement with relatives), with both categories receiving weekly allowances: Euro 312 under 12s, Euro 339 for 12 and over (2007); residential care 10 per cent; other arrangements 10 per cent (based on data for 2003).
- Destination of care leavers – no formal data.
- Number of care leavers – no formal data, although 250–300 per annum nationally would seem a reasonable estimate of those ageing out of care.

Key sources

- Children in Care Statistics (national for 2003), www.dohc.ie/publications/pdf/stats05_child.pdf.
- Department of Health and Children (2001a) *Youth Homelessness Strategy.*

Introduction

This chapter gives a brief introduction to issues relating to provision for care leavers in Ireland. This issue is relatively neglected in Ireland, despite some recent limited policy work. The absence of routine administrative data and the lack of a clear legal requirement to provide after care support are examples of this relative neglect. The chapter summarises the legal position, some empirical research that has been undertaken (mainly by postgraduate students), and some recent policy commentary and development work.

Case examples

Scenario one: a benign scenario

The most benign scenario probably involves a history of relatively stable placement in long-term care with a foster family, where the young person continues to live with or be a strong part of the family beyond the formal care leaving age of 18. While clear research evidence on this is awaited (research under way), the anecdotal evidence suggests that many carers do not expect the young person to leave at 18, even if no allowance continues. It should also be noted that it is not unknown in the Irish system for the placing agency to continue to pay the fostering allowance to a foster family beyond 18 for as long as the young person remains in full-time education or training, although practice varies widely in this regard.

Scenario two: a negative scenario

The most negative scenario might involve a young person (possibly entering care later) with a history of multiple placements and educational and behavioural problems. The young person might have poor relationships with carers (and their own parents) and may frequently run away from placements leading to a high risk and unstable lifestyle possibly involving illicit drug use and exposure to the sex trade.

Ireland's welfare regime

Putting it rather simply, Irish welfare state provision has been broadly conservative over time. Broadly, the Irish state seems to assume families will be responsible for their young people beyond 18 years of age, and does not really make adequate alternative provision where this proves not to be true.

Currently, the Irish welfare state may be characterised as resulting from a 'low tax, low spend' government position in the recent period of economic boom/growth (Timonen 2005). Previously, lack of available funds was also a factor in such a conservative approach to provision, yet such a characterisation understates the complexity and at times relative generosity of Irish provision. A recent major review of social protection and the Irish welfare state (National Economic and Social Council 2005) suggested that the Irish model reflects 'a hybrid welfare state undergoing multiple changes' (p.14) and that 'Ireland's current welfare state has disparate elements that resemble, respectively, the citizen-based Nordic welfare model, the social-insurance Continental European model and the residual Anglo-Saxon welfare model' (p.17). Many observers (including O'Donnell 1999 and Cousins 1997) see Esping-Andersen's (1990) three-way welfare state typology as offering a poor fit with the case of Ireland. Indeed, Cousins suggests, in response to Esping-Andersen's inconsistent approach to classifying Ireland, that the 'Irish welfare state is obviously a highly moveable feast but not one which Esping-Andersen attempted to digest' (p.226).

Legal and policy framework

A glimpse of the position of young people in Ireland

The following points give a glimpse into key aspects of young people's opportunities, situation and lifestyle in Ireland:

- Four in every five young people (82%) of school leavers in the 2002/3 cohort obtained their Leaving Certificate (at age 17–18). Less than 4 per cent of young people left school without qualifications (Gorby, McCoy and Watson 2005).

- The unemployment rate among school leavers averages 21 per cent (in 2004) (compared to an average unemployment rate for all ages of 4.4 per cent, www.cso.ie/statistics/sasunemprates.htm). The school leaver unemployment rate rises to 68 per cent for those with no qualification (Gorby *et al.* 2005).

- One in five children under 16 years of age (21.9%) face a risk of poverty (defined as below 60% of median income).

- Education participation rates (year 2000 data) at age 15 are 96.6 per cent; at age 16, 91.4 per cent; at age 17, 80.1 per cent; at age 18, 62.1 per cent; and at age 19, 48 per cent. The Irish participation rate for age 15–19 of 79.8 per cent is slightly above the OECD country average of 77.3 per cent.

Young people's access to services

The following points give some flavour as to some key features of Irish provision:

- Unemployed persons over 18 years actively seeking work may apply for means-tested weekly Job Seekers' Allowance currently worth €185.80 (2007) per week. In the case of persons up to age 24 living with their parents, a formula to take account of parental income is included in the means test.

- There are no school fees in publicly funded primary or secondary schools (attended by the vast majority of children and young people).

- There are no fees payable by EU university students for their first degree in Ireland.

- Any person aged 23 and over may make a 'second chance' application for a university or college place (with no fees payable), irrespective of previous educational attainment.

- There is free access to health care for the poorest third of the population and the option of subsidised access for the balance.

Legal framework and administrative structures relevant to leaving care

The Child Care Act 1991 governs the Irish child protection and welfare system. Provision for children in care is the responsibility of the public managed and funded (unitary) Health Service Executive (subsuming former regional health boards) which delivers health and social care on a national basis. At local level, services are provided at community care area level (broadly analogous to one larger or two smaller counties).

Section 45 of the Child Care Act 1991 gives powers to health boards – now the health service executive – to assist care leavers up to the age of 21, or until the young person completes a course of education. 'Assisting' may entail visiting, assisting, arranging completion of education, contributing to maintenance while in education, placing in a suitable trade, calling or business, arranging hostel or other accommodation, or cooperating with housing authorities in planning accommodation for young care leavers at 18 years of age.

The *National Standards for Children's Residential Centres* (Department of Health and Children 2001b) specify that 'young people up to a minimum age of 21 should be supported, as they request, by the after care service' and set out various measures that should be put in place (a similar document exists for foster care).

Secondary data

Secondary data on care leavers is almost non-existent in the sense of routine administrative data. The National Department of Health and Children publishes rudimentary data on the composition of the in-care population nationally from time to time.

Leaving care research

It has been possible to identify one funded study (Kelleher and Kelleher 1998) and three studies undertaken by postgraduate students (Hally 1999; Nee 1999; Wells 2005) that generate at least some evidence as to outcomes for care leavers.

Kelleher and Kelleher (1998) remains the most significant study published on the issue of the progress of young people leaving care. It reports on a sample of 56 young people discharged from the care of any of three regional health boards. The sample was based on all those young people aged 13 years or over, who had been in care for at least two months; two-thirds of the young people in the sample were aged 17 or 18 at the point of leaving care. The authors acknowledge that the sample identified probably does not capture all cases meeting the criteria, due to the absence of a database or records on care leavers (p.59).

One in three of the young people (36%) had had previous admissions to care; that is, in addition to the final care placement they had left. Almost half (45%) were leaving residential care. Over half (57.1%) had spent over two years in care; four out of five (80.4%) more than one year in care. Almost half (45%) had at least monthly contact with parents while in care.

On leaving care, a third (32%) returned home, one in four (27.5%) had accommodation in the private rented sector, and seven young people (12.3%) remained with their foster family (that is, more than half of a total of 13 whose last care placement had been in foster care). One in ten were in hostels or supported accommodation. The whereabouts of 12.5 per cent was unknown and three young people were either homeless (two) or in prison. According to the researchers, almost half (48%) of the transitions from care were 'crisis led'; that is, they 'were precipitated by the young person either walking out of the placement or by the placement breaking down in some other way' (p.73).

At six-month follow-up, 49 of the original 56 young people could be traced. Of the seven not contactable, one had died, one had emigrated and the whereabouts of the other five was 'unknown to the social services'. Twelve of the 18 who had moved home remained there, and another five had now gone home. Five of the seven who remained in their foster home were still there.

In terms of education, 10 per cent had sat the national Leaving Certificate examination (compared to 82% in the general population according to the researchers, p.82), and a further three (all in long-term foster care) had made it to third level courses. As to overall progress, social workers rated one in five (22.5%) as making 'poor' progress, 34.7 per cent as 'fair', 28.6 per cent as 'good' and 10.2 per cent as 'very good', with a final 4 per cent for whom there was no information. Of the 19 young people making 'good' or 'very good' progress, 12 were in the private rented sector, five lived in their foster home and two were living with their family of origin. All enjoyed 'intensive support from either a social worker, a residential child care worker or a foster parent'. Overall, social workers estimated that half of the young people were not getting the after care support they needed.

According to the researchers, the young people making 'good' or 'very good' progress tended:

- to be in the older age groups
- to have educational qualifications
- not to be involved in drugs
- not to have had a breakdown in their care placement
- not to be living at home
- to have had a planned transition from care.

(p.78)

As part of a study for her Masters degree dissertation, Wells (2005) used data extracted from case records to examine the progress of a sample of 164 care leavers referred to a regional after care service in the period December 2001 to December 2004 in a health board region. Three in five young people (61.6%) were living in foster care at the time of referral to the after care service, and at the time of the study (or case closure) almost half (46.5%) of the sample were living with their foster carers. One in ten were living in independent accommodation at the time of referral, a proportion that rose to 35.4 per cent at the time of the study (or case closure). Almost a third (30.5%) had experienced at least one episode of homelessness since leaving care. The likelihood of experiencing such homelessness was strongly associated with having a non-family-based placement as final placement ($p < 0.001$). One in eight of this sample had no educational qualification (12.2%). One in five (21.8%) had a Leaving Certificate, compared to 82 per cent in the general population (Gorby *et al.* 2005), a further 19.7 per cent had other qualifications, and for 13.4 per cent there was no information. Remaining in education beyond 18 years was strongly associated with family placement ($p < 0.001$). Four out of five of those who achieved a Leaving Certificate had a final placement in a family.

Using evidence on how they were faring overall in terms of accommodation, education/training/employment and health (relevant data available for 130 of the 164 cases) the young people were classified as 'doing well' (47.7%), 'doing moderately well' (43.3%) and 'doing poorly' (10%). Factors found to be strongly associated with more positive outcomes for the young people leaving care were:

- being admitted to care before the age of ten years ($p < 0.01$)
- being in their last placement before leaving care for more than three years ($p < 0.001$)
- having no children ($p < 0.05$)
- leaving care from a family based placement ($p < 0.001$)
- having regular contact with their former foster carers ($p < 0.001$).

(p.93)

Nee (1999, in Buckley 2002, p.178) interviewed 13 care leavers who had left the care of the same regional health board between 1995 and 1998. Of the 13, seven were still living with their foster families and two more made regular weekend visits to their former foster families. The young people reported that the main source of support was from their foster or birth families, with social work support having become less prominent in their lives. The importance of support from families for care leavers, however, was not a feature found by Hally (1999, in Buckley 2002, p.178) in his study of ten young women who had left the care of a residential centre in the juvenile justice system. These young women reported a diminishing and often low level of support from families on leaving care (despite family contact being active while they were in care).

A study of youth homelessness

Mayock and Vekic (2006) report on the first phase of a qualitative study of 40 cases (in the age range 12–22) of youth homelessness in Dublin using a longitudinal cohort design. Of the 40 cases in the study, 16 (40%) had a range of varied public care histories. On the basis of their data, the researchers identify three 'homeless pathways', of which having a care history is one. The themes of (1) deep disaffection with the idea of being in care and (2) general instability of living/care arrangements seem to run through the experience of these particular young people. Exposure to, or extending, 'hard' drug use was a live risk for all the young people in the sample, as was a risk of making the transition to 'chronic homelessness'.

Conclusion

There has been a gradual accumulation of support as evidenced in policy reviews and policy stances for recognising the needs of, and strengthening provision for, care leavers. Although, critically, three serious impediments remain. First, while the Child Care Act 1991 did empower the provision of after care, it did not *require* it of health boards (now the Health Service Executive). Second, linked to the first point, there is a clear lack of a national framework of guaranteed and consistent provision for young care leavers, irrespective of their location, leading to many young people 'leaving care in an unplanned way' (Social Services Inspectorate 2000, p.2). Third, there is an almost complete dearth of official data or evidence on outcomes for care leavers.

The Social Services Inspectorate (2004, p.48) called for after care to become a duty of the Health Service Executive (the body responsible for children in care) and also called on them 'to develop comprehensive after care policies and services clearly outlining all aspects of support and enti-tlement for the young person leaving care' (p.78), points further reinforced by the Children's Rights Alliance (2006, p.34), the UN Committee on the Rights of the Child in its comments on Ireland's country report (2006, pp.7–8) and the Social Services Inspectorate, (2005, p.9).

There is no shortage of aspiration and even commitment in relation to developing after care provision, but as indicated above the issue is really more one of closing the gap between rhetoric and reality and ensuring proper 'ownership' of the issue.

In 2004, national guidelines for health boards on 'Developing a Leaving and After Care Policy' were approved by the National Youth

Homelessness Strategy Monitoring Committee. In addition, the Social Services Inspectorate includes formal guidance on practice in relation to after care on its website. There is also explicit reference to after care for care leavers in the Youth Homelessness Strategy (Objective 4) and the National Children's Strategy (Office of the Minister for Children 2000, p.65).

While national policy guaranteeing provision for care leavers remains underdeveloped, the picture is more mixed than this might imply. Specific after care programmes and after care worker posts are beginning to emerge. But in the absence of a legal *requirement* to provide care, many young care leavers may not have their needs met, especially those with special needs or without the support of their (former) carers.

Key messages for policy and practice

There is a need:

- for an explicit statutory requirement to provide ongoing specified levels of support to young people ageing out of care, with particular reference to those in continuing education or training
- to extend the formal care leaving age to 21, with an early commitment to raise it to 19
- for annual data to be gathered in relation to numbers and outcomes for young care leavers
- for explicit pre-service and in-service training for carers and social workers in relation to the needs of care leavers
- for a research programme to:
  - ○ study the progress and needs of care leavers
  - ○ study the impact and effectiveness of different forms of support provision
  - ○ join in coordinated international efforts to monitor needs, outcomes and provision.

References

Buckley, H. (2002) *Child Protection: Innovation and Intervention.* Dublin: Institute of Public Administration.

Children's Rights Alliance (2006) *From Rhetoric to Rights – Second Shadow Report to the United Nations Committee on Rights of the Child.* Dublin: Children's Rights Alliance.

Cousins, M. (1997) 'Ireland's place in the worlds of welfare capitalism.' *Journal of European Social Policy* 7, 3, 223–235.

Department of Health and Children (2001a) *Youth Homelessness Strategy.* Dublin: The Stationery Office.

Department of Health and Children (2001b) *National Standards for Children's Residential Centres.* Dublin: The Stationery Office.

Esping-Andersen, G. (1990) *The Three Worlds of Welfare Capitalism.* New Jersey: Princeton University Press.

Gorby, S., McCoy, S. and Watson, D. (2005) *2004 Annual School Leavers' Survey of 2002/3 Leavers.* ESRI Report for the Department of Education and Science.

Hally, S. (1999) 'A Study of the Perspectives of Former Service Users and Their Carers.' Project submitted in partial fulfilment of the requirements of the Post-Graduate Diploma in Child Protection and Welfare, Trinity College Dublin. In H. Buckley (ed.) *Child Protection: Innovation and Intervention.* Dublin: Institute of Public Administration.

Kelleher, P. and Kelleher, C. (1998) *Out on Their Own – Young People Leaving Care in Ireland.* Dublin: Focus Point.

Mayock, P. and Vekic, K. (2006) *Understanding Youth Homelessness in Dublin City – Key Findings from the First Phase of a Longitudinal Cohort Study.* Dublin: The Stationery Office.

National Economic and Social Council (2005) *The Developmental Welfare State.* Report No. 113. Dublin: National Economic and Social Development Office.

Nee, L. (1999) '"Where Do I Go from Here?" The Young Person's Experience of After-care.' Project submitted in partial fulfilment of the requirements of the Post-Graduate Diploma in Child Protection and Welfare, Trinity College Dublin. In H. Buckley (ed.) *Child Protection: Innovation and Intervention.* Dublin: Institute of Public Administration.

O'Donnell, A. (1999) 'Comparing Welfare States: Considering the Case of Ireland.' In G. Kiely, A. O'Donnell, P. Kennedy and S. Quin (eds) *Irish Social Policy in Context.* Dublin: University College Dublin Press.

Office of the Minister for Children (2000) *National Children's Strategy: Our Children – Their Lives. 2000-2010.* Dublin: The Stationery Office.

Social Services Inspectorate (2000) *Social Services Inspectorate Practice Guidelines on: Leaving Care and Aftercare Support.* Cork: Health Information and Quality Authority. Accessed 09/09/07 at www.hiqa.ie/media/pdfs/sc_guidance_leaving_aftercare.pdf

Social Services Inspectorate (2004) *Annual Report 2004.* Dublin: Social Services Inspectorate. Accessed 31/03/08 at www.hiqa.ie/media/pdfs/news/ssi_ar_2004_en.pdf

Social Services Inspectorate (2005) *Annual Report 2005.* Dublin: Social Services Inspectorate. Accessed 31/03/08 at www.hiqa.ie/media/pdfs/news/ssi_ar_2005_en.pdf

Timonen, V. (2005) *Irish Social Expenditure in a Comparative International Context.* Dublin: Combat Poverty Agency and the Institute of Public Administration.

UN Committee on the Rights of the Child (2006) *Consideration of Reports Submitted by States Parties Under Article 44 of the Convention on the Rights of the Child. Concluding Observations: Ireland. Crc/C/Irl/Co/2.* Accessed 21/09/07 at www.childrensrights.ie/pubs/ IRLCONCOBS.pdf

Wells, J. (2005) *What Happens to Young Care Leavers? A Study of 164 Young People who have been in the Care of the Mid-Western Health Board/Health Service Executive Mid-Western Area.* Dissertation, submitted in partial fulfilment of the requirements of the MSc in Child Protection and Welfare. Dublin: Trinity College.

Chapter 8

Israel

Rami Benbenishty

Background and key statistics

- In 2005 there were about 2,537,000 children in Israel, more than a third of the total population (National Bureau of Statistics 2005); about 22.6 per cent of them were in the age range of 15–19.

- The rate of poverty among children is high – a third of them live in families under the poverty line (23.9% among Jewish children and 59.2% among Arabs) (National Council for the Child 2005, p.317).

- 330,000 children and youth are at high risk, 15 per cent of the relevant population; 165,000 do not get any services; 135,000 live with domestic violence; 144,000 suffer neglect; and 49,000 are victims of physical abuse (Schmid 2006).

- About 2.6 per cent of the non-religious population, 15.9 per cent of the religious population and 18.8 per cent of ultra-orthodox children are educated in out-of-home arrangements.

- Arab children constitute approximately 10 per cent of children in out-of-home arrangements (compared with their proportion in the total children population which is more than 20%).

- The number of children who reside out of home ranges between 60,000 and 70,000 children; about 9000 are placed by the Ministry of Welfare, about 80 per cent in residential care and the rest in foster families.

- In 2005 there were about 1700 children placed in foster families, with 8.4 per cent aged 0–4 and 38.9 per cent aged 13–18.

Key sources

- National Beueau of Statistics (2005).
- National Council for the Child (2005).

Introduction

Israel has been an independent state since 1948. The Charter of Independence declared that, on the basis of the historical roots of the Jewish People in Israel and the 1947 UN declaration, a Jewish and democratic state is established in the Land of Israel. Among the principles of the new state were the right of return to Israel of Jews from all over the world, freedom of worship to all religions, freedom, justice and peace, and complete social and political equality to all citizens.

Since its inception, Israel has been facing major challenges. Two of these are directly relevant to this chapter. First, the promise to become the state for all Jews resulted in massive waves of immigration from all over the world and its Jewish population increased dramatically from about 600,000 in 1948 to about 5,000,000 today. This immigration strengthened Israel, which has made tremendous gains in agriculture, industry, technology, science, cultural developments and education. At the same time, immigration also resulted in substantial difficulties for groups of new immigrants who are disempowered groups of first, second and third generation citizens, mostly on the geographical and social periphery. Second, the establishment of a Jewish State in the Middle East, in a country formerly inhabited mostly by Arabs and bordering with Arab states, is the source of major ongoing armed conflicts. A series of wars is having a major impact on the Israeli society. About 20 per cent of its population consists of Arab citizens who experience discrimination and lower socio-political-economic status. The conflict is a major source of stress on Israeli society and has many tragic ramifications. Specifically relevant to this chapter is the priority given to the security issue in the allocation of available resources and fewer resources and opportunities offered to Israeli Arab youths.

Case examples

Maya

Maya was born in a small village. Her mother committed suicide and her father died shortly afterwards, when she was nine. She has two older brothers who could not care for her. She was placed in a foster family in the village but did not get along with her new siblings or with the foster father. She was placed with another family in the village when she was 11. As an adolescent she had very low self-esteem, rebellious behaviour and slightly promiscuous brief encounters with older males. She had serious difficulties in her relationships with her foster siblings and many arguments and disagreements with her foster mother. Following this she became part of the foster family who treated her like one of its own. At the age of 18 she joined the military and is doing remarkably well. She lives next to her two older brothers who are themselves involved in low-level criminal activity. She will leave the military soon and will be looking for a job and a place of her own.

David

David was born in the Former USSR and when he was ten he came to Israel with his mother. She had mental health difficulties and could not care for him. He was placed in residential care. While he was in care she passed away. He is 18 now and has to leave the residential placement. He will be drafted to the military in six months. He was given the chance to live in a new type of 'flat in the community' as part of an experimental programme for youth leaving care with no family support. He currently lives there with six others, three of them already in the military. The worker is mediating between him and the military to ensure that he will be drafted to a meaningful military service. David is working part time in a car washing place. He received a vocational assessment. He was offered help in completing his final high school test, or taking a short course on how to use computers in office work. Currently, he is not interested in his studies or getting better work skills. He wants 'a break' and the worker who attends to the flat is trying to engage him in thinking about his future while in the military and after. David is grateful for the place, but is not interested in doing more.

Israel's welfare regime

Israel is a multi-party democracy. The first regimes were governed by parties with a socialist orientation. In the last decades Liberal and Neo-Liberal ideology is more prevalent and there is a strong trend towards privatisation and globalisation which is having a major impact on Israel's society and economy. The rhetoric of the founders of the state emphasised values such as equality and sharing of resources. Over the years Israel adopted a welfare state ethos characterised by attempts to employ universalistic criteria. In recent years there has been a gradual move away from these principles and towards a more conservative welfare regime. Currently, Israel may be considered as having a conservative (Stier, Lewin-Epstein and Braun 2001) or a 'corporatist' welfare regime (Lewin-Epstein, Stier and Braun 2006).

Legal and policy framework

Child welfare ideology in Israel emphasises the importance of growing up within the family. Practitioners try to avoid out-of-home placements and prefer community-based solutions for children at risk. In recent years this ideology has been strengthened with the recent policy emphasis on 'With the Face to the Community'. This is a major policy change in child welfare in Israel that aims to reallocate resources from out-of-home care to services provided to children and family in their community. Among other components, policy directives put limits on the length of stay in out-of-home care and provide means to redirect resources formerly put into out-of-home placements to use in building community-based services.

In general, Israeli children enter out-of-home care through two main channels – education and welfare. The educational component accepts children to residential junior and high schools. The population served is heterogeneous. The welfare track is used as a therapeutic intervention for youths at risk due to their parents' difficulties and for youths who present major behavioural and emotional difficulties. There are two main entry points to out-of-home welfare placements: a 'decision committee' and the juvenile court. Most welfare placements are made through a 'decision committee'. These local interdisciplinary committees, with the participation of the family (increasing over time) and the child, consider the needs of the child and family, including the available treatment options in the community and in out-of-home placements. Most of the assignments made by the welfare departments are done with parental approval (about 80%) and do not involve the legal system.

According to the Israeli Statistics Bureau, about 2.6 per cent of the non-religious population, 15.9 per cent of the religious population and 18.8 per cent of ultra-orthodox children are being educated in out-of-home arrangements, in these types of placements. It is common to estimate the number of children who reside out of home as ranging between 60,000 and 70,000 children. In 2004, of all the children in out-of-home care, there were 8651 children who were placed by the Ministry of Welfare. The majority (about 80%) were placed in residential placements designed for children at risk. In 2005 there were about 1700 children placed in foster families, with 8.4 per cent aged 0–4 and 38.9 per cent aged 13–18. Although a high proportion of Arab children are vulnerable and excluded they are under-represented in out-of-home placements (compared with the general population). Arab children constitute approximately 10 per cent of children living in out-of-home arrangements (compared with their proportion in the total children population which is more than 20%).

The relatively large number of children who are being educated out of home, and the small proportion of foster care placements compared with referrals to residential facilities, has evolved from the unique cultural and historical roots of education in institutional settings in Israel (see, for example, Jaffe 1982).

Most out-of-home placements made by the Welfare Ministry are in residential facilities. These institutions are considered to be on a continuum which pertains to the intensity of psychosocial care required – 'Educational', 'Rehabilitative' and 'Treatment'. In recent years a more intense form of care has been introduced – 'Post-hospitalisation' – that addresses the needs of children who require intensive psychological and psychiatric care. Care in out-of-home placements is provided mostly by non-government organisations and not-for-profit organisations. Supervision and funding are provided by the Welfare Ministry, although most facilities engage in additional independent fund raising.

Although recent figures are unavailable, there are many indications that out-of-home care in Israel is more stable and long term than in the United Kingdom and the United States. For instance, Benbenishty and Segev (2002) report that about 30 per cent of children in foster care stay more than four years in placement and the mean length of stay for children entering between the ages of 4–6 years is almost five years. Most placements are stable and disruptions are uncommon (Benbenishty and Oyserman 1995).

Currently there are no exact figures on the number of care leavers every year, although it has been estimated that there are about 350 youths who leave out-of-home care and have no family to back them up in independent living (Zilka and Schuman 2003).

Whereas young adults ageing out of care in Israel share much in common with their counterparts in other Western countries, there are certain issues that are more specific. Completing military service, and especially carrying out meaningful service that includes challenging roles (such as in combat or in technologically sophisticated units) and gaining promotion, is regarded as making an important contribution to future integration into society.

Care leavers frequently face challenges with regard to their military service which are not shared by most youth raised at home. The military prefers not to recruit care leavers, especially alumni of welfare placements, because of their difficult background (for example, criminal record, low educational attainment) and lack of skills. Furthermore, even after recruitment, many care leavers do not have the support and family resources required to overcome the difficulties of military service. Hence, the successful completion of meaningful military service can be an important asset for care leavers and lift their prospects for further integration into normative society. In contrast, failure to serve, especially following a stay in out-of-home care, may stigmatise them and limit severely their options in later life.

The relevant organisational structures in Israel may add to the potential difficulties of care leavers. As indicated earlier, youth in out-of-home care may 'belong' to either the Education or the Welfare Ministry. However, youths may fall between the cracks of these ministries and there is no planned continuity in care. They need to be in 'real trouble' in order to become clients of other services. Consequently, there is no national service provider that offers services to care leavers. Some not-for-profit philanthropic organisations do target this population and offer some services. However, each of these organisations picks and chooses the clients they prefer. Others are left without services and support.

Legal arrangements

The legal arrangements covering child welfare in general and out-of-home placements in particular consist of a series of laws and regulations, many of them outdated, and they provide only partial coverage of many central issues that have emerged over the years. For instance, there are no specific laws covering foster care.

In 1997 the Minister of Justice appointed a Committee for Examination of Fundamental Principles regarding the Child and the Law and their Legislative Implementation ('The Public Committee on Children and the Law'). This committee, headed by the Honourable Judge Saviona Rotlevy, had the mandate to examine all the legal aspects regarding children. The committee used the UN Convention on the Rights of the Child as its main guiding principle and submitted a series of reports and a draft law proposal in 2003. One of the subcommittees was in charge of out-of-home placement. This subcommittee was the first to propose a legal framework to deal with the needs of children who age out of care. The proposal addresses two issues:

1. A transition plan for youth in care upon reaching 17 years of age.

2. Assistance for youth transitioning out of care.

However, this proposal has not been accepted yet and presently there is no specific legal framework that addresses the needs of care leavers.

Secondary data

Welfare organisations in Israel have been slow in adopting advanced information technology. Most of the progress in this area is driven by managers who are concerned with financial issues. Hence, in recent years there are administrative databases that document activities in the child welfare system, most notably referrals to services that need to be funded and require transfer of funds to second and third sector service providers. Consequently, all out-of-home placements are documented in a central database that contains (minimal) information on the child and on entry to and exit from each placement. Unfortunately, however, this database is not available for analysis by researchers due to numerous problems and excuses – fear of public exposure, lack of resources to provide technical help, lack of legal arrangements and privacy issues. As the time of writing there are strong indications that this situation will change soon and a series of administrative databases will become available for analysis.

Another important relevant database is the RAF (Regulation, Assessment, Follow-up and continuous improvement of quality) information system. This system was developed to improve quality control and supervision of residential facilities. It is based on an annual data collection regarding the status of each child placed by the Ministry of Welfare in a residential facility and assessment of various aspects of the institution as a whole (see Zemach-Marom, Fleishman and Hauslich 2002 for further details). Despite some technical difficulties, this database is readily accessible and can provide important information. A recent doctoral dissertation examined the psychosocial and educational functioning of children and youth who reside in rehabilitative, therapeutic and post-hospitalisation institutions (Attar 2006). However, the richness of the RAF database has not been mined yet, although there seems to be some progress toward making it more accessible to researchers. Future studies should apply longitudinal designs to follow up on children in care and identify changes over time. It is also important to connect this database with other administrative databases on these children and their families.

The Israel Bureau of Statistics has the legal mandate to gather any data and receive all existing databases in all areas. The Bureau has extensive databases from many different government departments and is able to combine them to create gigantic databases that cover a wide range of spheres. For instance, we are in the process of designing a database of all children who were in out-of-home care for a period of time that will contain information on the children (e.g. issues of education, health, delinquency), their schools and residential facilities, and their parents and siblings (e.g. demographic background, income, delinquency, health, employment and more). Although the utilisation of such databases may be cumbersome, due to the need to meet many legal requirements, the potential for secondary analysis is enormous.

Leaving care research

There has been relatively little research on the status of alumni of out-of-home placements in Israel. The most comprehensive study was conducted by Weiner and her associates (Weiner and Kupermintz 2001; Weiner and Weiner 1990). This longitudinal study followed up (for 22 years) a group of children who were placed in early childhood (younger than six years old) in one institution in the Northern city of Haifa in Israel. In the third and final stage of the follow-up the authors interviewed 206 adults (ages 22–30). They found that 36 per cent were married, a third of them had children and none of them was in an out-of-home placement (Weiner and Kupermintz 2001). Only half of them completed high school and only 61 per cent served in the military, well below the proportion in the general population. More than half were employed, although mainly in 'blue collar' occupations. The study also showed that 10.2 per cent were assessed as 'not functioning', and 12.6 per cent as 'functioning with problems' (such as criminal activity and prostitution).

Benbenishty and Schiff (2003, and Schiff 2006) followed up 109 alumni of *Orr Shalom*, a large network of group homes in Israel. Overall, these alumni had positive experiences while in care and their stay in the group home may have protected them against malfunctioning in adulthood, given their disadvantaged childhood backgrounds. Phone interviews with these alumni revealed a mixed picture regarding their functioning in several areas. Just over half of the group had acquired at least 12 years of formal education, while most had completed exactly 12 years and a full or partial *Bagrut* (matriculation tests). The rate of military service among males was 60 per cent, similar to graduates of similar programmes but lower than the national average. One-third of the young people thought that they had fewer friends compared with most people. Half of the group felt that they could always talk with a close friend about a personal problem. However, almost one-fifth felt that they could not talk with friends about a personal problem or that they had no friends at all. A sizeable proportion of the young people had difficulties in integrating into normative society. Half of the males interviewed reported being involved with the law and about a third had a criminal record. It should be noted, however, that only 38 young people responded to this question. Life satisfaction among this group was positive, but somewhat lower than that of the general population, at least in comparison to studies in the United States.

The authors examined in detail alumni's retrospective evaluation of their experiences of leaving care and the transition phase. Ninety-four alumni (38 men and 56 women) were interviewed by phone. Results reveal major difficulties in transition. About half of the young people perceived their transition from care as quite hard or very hard. One-fifth of the group reported having no one to talk to during the first period of leaving care. Women described their transition as more difficult than men in the sample. The general retrospective evaluation of the group-home experience was very positive for both men and women. Better relationships between the child and the group-home parents while in care were associated with *more* difficult transitions to independent living. The *longer* the alumni (especially boys) stayed in care, the tougher they perceived their transition to independent living.

The only study completed regarding 'readiness for leaving care' among adolescents while they were still living in care was conducted by Benbenishty and Schiff (2004). The authors interviewed 66 adolescents in foster care, 47.6 per cent of them males with a mean age of about 17.3 years. The findings revealed that overall the adolescents felt they were ready for independent living and were quite confident regarding their skills in many aspects of functioning. However, as regards employment, 'getting around' and dealing with bureaucracy, military services and education, they felt they were less ready.

In recent years, a growing awareness of the needs of youth who age out of care, especially those who 'lack familial backing', has contributed to the evaluation of experimental services. Benbenishty is currently examining organisational issues (such as inter- and intra-agency coordination) and the views of policy makers, service providers and the young participants. The study employs a longitudinal design and is following up young participants, using information obtained through periodic interviews with the participants and service providers. The intermediate findings suggest that there is a clear need for such services for youth in transition from out-of-home care and the participants in these programmes are indeed the intended target population. There are strong indications that most of the participants do not have realistic plans for their immediate future and lack skills to help them carry out these plans. Youth see the services they receive as helpful and most of them are very satisfied with their participation in the programme.

Benbenishty's intermediate reports (December 2006; June 2007) suggest that organisational structures, such as division between welfare and education and service structures and age, are barriers to effective services in this area. He suggests that there is a need to redesign services for youth who are ageing out of care and create a continuum of care that would integrate services along the age continuum and among service providers and government offices. Presently there are some indications that the evaluation findings and recommendations are being considered seriously and changes will be introduced at least into the Ministry of Welfare services for youth. Some of these changes are aimed at integrating services for youth ageing out of care within new service centres designed for normative youth.

Conclusion

Growing up in out-of-home placement is more prevalent in Israel than in many countries. Whereas much effort has been invested in caring for children and youth in these placements, few services are directed to help young people in their transition from care and integrating them into normative society. The legal framework does not provide enough direction and support to develop services in this area. Research shows that there is a need for such services. Israel seems to be on the verge of addressing this situation and there are several developments suggesting that a new set of services will be made available to this group. These developments will be strengthened if advocacy brings about legal changes and research uses more effectively secondary and primary data in order to help design the new service system.

Key messages for policy and practice

- There is a significant need for help in transitioning from out-of-home care that is currently not being met.
- Lack of a legal framework is a major obstacle to improved service systems.
- Early results from experimental programmes are promising.
- There is a need for organisational changes to provide an integrated continuum of care.
- Secondary data should be used more effectively to help assess youth while they are in care and to estimate levels of need.
- Research should be carried out utilising, among other things, longitudinal designs to understand life trajectories of children and youth who spend significant parts of their lives in out-of-home care.

References

Attar, S. (2006) *Child, Family and Institutional Characteristics as Predictors of the Psychosocial and Educational Functioning of Children in Rehabilitative, Therapeutic, and Post-hospitalization Residential Facilities.* Dissertation. Jerusalem: Hebrew University.

Benbenishty, R. (2006) *A Bridge for Care Leavers with No Family Support – An Intermediate Report, December 2006.* Jerusalem: Hebrew University.

Benbenishty, R. (2007) *A Bridge for Care Leavers with No Family Support – An Intermediate Report, June 2007.* Jerusalem: Hebrew University.

Benbenishty, R. and Oyserman, D. (1995) 'Children in foster care: Their present situation and plans for their future.' *International Social Work 38*, 117–131.

Benbenishty, R. and Schiff, M. (2003) *A Follow Up Study of 'Orr Shalom' Graduates Ages 18 and Up – Research Report.* Jerusalem: Research Group of Mental Health and Well Being in Childhood and Adolescence, School of Social Work and Social Welfare, Hebrew University.

Benbenishty, R. and Schiff, M. (2004) *Adolescents' Status in Foster Care and the Perception of Readiness for Independent Life – Research Report.* Jerusalem: Research Group of Mental Health and Well Being in Childhood and Adolescence, School of Social Work and Social Welfare, Hebrew University.

Benbenishty, R. and Segev, D. (2002) 'Characteristics and predictors of length of stay in foster care in Israel.' *Mifgash L'avoda Chinoochit-Sozialit 16*, 93–114.

Jaffe, E.D. (1982) *Child Welfare in Israel.* New York: Praeger.

Lewin-Epstein, N., Stier, H. and Braun, M. (2006) 'The division of household labor in Germany and Israel.' *Journal of Marriage and the Family 68*, 5, 1147–1164.

National Bureau of Statistics (2005) *Statistical Abstract of Israel – No. 56.* Jerusalem: National Bureau of Statistics.

National Council for the Child (2005) *Children in Israel: Annual Statistics.* Jerusalem: National Council for the Child.

Schiff, M. (2006) 'Leaving care: Retrospective reports by alumni of Israeli group-homes.' *Social Work 51*, 4, 343–353.

Schmid, H. (2006) *The Public Committee Report for the Situation of Children and Youth at Risk.* Jerusalem: The State of Israel.

Stier, H., Lewin-Epstein, N. and Braun, M. (2001) 'Welfare regimes, family supported policies, and women's employment along life-course.' *American Journal of Sociology 106*, 6, 1731–1760.

Weiner, A. and Kupermintz, H. (2001) 'Facing adulthood alone. The long-term impact of family break-up and infant institutions: A longitudinal study.' *British Journal of Social Work 31*, 2, 213–234.

Weiner, A. and Weiner, E. (1990) *Expending the Options in Child Placement: Israel's Dependent Children in Care from Infancy to Adulthood.* Lanham: University Press of America.

Zemach-Marom, T., Fleishman, R. and Hauslich, Z. (2002) 'Improving Quality of Care in Residential Settings in Israel through the RAF Method.' In P.M. Bergh, E.J. Knorth, F. Verheij and D.C. Lane (eds) *Changing Care: Enhancing Professional Quality and Client Involvement in Child and Youth Care Services.* Amsterdam: SWP Publishers.

Zilka, E. and Schuman, S. (2003) *Youth Lacking Familial Backing – Research Report.* Jerusalem: JDC, Brookdale Institute.

Chapter 9

Jordan

Rawan W. Ibrahim

Background and key statistics

- Population: 5.5 million (2,584,100, approximately 47 per cent of the population, are children under the age of 18; 69 per cent of the population are 29 years of age or below).

- Youth[1] admitted to the child welfare system (2006): 10,919 (categorised below).

  - Child abuse and neglect: 3798 (1950 home supervision, 129 admitted to care homes, 1719 closed cases).

  - Peddling:[2] 710.

  - Delinquency: 5300 (3221 admitted to rehabilitation centres,[3] 2079 pending/closed cases).

  - Youth admitted to residential care homes[4] for care and protection (main form of substitute care): 1114.

- Care leavers usually live independently at much younger ages than peers without a history of living in substitute care (usually age 18).

- Care leavers 2005–2006: 163.

Key sources

- Arab Urban Development Institute (2004).
- Department of Statistics (2006a, 2006b).

- Ministry of Social Development (2006).
- United Nations Development Programme (2004).

Introduction

The Hashemite Kingdom of Jordan is located in southwest Asia, bordering occupied Palestine, Syria, Iraq and the Kingdom of Saudi Arabia, with portal access to the Red Sea from the Gulf of Aqaba. Administratively, it is divided into 12 'governorates'; each is also sub-divided into districts, headed by appointed officials. Since the Kingdom's independence from the British Mandate in 1946, Jordan has been a constitutional monarchy whereby powers are divided into three branches: executive, legislative and judicial. The central government is made up of the cabinet (Council of Ministers) and headed by the prime minister, who is appointed by the King (subject to parliamentary approval). The cabinet's responsibility varies, ranging from infrastructure development, education and social welfare to national defence.

The governmental body responsible for youth involved in the national child welfare system is the Family and Childhood Directorate within the Ministry of Social Development (MOSD). The directorate is further divided into three sub-units, with 40 branches distributed among 'governorates'. This chapter focuses on youth admitted to residential care and not youth in conflict with the law, or those involved in peddling (unless they were admitted to care homes).

According to the Department of Statistics, between 1951 and 2004 the Jordanian population grew ten-fold from half a million to 5.10 million (Department of Statistics 2004). This was due to the steady growth rate (Population and Development Council and Jabre 2002, p.3; United Nations Development Program 2004), forced migration of Palestinian refugees following Arab-Israeli wars reaching 1.7 million (United Nations Relief and Works Agency for Palestine Refugees 2006), the influx of Iraqi refugees and returning Jordanian expatriates following the Gulf wars, and migrant workers (United Nations Development Programme 2004).

Among the most distinct demographic features of Jordan is its youthful population – 69 per cent of the population are under the age of 29

(Department of Statistics 2006b). This, coupled with high growth rates, is a 'double-edged sword', being Jordan's 'greatest asset and its most pressing challenge' (United Nations Development Programme 2004, p.18). The vast numbers of youth provide human capabilities for future economic and social development. However, with so many youth entering the reproductive age, the high growth rate will not significantly decline, and their need for employment opportunities will be a great strain on already-scarce resources (United Nations Development Programme 2004).

Case examples

Nashmi

Nashmi's parents were divorced; his mother remarried and left the country. He was admitted to care at age nine as a result of abuse by his father. Due to gender separation after a certain age, and the limited age group of each home, he had four placements. The homes did not provide counselling and the quality of care varied, in the absence of minimum standards. He also changed school six times during his time in care, as a consequence of changing homes and stigma within schools. At age 15 he was discharged from care under the pretence that he would live with his maternal family, which he did initially, but he felt he was a burden. He does not have health insurance and is suffering from a heart murmur and depression. He is currently 17 years old, living alone with his younger brother who was also in care. Nashmi is still attending school but is struggling with balancing work, finances and education. There was no follow-up from his last placement. His extended family supports him morally and aids him financially when they can.

Mukhtar

Mukhtar was admitted to one of the few homes that serve children from infancy to age 18. He witnessed negative outcomes when surrogate siblings in care contacted their families, and therefore, to protect himself from disappointment, Mukhtar decided to avoid establishing contact with his family. Preferring vocational training, he obtained carpentry qualifications. With the aid of the home, upon discharge Mukhtar was employed, had accommodation with a surrogate brother, and savings in a personal bank account from sponsors during care. After a year, the carpentry shop closed. Mukhtar was unemployed, had problems with his landlord and financial difficulties. Unsatisfied with menial jobs and unable to secure better accommodation, Mukhtar requested aid from the home, and some of its previous employees who maintained contact with him. He was supported in securing another job in carpentry, and better accommodation. Recently, Mukhtar married a woman who was also in care. The home supported the couple with the wedding, as well as providing family planning guidance. Mukhtar is also informally aiding the home in preparing his surrogate siblings prior to discharge.

Jordan's welfare regime

Western welfare systems are generally sustained by domestic tax collection where citizens are repaid through necessary services (e.g. education, cash payments during unemployment). The case in Jordan is different for two main reasons: formally for having been a semi-rentier[5] state, and informally because societal norms play a vital role in addressing welfare issues. Formal provisions of welfare services were not based on tax collection, but rather, 'enacted during periods of government budget surpluses and contributed to deficits during periods of reduced revenues' (Al Khouri 2000, p.2). The main economic driver, employer and supplier of social services was the Jordanian public sector, and still is, to a lesser degree (Al Khouri 2000; Brynen 1992; Piro 1998). Consumer goods were subsidised, and by 1986 46.7 per cent of the labour force were state-employees in various sectors and state-owned enterprises (Abu Jaber, Buhbe and Smadi 1990).

Informally, Jordanian society is very much family-based. For example, regardless of financial strains, it is not uncommon to find three generations living in one home, as the use of retirement homes is not socially acceptable. Moreover, transitioning of young adults in Arab culture is much more extended in comparison to the West. Young adults only leave the parental or family home (temporarily and usually with continuous support) for educational and employment purposes, or if they are married. It is not unusual for couples to begin their life living with their in-laws, until they can financially manage otherwise. Family support also extends to other relatives, when for example children lose their parents.

Due to sharp declines in oil prices during the 1980s, and the consequently deteriorating economy, Jordan was obliged to begin the implementation of Structural Adjustment Programmes (SAPs) (Baylouny 2006; Piro 1998). As a result of SAP policies, wages of nearly half the labour force (state-employees) were capped, state employment was cut, subsidisation of consumer goods was ceased and prices were said to have 'sky rocketed' (Baylouny 2006, p.352). The overall standard of living sharply deteriorated; 'poverty declared by the World Bank effectively eliminated in the 1980s was 30 per cent by 2000' (Baylouny 2006, p.352).

In positioning the welfare regimes of developing countries, Gough *et al.* (2004) expand the concepts used by Esping-Andersen (1990). Due to the nature of developing countries, Gough *et al.* have stretched Esping-Andersen's triangle of state, market and family into a square, adding the community and global dimension. They consider the fact that non-rich countries greatly rely on international actors,[6] and transfers of resources, whereby all four domains are linked (Gough *et al.* 2004, p.5). Gough *et al.* propose three main 'families of regime': welfare state regimes, informal security regimes and insecurity regimes (p.33). They sub-divide and explain these as follows (p.44):

1. Actual or potential welfare state regimes. High state commitments and relatively high welfare outcomes.

2. More effective informal security regimes. Relatively good outcomes achieved with below average state spending and low international flows.

3. Less effective informal security regimes. Poor levels of welfare coupled with low public commitments and moderate international flows.

4. Externally dependent insecurity regimes. Heavy dependency on aid and on remittances with very poor welfare outcomes.

According to this model, Jordan is an example of an externally dependent insecurity regime, having a medium high Human Development Index (HDI)[7] score, high public spending and very high international flows[8] (Gough *et al.* 2004, p.44). The World Bank noted that despite the difficulties imposed by the turbulent political situation, and lack of resources, 'Jordan has achieved above average development outcomes compared to other lower middle-income countries' (World Bank 2006, p.1). Notwithstanding improvements at the macro level, per capita income has not caught up. Poverty and unemployment (aggravated by high growth rates) are Jordan's main challenges[9] (Arab Urban Development Institute 2004; World Bank 2006).

As a consequence of declining living standards, the implementation of SAPs and state withdrawal from social provisions, families have been under strain and unable to continue offering as much support to both nuclear or extended family, as was traditionally the case. Consequently, individuals have become increasingly reliant on external support, but although the competitive market is growing, it is not yet able to accommodate the needs of an increasing youth population.

Legal and policy framework

According to Shteiwi (2003), social policies in Jordan were developed through four phases. The time frame of each and main characteristics are summarised below (Shteiwi 2003, pp.12 and 117).

Phase 1

Noted to span from the establishment of the Jordanian state prior to independence from the British Mandate until the late 1940s.

- No identified policies.
- Social aid was provided through Christian and Muslim charitable organisations.

Phase 2

Early 1950s–late 1960s.

- Institutionalisation of social work, through the establishment of General Unions for Voluntary Societies.
- Expanding provisions in healthcare, education and aid for special needs.

Phase 3

1970s–late 1980s.

- Increased change and development in orientation and scope; growth of social services, health and education were further expanded and became the benchmark of social policies (Shteiwi 2003, p.12).
- Beginning of subsidisation of consumer goods.
- Establishment of the National Aid Fund (major government poverty-alleviation programme).
- Significant state role in guaranteeing employment, enhancing social justice and distributing wealth to meet the basic needs of its people.

Phase 4

From 1990s–present.

- Marked by the sharp economic decline with increasing pressures for implementing SAPs and state withdrawal from previous social policies.

Current policies aim to ameliorate the general socio-economic situation. They include policies to reduce high growth rates, alleviate poverty, reduce unemployment, improve social protection, health and education, and empower women (Shteiwi 2003, p.116). Analysts criticise the programmes generated by these policies as being fragmented, ineffective and lacking clear targeting and distribution between pockets of poverty and disadvantaged populations (Arab Urban Development Institute 2004; Shteiwi 2003).

Jordan ratified several regional and international conventions.[10] For Jordanian legislation to be consistent with the principles of the UN Convention on the Rights of the Child (UNCRC), several amendments have been implemented. These include the guaranteed right and mandatory completion of basic education, prohibition of hazardous employment prior to age 18, and amendments to laws linked to disabilities, child protection, health and culture (Arab Urban Development Institute 2004, p.10; National Council for Family Affairs 2004). The UNCRC was the main driver for prioritising children's rights. As a result, developments in legislation concerning children and youth are ongoing. Currently, the draft Jordanian Child Rights Bill 2004 is awaiting parliamentary approval (National Council for Family Affairs 2006). The Bill includes 30 articles to reduce gaps between the UNCRC and national legislation, safeguarding children's rights especially regarding participation and improving protection (mainly for those in difficult circumstances, e.g. abuse). The Bill also aims to unify protective legislation, and unite national efforts to prioritise children's benefits from all economic, social and development programmes (National Council for Family Affairs 2006, pp.4–6). Currently there is no legislation or policies focusing on youth leaving residential care.

Although leaving care may not be a political or legislative priority, it could be argued that this is not so different to the situation until recently in countries such as the United Kingdom and the United States (Biehal *et al.* 1995; Collins 2000; Stein 2004). Despite the current lack of priority, there are possibilities to assist young people within the current legal and welfare system. For example, officials from the MOSD stated that, although no formal legislation exists, upon recommendations from managers of government residential homes, legal extensions postponing the discharge of youth from care (up to age 20) can be granted. Examples include youth with exceptionally difficult circumstances, those who are still in school or in vocational training, and those who have no immediate or extended families to return to (which are considered to be a minority group among all youth in residential care). Youth who have no family have requested support after discharge and were aided by the ministry in securing accommodation, employment and training. As part of internal policies and despite limited resources, informal aftercare support was also provided by some non-governmental organisation (NGO) homes. In addition, there is an initiative (Al Aman Fund) which aims to secure educational and vocational training funds for orphans, including those who left residential care at the age of 18 after three years of residency. The Al Aman Fund also offers career guidance and development, as well as practical aid and counselling to those who qualify.

Initiatives directly targeting youth in residential care were included in the Jordanian National Plan of Action for Children (NPA 2004–2013).[11] They include improvements in the scope and quality of holistic services (including the establishment of minimum standards), as well as capacity building of all staff working with youth in homes. Moreover, there are proposals for improved reintegration measures prior to leaving care, support for families at risk and an enhancement in kinship care. These measures reflect an increased awareness of preparation for leaving care, to aid youth. Another reflection of social awareness is the increasing profile of care leavers in recent media coverage. A number of interviews in newspapers and on national television have taken place with care leavers that depicted their experiences.

In parallel, there are broader policies and national aims to strengthen social safety nets while combating the country's main challenges (e.g. high rate of population growth, high rates of poverty and unemployment). These policies have an impact on the population at large, including all youth transitioning to adulthood. Some national initiatives that could *potentially* be used as post-care support include access to health care, enrolment in social security, employment and vocational training, educational loans, and higher education[12] (National Council for Family Affairs 2004; Shteiwi 2003; United Nations Development Programme 2004).

Apart from potential services found within broader policies, numerous national and international NGOs provide services for various segments of the population in need, including youth. Provisions include medical and legal services, financial aid, access to vocational training and employment, academic scholarships and loans, and mentoring (provisions of various services by NGOs can be found in the NCFA study of 2004).

As noted above, all of these provisions can assist post-care support, if care leavers have access to them, and they are not just directed at youth in conflict with the law, or those involved in child labour. Access should be facilitated to care leavers through the MOSD and NGO homes in coordination with these service providers.

Secondary data

Data currently found at the Family and Childhood Directorate are administrative by nature, detailing numbers of children in governmental and NGO homes by broad age groups, gender and general reasons for admission.[13] Youth are admitted into care voluntarily (subject to approval by the MOSD) or through a court order. In either case, the formal assessments largely appear to be based on family means and risk factors. Official data also include the numbers of youth leaving care. However, youth may enter care temporarily (some for a few days) and others from birth until they reach the legal age of adulthood. Numbers of those leaving care do not differentiate between the length of time spent in homes. Youth who generally remain the longest in care are those with unknown parents and orphans. Residential care homes are distributed throughout the country according to age groups and gender. Most likely, this subgroup would therefore move between at least two or three homes (and therefore schools).

Leaving care research

Only one evaluative study investigating residential care homes in Jordan has been conducted. The outcomes of this study were disturbing. It found that 86 per cent of NGO homes did not provide psychological services; there were no individual care plans for children and young people; incidents of abuse took place within and outside of homes; and there was a lack of adequate preparation to leave care and a lack of academic and vocational support (United Nations International Children's Emergency Fund and Allayan 2002). The results of this study have contributed to an awareness of the measures needed to improve the situation. However, there is also the possibility that the study might over-generalise negative aspects to all homes. There is practice evidence that some NGO homes strive to aid youth during and post care and these positive experiences should be researched, as they too would provide great insight in to what is working in Jordan. Thus providing positive models, or, at minimum, building blocks to work from. However, there is a lack of research, most probably due to the relatively small number of youth residing in care homes, and the assumption that they are likely to be united with families post care. It would be very useful to have more in-depth research data exploring young people's progress across their life path: from their pre-care experiences, while they are living in care, at the time of leaving care, and following them up for several years after care.

A starting point for Jordan would be considering the use of the seven dimensions[14] developed in the UK and used as part of the national *Framework for the Assessment of Children in Need and Their Families* (Department of Health, Department for Education and Employment and Home Office 2000; Parker *et al.* 1991). These dimensions have been used internationally, and could be used as measurements to assess the progress of children (from birth to age 18), as well as the quality of care provided. They function as a tool 'to contribute to the understanding necessary for appropriate planning' (Compton and Galaway 1989), and are based on principles of 'reasonable parenting' as well as the 'promotion of children's welfare', rather than focusing on solving problems as they arise. They also have the potential to incorporate additional dimensions for the post-care period, including: identifying trans-generational institutionalisation; benefit dependency; vocational and academic qualifications on leaving care; participation in education and employment; conflict with the law; homelessness; juvenile prostitution; managing finances; housing; and managing relationships and parenthood. It may be thought that the collection of such data is very ambitious, but it should be manageable due to the relatively small numbers of youth in care. Such research will be vital in light of the wealth of information and lessons it can provide, especially in comparing factors found in successful and unsuccessful cases.

Unfortunately, there is no research that focuses on care leavers in Jordan. I hope to redress this situation. My doctoral research study is exploring the experiences of Jordanian care leavers, and how prepared they were upon leaving homes – thus for the first time giving them a voice.

Conclusion

Jordan can be classified as an externally dependent insecurity regime, dependent on aid with poor welfare outcomes (Gough *et al.* 2004). Despite macro-level achievements, poverty and unemployment remain relatively high: 53.8 per cent of the unemployed are between the ages of 15 and 24; that is, during the critical transitioning phase to adulthood. Additionally, within this context, there is an absence of a legal and policy framework to support young people leaving care; this is coupled with lack of preparation and vulnerability highlighted in the only evaluative study of care homes carried out in Jordan. Practice evidence suggests that care leavers were assisted in various ways by some homes, although assistance appears to be dependent on the presence of individuals, or the internal policies of selected homes, not on established or comprehensive policies. Secondary data is limited and administrative by nature, but includes information on reasons for admission, age groups, gender and annual number of youth in care. Research into young people leaving care in countries such as the United Kingdom has made a positive contribution to both policy and practice (e.g. Children [Leaving Care] Act 2000 – Department of Health 2001). Jordan can greatly benefit from learning about this Act as well as developments supporting care leavers in various countries. Consideration and guidance of future policies and services within the Jordanian context must be based on in-depth research with care leavers, especially in view of their vulnerability upon leaving care, and their high risk of being socially excluded within the current socio-economic context.

Key messages for policy and practice

- Minimum standards for residential care homes to include individual care plans incorporating the seven developmental dimensions and family assessments. Returning to families may not be suitable; their presence should not be taken for granted. Standards should include criteria for 'discharge eligibility', namely academic/vocational qualifications, health care insurance, secured accommodation, employment/academic participation and quality of familial relationships.

- Establishment of formal links between the homes and national initiatives aiming to strengthen safety nets, and NGO initiatives targeting youth.

- A research-based policy in support of care leavers must be established with specified follow-up criteria for an extended time frame (e.g. to age 24).

- Expansion of the services of the Al Aman Fund to become a 'leaving care' centre where support is not limited to qualifying candidates aged 18–21. It is recommended that the fund becomes a base for care leavers offering guidance and comprehensive support (including emotional, practical and social needs). It would be most advantageous if career guidance and development from the fund began while youth were still in care and as part of the preparation process in the homes.

- Establishment of minimum standards and qualifications for all staff working in residential homes and those providing post-care support.

- Establishment of an independent 'monitoring and evaluation' body (M&E) especially for youth admitted to care, to ensure adequate implementation of minimum standards, unite and evaluate the quality of services provided (during and post care), promote the welfare of both youth in and post care, as well as continuing to develop policies and services. The M&E body should have public awareness programmes to ameliorate the stigma experienced by children in care, especially in schools.

Notes

1. The term 'youth' is used throughout the document, encompassing both children and youth in care and until discharge. The term may be used intermittently with young people.
2. A form of selling goods on the streets or begging.
3. Rehabilitation centres for youth in conflict with the law: a total of five. All are governmental; four are for males and one is for females.
4. Residential care homes: a total of 24, of which 22 are private and two are governmental. All serve youth 'in need of care and protection' from birth to age 18 (in some

circumstances, extended to 21). The homes are licensed and monitored by the Family and Childhood Directorate within the Ministry of Social Development.

5. Semi-rentier state: oil-producing countries (e.g. Saudi Arabia) were classified as rentier states. In short, 'income derived from externally generated rents are available due to the gap between cost of production and the price of commodity. Financial resources generated are directly acquired by externally produced rents rather than through domestic means like taxation' (Piro 1998, p.11). Jordan has been classified as a semi-rentier state because it is not an oil-producing country and therefore not dependent on a single resource but a 'combination of foreign aid and labour remittances' (Piro 1998, p.11; also see Brynen 1992, pp.71–2), thus contributing to the ill development of a sound foundation of economic production that is highly vulnerable to the turbulent regional political system (Beblawi and Luciani 1987 in Brynen 1992 and Piro 1998).

6. International actors such as the World Bank (WB), World Trade Organisation (WTO) and the International Monetary Fund (IMF).

7. The Human Development Index is a composite indicator used to estimate well-being and developed by the United Nations Development Programme (UNDP). Calculations are based on measurements of three factors: standard of living (measured by gross domestic product (DPG) per capita in purchasing power according to standardised price levels), life expectancy and educational attainment (measured by adult literacy and enrolment ratios) (United Nations Development Programme 2004, pp.15–16, 131).

8. It is important to note that Jordan's reliance on aid is changing; it now largely depends on three forms of taxes (sales, income and custom taxes). In terms of welfare outcomes, 98.5 per cent have health care access (United Nations Development Programme 2004). The literacy rate is 89.9 per cent (Department of Statistics 2006b), expenditure on health and education of GDP is 16.1 per cent, and the annual government public expenditure on poverty alleviation is 3.26 per cent (Shteiwi 2008). All of these reflect the government's high commitment to encourage positive welfare outcomes and supporting the poor.

9. While the annual GDP growth rate remained constant at 3.2 per cent, the population has increased at a rate of 2.3 per cent (increasing the number of the poor); 14.7 per cent of the population is below the poverty line (Department of Statistics 2006b). The general poverty line adopted by the World Bank was based upon the cost of a minimum standard of both food and non-food items (*annual* JD 504 per person approximately $709). Of the total poor, 13.1 per cent are in urban, and 22.8 per cent in rural, areas (Department of Statistics 2006b). However, due to high urbanisation rates (78.3% of the total population at that time), the number of urban poor are said to be three times that of rural poor (Arab Urban Development Institute 2004). Currently the urban population has increased to 82.3 per cent (Department of Statistics 2006b). Unemployment has been 14.8 per cent (Department of Statistics 2006a); of the overall unemployed, 53.8 per cent are 15–24-year-olds (Department of Statistics 2006a).

10. Jordanian ratification of Arab and international conventions in 1984 and 1991 such as the UN Convention on the Rights of the Child (UNCRC), ILO Convention No. 138 and No. 182 (minimum age to employment entry and the prohibition and elim-

ination of the worst forms of child labour), in addition to two optional protocols adopted by the UN General Assembly dealing with the sale of children, child prostitution and child pornography. Jordan ratified the UNCRC with reservations to articles 14, 20 and 21 whereby any child born without known parental lineage does not have the right to choose his religion and is therefore Muslim; if a family would like to foster a child there are national laws and specified eligibility criteria to abide by, under Muslim Shari'a law. The same applies to adoption, which is much respected and encouraged, but only allowed following Islamic laws (Kafala or adoption in Islam) (Arab Urban Development Institute 2004; National Council for Family Affairs 2004).

11. National Plan of Action (NPA) 2004–2013 was devised by the National Council for Family Affairs (2004). NCFA is a semi-governmental organisation, established by a special law following a royal decree; under its umbrella, it unites efforts of all private/public institutions. Along with its partners, it develops policies and initiatives concerning all matters for the welfare of children and families in Jordan, including children in residential care (up to age 18), youth in conflict with the law, etc. The guiding framework of NPA 2004–2013 was based on accomplishments of the previous NPA (1997–2003) and subsequent to a number of regional and international conferences that were all based on the commitment and declaration to children (A World Fit for Children). The current NPA has five main components that are all related to the well-being of children beginning from neonatal care to monitoring and evaluating of services and the role of the media.

12. Access to education, vocational training and employment may be facilitated through NAF. Health care may also be through NAF or employers in the formal sector. Higher education could be obtained through the reserved quota in universities for unprivileged students; educational loans are also provided to families enrolled in NAF. Employment could be assisted by the National Employment Centre.

13. The identified broad reasons are: broken homes resulting from divorce, separations such as jail where parents are no longer capable of caring for their children, unknown parents, orphans and abuse including neglect.

14. The dimensions are: (1) Health; (2) Education; (3) Behavioural and emotional development; (4) Family and peer relationships; (5) Self-care and competence; (6) Identity; and (7) Social presentation.

References

Abu Jaber, K., Buhbe, M. and Smadi, M. (eds) (1990) *Income Distribution in Jordan.* Boulder: Westview Press.

Al Khouri, R. (2000) *The Welfare State, Globalization, and Middle East Peace: The Case of Jordan.* Paper presented at the Middle East Virtual Community (MEVIC, August 2000). Accessed 01/09/07 at www.mevic.org/papers/welfare-state.html

Arab Urban Development Institute (2004) *MENA Child Protection Initiative: The Report on Amman.* Commissioned by the Arab Urban Development Institute and conducted by the Information and Research Centre at the King Hussein Foundation. Jordan: IRC.

Baylouny, A.M. (2006) 'Creating kin: New family associations as welfare providers in liberalizing Jordan.' *International Journal of Middle East Studies 38*, 349–368.

Beblawi, H. and Luciani, G. (eds) (1987) 'The Rentier State.' In R. Brynen (1992) 'Economic crisis and post Rentier democratization in the Arab world: The case of Jordan.' *Canadian Journal of Political Science 25*, 1, 69–97.

Biehal, N., Clayden, J., Stein, M. and Wade, J. (1995) *Moving On: Young People and Leaving Care Schemes.* London: HMSO.

Brynen, R. (1992) 'Economic crisis and post Rentier democratization in the Arab world: The case of Jordan.' *Canadian Journal of Political Science 25*, 1, 69–97.

Collins, M.E. (2000) 'Transition to adulthood for vulnerable youths: A review of research and implications for policy.' *Social Service Review 75*, 271–291.

Compton, B.R. and Galaway, B. (1989) *Social Work Processes.* Pacific Grove: Brookes Cole.

Department of Health (2001) *Children (Leaving Care) Act 2000: Regulations and Guidance.* London: The Stationery Office.

Department of Health, Department for Education and Employment and Home Office (2000) *Framework for the Assessment of Children in Need and Their Families.* London: The Stationery Office.

Department of Statistics (2004) *Population and Housing Census 2004.* Jordan: Department of Statistics. Accessed 07/09/07 at www.dos.gov.jo/dos_home_e/main/index.htm

Department of Statistics (2006a) *Appraisal of Poverty Indicators Based on the Household Expenditure Survey 2005.* Jordan: Department of Statistics. Accessed 01/09/07 at www.dos.gov.jo/dos_home_e/appraisal%20of%20poverty%20indicator.pdf

Department of Statistics (2006b) *Jordan in Figures 2005. Issue 8, May 2006.* Jordan: Department of Statistics. Accessed 01/09/07 at www.dos.gov.jo/dos_home/jorfig/2005/jor_f_e.htm

Esping-Andersen, G. (1990) *The Three Worlds of Welfare Capitalism.* New Jersey: Princeton University Press.

Gough, I., Wood, G., Barrientos, A., Bevan, P., Davis, P. and Room, G. (2004) *Insecurity and Welfare Regimes in Asia, Africa and Latin America.* Cambridge: Cambridge University Press.

Ministry of Social Development (2006) *Annual Report of the Family and Childhood Directorate.* Unpublished. Jordan: Ministry of Social Development.

National Council for Family Affairs (2004) *Jordan Country Study of Disadvantaged Children.* Unpublished study completed for the World Bank with the National Council for Family Affairs. Jordan: National Council for Family Affairs.

National Council for Family Affairs (2006) *The Non-Governmental Supplementary Report on the 3rd Jordanian Official Report on CRC.* Unpublished report. Jordan: National Council for Family Affairs.

Parker, R., Ward, H., Jackson, S., Aldgate, J. and Wedge, P. (1991) *Looking After Children: Assessing Outcomes in Child Care.* London: HMSO.

Piro, T. (1998) *The Political Economy of Market Reform in Jordan.* New York: Rowman and Littlefield.

Population and Development Council and Jabre, B. (2002) *Proposal for Consolidation of Family Planning: Reproductive Health Programme in Jordan.* Report submitted as part of the Jordan Poverty Alleviation Program. Jordan: Ministry of Social Development and JPAP.

Shteiwi, M. (2003) *Social Policies in Jordan: The Social Development Report for Jordan, 2003.* Jordan: Jordan Center for Social Research (JCSR) and the Friedrich Ebert Stiftung Foundation.

Shteiwi, M. (2008) *Poverty and Unemployment in Jordan: The Social Development Report for Jordan 2006.* Forthcoming. Jordan: JCSR.

Stein, M. (2004) *What Works for Young People Leaving Care?* Essex: Barnardo's.

United Nations Development Programme (UNDP) (2004) *Jordan Human Development Report 2004: Building Sustainable Livelihoods.* Jordan: Ministry of Planning and International Cooperation and United Nations Development Programme.

United Nations International Children's Emergency Fund and Allayan (2002) *Evaluation of Rehabilitation Centers for Juveniles and Care Centers in Jordan.* Unpublished study. Jordan: UNICEF.

United Nations Relief and Works Agency for Palestine Refugees (2006) *Jordan Refugee Camp Profiles.* Amman: UNRWA. Accessed 01/07/09 at www.un.org/unrwa/refugees/jordan.html

World Bank (2006) *Country Assistance Program for the Hashemite Kingdom of Jordan 2006–2010.* Jordan: MENA, Jordan Country Management Unit and International Finance Corporation.

Acknowledgements

Special thanks to the following for their valuable input: Dr Jonathan Dickens, Dr Musa Shteiwi, Dr Hala Hammad, Deena Kalimat, Lina Kopty, Lina Mola and the SOS Villages in Jordan, Riad Al Khouri and Roxana Anghel. From the Ministry of Social Development, special thanks to Mohamad Kharabsheh and Khitam Jaber. Most importantly, my No. 1 teachers, the care leavers themselves.

Chapter 10

The Netherlands

Erik J. Knorth, Jana Knot-Dickscheit and Johan Strijker

Background and key statistics

- The Netherlands is home to well over 16.3 million people, approximately one in four (24.2%) of whom are children and young people under the age of 20 years (Centraal Bureau voor de Statistiek 2007).

- 21 per cent of these young people are of foreign descent and mostly of non-western origin.

- In 2003/2004 nearly 44,000 young people were placed in family foster care or residential settings.

- The most common placement type is residential care, accounting for around 60 per cent of all placements. In January 2006, some 3500 young people were on a waiting list (> two months) for a foster care or a residential placement.

- Residential placements are spread over three sectors: youth welfare services (2/3), in-patient mental health services (1/8) and residential provisions on a court order (1/5).

- The number of young people leaving care each year is unknown.

Key Sources

- Centraal Bureau voor de Statistiek (2007).
- Expertisecentrum Jeugdzorg NIZW (2006).
- Knorth et al. (2008).
- Strijker and Zandberg (2005).

Introduction

In the Netherlands some 220,000 young people (5.6% of 0–19-year-olds) are in touch with social services in a welfare, mental health and/or judicial context, a fifth of them (44,000) using out-of-home care services (Knorth 2005a). This chapter will focus on youths living in and leaving care. From our analysis it emerges that residential provision on court orders (correctional placements) alone provides a legal framework for providing after care and re-integration services for young care leavers. It was found that there are few Dutch studies on leaving care.

Case examples

Charles

Charles' mother died when he was five. His father was not able to take care of his son. The child protection board intervened when Charles was eight and arranged for a short stay in a foster family placement. After two months he was moved to a long-term foster family with four other children. It took him half a year to settle down. After a few relatively peaceful years Charles became more and more aggressive after his 15th birthday. According to his foster parents his friends were a bad influence on him and drank a lot of alcohol. He took an intermediate vocational training course on retail trade, but he failed his exams. When he was 17 the situation in the foster family became intolerable and Charles moved to a training centre for independent living.

Doreen

Doreen (16) was placed in secure accommodation (a correctional placement) because, among other things, she was forcing young boys to have sex with each other. The Education and Training Programme (ETP) in the institute included psychological goals, schooling, job orientation, social skills training and creative expression. After six months Doreen drew up a plan with agreements on how she would spend her leisure time and on her school performance. Her therapist focused on enhancing her self-esteem and exploring issues, including identity, sexual orientation, friendships and Doreen's role in the family. She visited trainee posts and contacted the Centre for Work and Income (CWI). Once she had left care she participated in a six-month aftercare programme, especially aimed at supporting her to find and keep a job. Alongside this, a probation officer provided assistance with financial and household matters.

The Dutch welfare regime

Pinkerton (2005) typifies the Dutch 'welfare regime' as *social democratic,* a finding that was based on Esping-Andersen's work (1990). However, in the last 10 to 15 years this 'regime' has increasingly been showing *liberal* tendencies. In the last two decades, for instance, there have been major cuts on more expensive provisions (such as residential youth welfare services). There is also growing support for the proposition that youth care services with proven effectiveness (including cost-effectiveness) alone can count on government support (Knorth 2005a).

Youth care is largely financed by government funds. In 2005 the expenditure for Dutch youth care services amounted to 1.6 billion euros (Expertisecentrum Jeugdzorg NIZW 2006). This is somewhat less than a tenth (9.2%) of the joint budgets of the ministries involved, notably Public Health, Welfare and Sport (PHWS) and Justice. Educational services are not included. The implementation of services is almost solely in the hands of non-governmental organisations. Taking into account the Dutch Gross National Product (GNP) of more than 495 billion euros the Dutch state spent 0.32 per cent of its GNP on child and youth care in 2005.

Legal and policy framework

In the 19th century numerous private institutions for 'neglected children' were founded all over the Netherlands. Juvenile offenders were accommodated in separate detention centres. The Children Act in 1901 (Van der Linden, Ten Siethoff and Zeijlstra-Rijpstra 1999) introduced government regulations for intervening in family relationships and this provided a legal framework for the institutions mentioned above. 'Re-education' became the core concept. In 1921 the Court Supervision Order was introduced as a child protection measure for children whose moral and/or physical development was threatened. The same year saw the appointment of separate juvenile court magistrates (Kruithof 2005).

After World War II, government subsidies for youth care gradually increased and the role of the government became more and more important. There was, however, a lack of national policy development and coordination. As a consequence, all the ministries involved – notably public health, social work, justice and education – started developing their own types of services and provisions from their own perspectives.

In the mid-1960s, youth care services started focusing on involving the family in the provision of care. Children's homes were introduced with a homely atmosphere with the aim of offering the child a situation to grow up in that resembled the family situation as closely as possible (Van Lieshout 1984). In the 1970s, care workers started realising the importance of children's rights, the participation of those seeking care and – most importantly – the prevention of developmental and rearing problems (Tilanus and Van Montfoort 2005).

Youth Care Act 1989

In the 1980s, the greatest change in post-war government policy came about. The government started emphasising the need for 'ambulant care' and presented youth care as a 'social concern'. The aim was (and still is) to help young people in their own home situation as long as possible in order to prevent the need for an out-of-home placement (Knorth, Knot-Dickscheit and Tausendfreund 2007). This policy was called the *zo zo zo beleid* which was legalised in the Youth Care Act of 1989. Youth care had to be given *as* lightly as possible, *as* close to home as possible and for *as* short a time as possible. Later on a fourth 'as' followed, which was: care should be offered *as* fast and timely as possible (Knorth 2005a).

In the same period decentralisation of responsibilities and tasks within youth care took place. The overlap of tasks and responsibilities between three layers of government[1] and the fact that more organisations developed additional provisions led to lack of clarity and integration of services in youth care in the Netherlands. The Youth Care Act 1989 aimed to provide more cohesion but was not successful in achieving this; a new law proved necessary (Tilanus and Van Montfoort 2005).

Interlude: chain approach

An important source of inspiration for initiatives to establish more cohesion in youth care policy was detailed in the paper *Vulnerable Youths and Their Future* (Schuyt 1995), which was directed to the central govern-

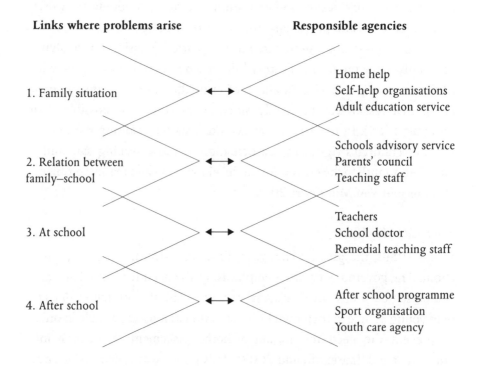

Links where problems arise   **Responsible agencies**

1. Family situation

Home help
Self-help organisations
Adult education service

2. Relation between family–school

Schools advisory service
Parents' council
Teaching staff

3. At school

Teachers
School doctor
Remedial teaching staff

4. After school

After school programme
Sport organisation
Youth care agency

Figure 10.1: Exemplary outline of course of life links and chain approach

ment. The author's analysis started from the child's life course perspective, entailing a number of crucial elements or phases in each child's life. Every phase could be the starting point of developmental problems or stagnation. Schuyt distinguished ten chain elements in a person's course of life, notably family; relation between family and school; at school; after school; between school and work: drop-out; between school and work: preparing for a job; getting a job; on the job; underway and unemployed; and in society. The author proposed, as a first step before any intervention, to identify the responsible party for dealing with the problems in each separate chain element (which together formed an entity of so-called *chain care*). Figure 10.1 illustrates the first four elements of the chain approach.

The concept of 'chain care' has been translated to youth care and might be useful in analysing the problems that care leavers encounter on their way to independence.

Youth Care Act 2005

When the Netherlands signed up to the UN Convention on the Rights of the Child (UNCRC) in 1995 a new impulse was given to youth care policy, particularly concerning youth participation (NIZW International Centre 2001). 'Youth participation in the Netherlands is mainly defined nowadays in terms of active involvement and shared responsibility of children and youths in their own environment' (ibid, p.4). This changed youth policy and also focused more attention on the protection of children and youths. The new Dutch Youth Care Act, in succession to the 1989 Act, was introduced on 1 January 2005. The new Act has strengthened the client's legal position. *Bureau Jeugdzorg* (BJz, i.e. Youth Care Agency) has become the central access gate for the more intensive forms of guidance and treatment (Knorth *et al.* 2003). In addition, child and youth care on a local level (municipalities) has been strengthened, aimed at prevention and providing easily accessible care.

Secondary data and research

It appears from research that the majority of young people in the Netherlands are faring well (Bakker 1999a). Ten to fifteen per cent of young people are regarded as 'problem youths' (Bakker 1999b; Schuyt 1995). In about 2 to 5 per cent of these youngsters the problems are so severe that long-term and intensive care is necessary (Hermanns et al. 2005). In the 1990s, 'problem youths' became a much debated topic. There was more and more concern about the growing gap between 'successful' and 'unsuccessful' youths (Bakker 1999a). It became clear that society was seeing an increasing group of deprived youths with bleak prospects, especially in relation to school drop-out and a lack of qualifications to get started in society. Moreover, research results showed an increase in high-risk behaviour such as alcohol and drug intake and smoking in Dutch youths (NIZW International Centre 2001). Although there was little increase in juvenile delinquency, the extent of their criminal behaviour was becoming more serious (Van der Laan 2001). Furthermore we also saw an increase in the number of homeless young people (Noom, Roorda-Honée and Heydendael 2003).

Latest figures (Expertisecentrum Jeugdzorg NIZW 2006) reveal that in 2004 more than 100,000 young people were registered at the BJz as new clients. In 32,500 cases the BJz applied for intensive care. In all other cases care workers were consulted at the agency. An equal number of youths (33,000) were referred to mental health care provisions by their general practitioners. In addition, 4700 youths were placed in residential institutes as a result of court orders.

At the end of 2004 nearly 11,000 youths resided in foster families (Bureau Landelijke Voorlichting Pleegzorg 2006). The same source of information reported a total of 17,500 *users* of foster care. In 50 per cent of these cases a stay lasted no longer than six months. The number of children in foster care is gradually growing. Since 1999 there has been a 75 per cent increase (Van Wijngaarden 2005). More under five-year-olds are now in foster care than before. Fewer adolescents are placed in foster families and their numbers are dwindling; in 2005 only 13 per cent of all newly placed children in foster care were aged 15 years or above. According to Bureau Landelijke Voorlichting Pleegzorg (BLVP) (2006) this tendency can be explained by the high risk of breakdown in the age group of 14-year-olds and older. According to Strijker and Zandberg (2005) the percentage of placement breakdowns for this age group stands at 45 per cent.

Dutch youth care policy concerning out-of-home placements shows a preference for foster family placements over residential placements. The reality is that there are more youths in residential care than in foster families. At the end of 2003 the number of residential placements amounted to about 11,600 (Expertisecentrum Jeugdzorg NIZW 2006). The number of *users* of residential care was much higher: more than 26,000. The difference can be explained by the fact that stays in residential care amount to a length of six months on average (short stays included). If short-stay placements are not taken into account the average length of stay amounts to 10.5 months (Knorth 2005a). The average age of the youths admitted is 14 and the percentage of breakdowns is 35–50 per cent (Knorth 2005b).

Up to the present day there is no legal framework covering aftercare for foster children. The only kind of aftercare is given under the Provisions for Foster Care by way of evaluation sessions after the child has (prematurely) left his or her foster family. The same applies to young people in residential welfare homes or child and youth mental health or psychiatric institutions. There are no legal regulations for aftercare. The situation is different for juvenile correctional facilities. The Act for Juvenile Correctional Institutions stipulates that youths should be able to participate in Education and Training Programmes (ETP) that help them prepare for leaving and afterwards (Van der Linden *et al.* 1999).

Leaving care research

Hardly any (recent) research has been conducted in the Netherlands on how care leavers fare in reality after leaving a children's home or foster family.

Residential care leavers

A review by Smit (1994) presented an overview of ten Dutch empirical studies in the years 1980–1990 concerning the situation of former residents of youth homes. The follow-up period was (with one exception) at least six months. The minimum age of the children in the sample was 15, although most of them were older. The percentage of young people not attending school or without a job varied between 17 and 47 per cent. In spite of occasional housing problems and a good deal of mobility, many former residents were quite happy with their housing situations. The majority of the youngsters had financial problems and were not able to cope with financial obligations on their own. Most of the young people did spend their leisure time in a relatively passive and unstructured way; membership of clubs (for instance, in sports) was relatively rare.

Many boys and girls experienced problems in their social relations with others, including parents, other family members and peers (see also Buysse 1997). Consumption of hard drugs was seen in a maximum of 10 per cent of the former residents. The number of young people using soft drugs and/or misusing alcohol was at a much higher level. The degree of recidivism among former juvenile delinquents who had been placed in closed institutions varied between 10 and 72 per cent, depending on variables such as sex and length of time of the follow-up. Looking at the total scores in the different studies Smit concluded that between 50 and almost 90 per cent of the former residents functioned 'reasonably to quite well' (p.18). At the same time she also concluded that the outcomes for boys, young people with a foreign background (immigrants) and especially early care leavers (drop-outs) were unfavourable compared with the outcomes of girls, those from the Netherlands, and regular care leavers.[2]

Foster care leavers

There are no (recent) Dutch research publications with follow-up data on foster care leavers. To obtain some indication of the characteristics of youths leaving foster care, we have consulted a recently designed data file of our own research work in progress (Strijker 2006). The file counts 165 children, aged 16 years and older. From these children 104 have left foster care and 46 of these (44%) have left foster care prematurely ('breakdown'). The most common reasons for their leaving prematurely were: 'child's own choice' (45%); 'child showing problem behaviour' (19%); and 'child is in conflict with foster parent' (18%). The remaining 58 foster children from the group of leavers (56%) were written out on account of having reached the age of 18. Nevertheless, they stayed with their foster family. Whether or not they were well prepared by their foster parents for independent living is unknown. Children in the category 'breakdown' experienced significantly more problems and had more former placements than those in the category of children still in foster care. Children who left early ('breakdown') went to their birth family (32%), independent living (32%), a residential facility (14%) or another foster family (12%) (10% residual category). The follow-up characteristics of foster children who went to supervised living and residential facilities correspond most likely with those of the residential care leavers described above.

Social (re)integration

Smit (1993) conducted empirical research, specifically on youths leaving residential care. She concluded that there were few predictors of the situation after leaving care. In the group of youngsters who returned after care, those who had a positive attitude towards leaving fared best. In the group of young people living independently, the ones who were given support were the ones who did best.

In the Netherlands there is limited experience in preparing youths for leaving a residential home. Two programmes are known to work on this issue: Exit Training (ET) and Work-Wise (WW). *Exit Training* aims to minimise residential youths' chances of becoming homeless and living on the fringes of society (Spanjaard 2006). The main focus of this skills training programme is on practical and material issues, personal competences (social skills) and creating a network. The criterion for success is fulfilment of four of five key targets. It emerged that three of the four youths met this criterion – at the end of ET and six months later (Spanjaard, Van der Veldt and Van den Bogaart 1999).

Another specific method is *Work-Wise* (Klomp 2005). WW comprises of a number of integrated activities in the area of assessment, education and training, work experience and housing. Besides these aspects, attention also focuses on debt reduction, restoring relationships, social skills, creating social networks and leisure time activities. Small-scale research shows that 'after completing the WW project the majority of youths are able to cope independently in society' (Klomp 2005, p.419). The management of correctional centres may decide that their young residents should participate in an Education and Training Programme (cf. the case example of Doreen, p.132) and leave on probation. It appears from a recent survey that in practice only a few youths from residential centres participate in ETPs, and leave on probation (Inspectie Jeugdzorg 2006).

Conclusion

In the Netherlands some 44,000 children and youths utilise foster care and residential care services every year. For a proportion of them, notably 16–18-year-olds, their stay in a residential or foster home is the stepping stone to independent living. Crucial to the question of whether they succeed or not is (among other things) the amount of social support they receive on their way to independence (cf. Curry 1991; Smit 1993). Research shows that for care leavers there is a greater chance of succeeding if they have a supportive (family) network (cf. Munro, Stein and Ward 2005). A breakdown in care – a relatively frequently occurring phenomenon in out-of-home placements for youth – increases the risk of negative developments.

Research on intervention programmes aimed at supporting care leavers' integration into society shows indications of positive outcomes. Effect studies, based on concrete evidence (by applying experimental or quasi-experimental research designs), are, however, still lacking. In addition, there is little insight into longer term developments, given the brief follow-up periods in the research discussed above. The implementation of aftercare and re-integration programmes is to a limited extent legally regulated (only in the judicial sector). However, in practice programmes have not yet been fully implemented.

Our findings point to the conclusion that the situation of care leavers in the Netherlands is not given high priority in policy, practice or research. The outlined 'chain approach' may prove to be an interesting point of departure for developing aftercare and re-integration programmes in the long term.

Key messages for policy and practice

- Research in the Netherlands on residential child care indicates that at least 50 per cent of former residents function reasonably to quite well six months after leaving care.

- Outcomes for boys, young people with a foreign background (immigrants) and early care leavers are unfavourable compared with the outcomes of girls, natives and regular care leavers.

- Given the rate of placement breakdowns in residential and foster care (up to 50%) research concerning determining factors should be intensified.

- (Scarce) research on programmes aimed at supporting care leavers' integration in society shows indications of positive outcomes.

- A legal framework for providing aftercare services only exists in the context of correctional placements for young people with antisocial behaviour.

- (Research on) leaving care is a neglected concern in the Netherlands.

Notes

1. The *national government* was understood to be the primary governing body, responsible for youth care policy in general; the ministry of PHWS fulfilled a coordinating role. The *provinces* became responsible for managing and distributing the budget for regional youth care and their task was to support the organisations that provided care and protection to children and youths. The *municipalities'* aim was to shape youth policy with the emphasis on prevention at a local level. This division of responsibilities also represents the current situation.

2. A small proportion of the drop-outs – according to Scholte and Van der Ploeg (2006) ± 4 per cent of adolescent inhabitants – ends up as homeless youth. Noom's survey among homeless youngsters (cf. Noom *et al.* 2003) showed that 40 per cent of his sample ($n = 190$) had lived before in residential homes. Many interviewees appeared to be ambivalent when asked about their attitude towards care provisions to help them towards integrating into society; care in a practical sense is appreciated (help for financial and housing problems), but they often rejected care concerning psychosocial problems, stating that people should 'mind their own business' (cf. Noom, De Winter and Knorth 2008). A meta-analysis on outcomes of residential youth care programmes in general (Knorth *et al.* 2008) shows a (weighted) mean

effect size (ES) of .60 as to general problem behaviour and externalising behavioural problems. The results as to internalising behavioural problems show a mean ES of .45. It concerns short-term effects. The authors suggest that long-term effects can be positively affected by intensive aftercare programmes.

References

Bakker, K. (1999a) 'Inleiding.' ['Introduction.'] In K. Bakker, M. Pannebakker and J. Snijders (eds) *Kwetsbaar en Competent. Sociale Participatie van Kwetsbare Jeugd. Theorie, Beleid en Praktijk.* Utrecht: NIZW.

Bakker, K. (1999b) 'Sociale kwetsbaarheid en sociale competentie: een kaderstelling.' ['Social vulnerability and social competency: a frame of reference.'] In K. Bakker, M. Pannebakker and J. Snijders (eds) *Kwetsbaar en Competent. Sociale Participatie van Kwetsbare Jeugd. Theorie, Beleid en Praktijk.* Utrecht: NIZW.

Bureau Landelijke Voorlichting Pleegzorg (BLVP) (2006) *Factsheet Pleegzorg 2005. [Factsheet Foster Care 2005.]* Accessed 18/08/06 at www.pleegzorg.nl/tekst-algemeen/2005_Factsheet_Pleegzorg.pdf

Buysse, W.H. (1997) *Personal Social Networks and Behavior Problems in Adolescence.* PhD Dissertation. Leiden: Leiden University.

Centraal Bureau voor de Statistiek (CBS) (2007) *Kerncijfers. [Base Figures]* Accessed 08/03/07 at www.cbs.nl/nl-NL/menu/cijfers/kerncijfers/default.htm

Curry, J.F. (1991) 'Outcome research on residential treatment: Implications and suggested directions.' *American Journal of Orthopsychiatry 61*, 348–357.

Esping-Andersen, G. (1990) *The Three Worlds of Welfare Capitalism.* New Jersey: Princeton University Press.

Expertisecentrum Jeugdzorg NIZW (2006) *Feiten en Cijfers. [Facts and Figures.]* Accessed 18/08/07 at www.jeugdzorg.nl/smartsite.dws?id=2002

Hermanns, J, Van Nijnatten, C., Verheij, F. and Reuling, M. (2005) 'Ten geleide.' ['Foreword.'] In J. Hermanns, C. van Nijnatten, F. Verheij and M. Reuling (eds) *Handboek Jeugdzorg. Deel 1: Stromingen en Specifieke Doelgroepen.* Houten: Bohn Stafleu van Loghum.

Inspectie Jeugdzorg (2006) *Een Betere Terugkeer in de Maatschappij. De Uitvoering van STP en Proefverlof in de Praktijk. [A better return in society. The implementation of ETP and probationary release in practice.]* The Hague: Inspectie Jeugdzorg.

Klomp, M. (2005) 'Arbeidstoeleiding.' ['Steering to the labour market.'] In J. Hermanns, C. van Nijnatten, F. Verheij and M. Reuling (eds) *Handboek Jeugdzorg. Deel 2: Methodieken en Programma's.* Houten: Bohn Stafleu van Loghum.

Knorth, E.J. (2005a) 'Wat maakt het verschil? Over intensieve orthopedagogische zorg voor jeugdigen met probleemgedrag.' ['What makes the difference? Intensive care and treatment for children and adolescents with serious problem behaviour.'] *Kind en Adolescent 26*, 4, 334–351.

Knorth, E.J. (2005b) 'Uithuisplaatsingen' ['Placements out-of-home.'] In J. Hermanns, C. van Nijnatten, F. Verheij and M. Reuling (eds) *Handboek Jeugdzorg. Deel 2: Methodieken en Programma's.* Houten: Bohn Stafleu van Loghum.

Knorth, E.J., Harder, A.T., Zandberg, Tj. and Kendrick, A.J. (2008) 'Under one roof: A review and selective meta-analysis on the outcomes of residential child and youth care.' *Children and Youth Services Review 30*, 2, 123–140.

Knorth, E.J., Knot-Dickscheit, J. and Tausendfreund, T. (2007) 'Zorg voor jeugdigen: ambulant én niet-ambulant. Ontmoetingen aan de voor- en achterkant of ook gaande door het pand?' ['Child and youth care: ambulant and non-ambulant. Meetings at the front and back door or also on the floor?'] *Tijdschrift voor Orthopedagogiek 46*, 3, 115–129.

Knorth, E.J., Metselaar, J., Josias, H.J., Konijn, C., Noom, M.J. and Van Yperen, T.A. (2003) 'Indications for treatment in child and youth care: Results from two complementary studies.' *International Journal of Child and Family Welfare 6*, 4, 167–184.

Kruithof, B. (2005) 'Kinderbescherming.' ['Child protection.'] In J. Hermanns, C. van Nijnatten, F. Verheij and M. Reuling (eds) *Handboek Jeugdzorg. Deel 1: Stromingen en specifieke doelgroepen*. Houten: Bohn Stafleu van Loghum.

Munro, E.R., Stein, M. and Ward, H. (2005) 'Comparing how different social, political and legal frameworks support or inhibit transitions from public care to independence in Europe, Israel, Canada and the United States.' *International Journal of Child and Family Welfare 8*, 4, 191–201.

NIZW International Centre (2001) *Jeugd en beleid in Nederland: Overzicht van tien jaar. [Youth and policy in the Netherlands: A review of ten years.]* Utrecht: NIZW International Centre.

Noom, M.J., De Winter, M. and Knorth, E.J. (2008) *'Please help me!' 'Please leave me alone!: Matching needs and services for homeless youth* (under review).

Noom, M.J., Roorda-Honée, J. and Heydendael, P. (2003) *Thuisloosheid bij Jongeren en Volwassenen. [Homelessness of Young People and Adults.]* Houten: Bohn Stafleu van Loghum.

Pinkerton, J. (2005) *Welfare Regimes. Structuring the Space for Care Leaving?* Briefing paper presented at the 'Transitions to Adulthood for Care Leavers International Comparisons Seminar', 3–5 November, Queens University Belfast, Northern Ireland.

Scholte, E.M. and Van der Ploeg, J.D. (2006) 'Residential treatment of adolescents with severe behavioural problems.' *Journal of Adolescence 29*, 641–654.

Schuyt, C.J.M. (1995) *Kwetsbare Jongeren en Hun Toekomst. [Vulnerable Youths and Their Future.]* Rijswijk/The Hague: Ministry of Public Health, Welfare and Sport.

Smit, M. (1993) *Aan Alles Komt een Eind. Een Onderzoek naar Beëindiging van Tehuishulpverlening. [Everything Comes to an End. Research on Termination of Residential Youth Care.]* PhD Dissertation. Leiden: Leiden University.

Smit, M. (1994) *Stand van Zaken van Follow-up Onderzoek op het Gebied van de (Residentiële) Jeugdhulpverlening: Verslag van een Literatuurstudie. [State of the Art Concerning Follow-up Research on (Residential) Youth Care: Report on a Review of the Literature.]* Voorhout: Bureau WESP.

Spanjaard, H.J.M. (2006) *Handleiding bij De Vertrek Training. Intensief Ambulante Hulp Gericht op Competentievergroting en Netwerkversterking. [Manual of Exit Training. An Intensive Training Directed at Enhancement of Competencies and Network Support.]* Amsterdam: Uitgeverij SWP.

Spanjaard, H.J.M., Van der Veldt, M.C.A.E. and Van den Bogaart, P.H.M. (1999) 'Exit training for youngsters in residential care: Treatment to prevent homelessness.' *International Journal of Child and Family Welfare 4*, 2, 130–148.

Strijker, J. (2006) *Placement Dynamics in Long Term Foster Care*. (Data File). Groningen: Department of Special Education and Child Care, University of Groningen.

Strijker, J. and Zandberg, Tj. (2005) 'Breakdown in foster care.' *International Journal of Child and Family Welfare 8*, 2/3, 76–87.

Tilanus, C.P.G. and Van Montfoort, A.J. (2005) 'Jeugdzorg.' ['Child and youth care.'] In J. Hermanns, C. van Nijnatten, F. Verheij and M. Reuling (eds) *Handboek Jeugdzorg. Deel 1: Stromingen en Specifieke Doelgroepen*. Houten: Bohn Stafleu van Loghum.

Van der Laan, P.H. (2001) 'Antisociaal gedrag en jeugdcriminaliteit: Aard, omvang en ontwikkeling.' ['Antisocial behaviour and youth criminality: Nature, magnitude and development.'] In E.J. Knorth, T.A. van Yperen, P.H. van der Laan and G.A. Vlieger-Smid (eds) *Gedrag Gekeerd? Interventies in de Jeugdzorg bij Antisociaal Gedrag en Jeugdcriminaliteit.* Houten/Diegem: Bohn Stafleu van Loghum.

Van der Linden, A.P., Ten Siethoff, F.G.A. and Zeijlstra-Rijpstra, A.E.I.J. (1999) *Jeugd en Recht. [Youth and Justice.]* Houten/Diegem: Bohn Stafleu van Loghum.

Van Lieshout, J. (1984) *Gezinshuizen: Model en Methodiek. [Family Homes: Model and Methods.]* Amsterdam: Sociaal-agogisch Centrum Het Burgerweeshuis.

Van Wijngaarden, A. (2005) 'Thema: Pleegzorg in de tijd. Pleegzorg 2003 in cijfers.' ['Theme: Foster care in the course of time. Foster care 2003 in numbers.'] *Mobiel 31,* 6, 14–15.

Chapter 11

Norway

Jan Storø

Background and key statistics

- The total population of Norway on 1 January 2006 was 4,640,200.

- About 1,078,000 of these Norwegians were under the age of 18.

- In 2005, a total of 39,200 children and youths received assistance from the Norwegian Child Welfare Service, which represents 25.2 per 1000 children.[1] This is an increase of 4.2 per cent from the year before.

- The number of recipients of assistance from the Norwegian Child Welfare Service is increasing in all age groups, but the largest increase in the last few years has taken place among youths aged 18–22. Between 2004 and 2005 this group increased by 300 to a total of 4100, an increase of 7.7 per cent.

- Most young people leave care at the age of 18, 19 or 20.

- Norwegian Child Welfare Services seem to work with a larger number of young people as they leave care than they used to. It is natural to assume that one of the reasons for this is the legislative change that took place in 1998 (see below).

Key sources

- Clausen (2000).
- Statistisk sentralbyrå (Statistics Norway): www.ssb.no.

Introduction

Norway is a country with a relatively homogeneous population, and this has been the situation for most of the last century. We have traditionally had small relative differences in income, a short immigration history and low rates of unemployment. However, differences in income are increasing.

Norway is not more than 101 years old as an independent state. During the last 50 years it has grown wealthy, in the main due to the oil and gas deposits in the North Sea. In the present century Norway has been governed by shifting coalitions based either in the labour party or the moderate right wing party. A large neo-liberalist party has also had strong influence, although it has not yet been included in any coalition. The civil rights of the individual have a strong profile in Norwegian consciousness. A 'child perspective' is quite common in Norwegian legislation and current culture, but this perspective is not always converted into legal rights. The Norwegian people have through two referendums decided that the country should not join the EU.

The Ministry of Children and Equality is the government department responsible for the Child Welfare Act and Child Welfare Services. The locally based Child Welfare Services are responsible for most child welfare work, except for running institutions and recruiting foster family homes. These two areas are taken care of by the *Bufetat*, a municipal authority organised in five regions under a central leadership. This implies that leaving care services are mostly the responsibility of the local Child Welfare Services. Four main reasons for child welfare interventions can be identified: domestic conditions at the home of the child; child neglect; children displaying behavioural disorders; and child abuse (Clausen 2000).

Most children receiving assistance from Child Welfare Services, about 32,000, receive assistance while living at home, for example through home visits, supervision of the parents, kindergartens and support for the child. These types of assistance are most common for small children, whereas young people of more than 13 years are often placed directly (Clausen 2003). About 7100 children and youths were under the protective care of the Child Welfare Service during the year, and 83 per cent of these children were placed in foster homes. Clausen (2000) found that 56 per cent of all children experiencing at least one placement were placed for one or two years.

My own adaptation of figures from Statistisk sentralbyrå (Statistics Norway)[2] revealed that in 2003 there were 2234 young people aged 17 years receiving Child Welfare Services. The same year, 973 young people aged 19 and 244 aged 21 were receiving services. This indicates that young people are choosing to end their career of receiving help from Child Welfare Services when they are 18, 19 or 20 years old. Figures from previous years confirm this tendency. The largest decrease in services occurs from 18 to 19; almost half of the 18-year-olds in 2002 were not receiving child welfare services the year after. A more thorough investigation of these figures indicates that young people in foster care stay longer than those in residential care. The total number of young people aged 18–23 receiving child welfare services in 2003 was 3730.

Case examples

Anders

Anders was taken into care at three years of age. He had been living with his mother after his father died. In the following two years, Anders' mother had taken up drinking and the child welfare worker supervising the home had growing concerns about Anders' situation. After receiving several support measures, including respite care at home, Anders' mother agreed to a care order. Anders was first placed in a residential unit for assessment, and after two months he was permanently placed in a foster home.

Marianne

Marianne is living in a youth residential unit. She has just turned 18. The residential unit has offered her a supported flat for the next 6–12 months.

After that she has the option of renting a flat from social services, with the rent paid by Child Welfare Services. She will receive support from her contact staff in the residential unit once a week, as long as she lives in the supported flat. One member of staff has taken special interest in Marianne, and has promised to help her with her school work. Marianne's main concern is whether this support will end when she finishes school at 19.

Norway's welfare regime

Norway's welfare regime is best described as a model with a high level of decommodification and redistribution. This is close to Esping-Andersen's (1990) concept of the 'social democratic' model. A main objective for Norway's welfare state is to protect members of society from unintended impacts of market forces. Norwegian society is built on the desire to create equality between the citizens, and universalism is the main guiding principle for services from the authorities. Services from the state are financed by taxes. They are (at least to a large extent) run by the authorities and are guided by political decisions. The social democratic model is under pressure in Norway as during the last 20 years a market economy rationale has been introduced into public administration.

Legal and policy framework

The first modern Norwegian child welfare Act, implemented in 1954, had provisions for after care up to the age of 23. These were dropped when *Stortinget*[3] announced new legislation in 1992. One of the reasons for this change was media criticism of child welfare work during the 1980s. A common view was that the child welfare system intervened too often and too soon. This led to legislation that reduced the power of child welfare workers and increased that of the clients or users of services.

At the same time a municipal court-system for child welfare and other social matters was introduced. It was also decided that young people should get the opportunity to manage on their own when they reached the age of 18, without interference from workers, staff or carers. This led to a passive child welfare sector when it came to leaving care services. Workers generally accepted the new signals from the politicians even if they were politically rather than empirically based.

The term 'aftercare' disappeared from Norwegian child welfare for the next few years. When experiencing the problems created by the new Act, several workers and organisations began to discuss the problems relating to young people being sent out into society, having been in care, without proper preparation and support. One of the most important organisations in this discussion was the organisation of young people in care, *Landsforeningen for barnevernbarn* (LFB), which was started in 1997. They decided that their first goal would be to contribute to a change in the legislation in order to bring back leaving care services in Norwegian child welfare. The organisations, among them also the national organisation of foster carers, *Norsk Fosterhjemsforening* (NFF), and the union of social workers and child welfare workers, *Fellesorganisasjonen for barnevernpedagoger, sosionomer og vernepleiere* (FO), joined in a committee to arrange a major conference about leaving care in October 1997.

All the organisations also used their ordinary political channels to promote the issue. In the early summer of 1998 the Norwegian Parliament agreed upon a change in the legislation. The Ministry made it clear that the many messages they had received from workers, young people and others about the need for leaving care services were a major reason for the revision of legislation.

The changes to the Act were implemented on 1 September 1998, and sections 1–3 state:

> When the child approves, services implemented before the child reaches the age of 18 can be maintained or substituted by other services mentioned in this Act until the child has reached the age of 23.

The changes demonstrated a recognition of young people's need to have support after care, that the transition from care to adulthood in a modern society can be difficult and that the young person may need support over several years. The actual text in the Act does not refer specifically to the concept of aftercare, but says that any service offered by local authorities, and mentioned in other parts of the Act, can also be offered to young people leaving care. Normally this would include social support, financial support, help in finding accommodation, education and/or work, therapy, access to a support-person and a prolonged stay in a foster home or institution up to the age of 20 years. It also states that young people of 20 years or more cannot be given accommodation in an institution as a leaving care service.

Leaving care services are developing in Norway. It remains to be seen how local authorities in Norway will undertake this work in the future. They may provide direct services offered by social workers or they may pay foster carers or ask residential establishments to deliver the actual leaving care work. Specialist schemes are not very common in Norway. The other important change in the legislation concerns preparation. It was formulated as a new section, 4–15:

> The local authorities shall, in due time before the child reaches the age of 18, evaluate whether the placement (in an institution or a foster home) shall be prolonged or the child shall receive other services after having reached 18 years. If the child approves to receiving further services, the local authorities shall work out a plan for future services. The plan can be changed.

Under this regulation the local authorities have a duty to make a needs assessment at a stage where there still is time to prepare the young person for life after care. The Act says nothing specific about preparation, so workers have to decide what is good practice without formal guidance.

The organisation of young people in care, LFB, has suggested leaving care services should be a right that the Act should ensure for each individual young person. The Ministry has not agreed to this, but says that any young person being sent out of care without receiving leaving care services can make a complaint to the County Governor. This is meant to ensure young people all over the country receive equal possibilities in the transition. A study of such complaints to the County Governor identified 14 complaints in the year 2000 and 25 the year after (Storø 2004). It is debatable whether the right to complain contributes to good enough access to leaving care services. Young people also demanded a right to (return to) the service and ask for assistance even if they rejected support previously. The Act says that services can be given to young people after their 18th birthday even if they said no to the support when they still were minors. We have no substantial research on this, and the debate goes on as to whether Child Welfare Services will support young people in this situation or take the opportunity to close the case in order to save money. The last sentence of the insert refers to the possibility of changing the service a young person receives in line with his or her needs at any time (also after the age of 18). The Ministry states that all aftercare services should be based on the aim that the young person shall manage his or her own life without help from any authority. In this process most young people will need different services at different stages.

When young people become independent and end their contact with Child Welfare Services, they are entitled to help from NAV, which is the Norwegian Labour and Welfare Organisation. This organisation is a merger of three former organisations: the National Insurance Organisation, the National Employment Service and the Social Welfare Service. NAV's main objective is to provide work for its users.

The existing political debate on the situation of care leavers is paradoxical. Norwegian politicians demonstrate agreement on the need for action, but also a lack of political will to put through new legislation or other substantial changes. During the last year *all* parties in the parliament have spoken up for young people in the transition from care, but they have not reached an agreement on what should actually be done about the issue.

Secondary data

There is a lack of targeted information on care leavers. It is possible, via the personal identification number, to connect data about income, work, education, health, social security, child welfare services and so on. But this kind of comprehensive research is expensive and the demand to protect privacy also sets limitations. However, it would be naïve to suggest that these are the only reasons for the lack of research. Also, it may be that care leavers have not been a large enough group to demand the attention of researchers in Norway. Other areas such as general research on young people, research on the quality of child welfare services and research on disadvantaged groups visible in the media seem to dominate. Sometimes a possible area of research needs to be made visible by a certain event or media presentation. This has not yet happened in Norway when it comes to care leavers. Care experiences have been visible in the most central media for the last ten years, but this has not led to increased research interest on leaving care. It seems that care leavers are marginalised not only in society, but also when it comes to research.

Leaving care research

One research group has carried out research on children and young people in care in a way that can help us to learn more about care leavers. Kristoffersen (2005) and Clausen (2003) have conducted a longitudinal study on client careers for all children and young people in care and those receiving assistance while living at home between 1990 and 2006. This is important work as the annual statistical data do not say anything about care careers. The annual population of children in care and in contact with Child Welfare Services has doubled between 1990 and 2002 (Kristoffersen 2005); 10.4 per cent of all these children had lived in residential care and about half of them had been in care for less than one year; 11.7 per cent had lived in a foster home and about half of these children had lived there more than four years. Residential placements were mostly in use for young people.

This group of researchers have also found that about three-quarters of all young people with a care career will at some point be clients of the social welfare system (Clausen 2008). Kristoffersen's (2005, p.90) research also highlights the potential vulnerability of children and young people in care and having left care during the period 1990 to 2003:

> They have an obviously larger portion of disability benefit compared with children and young people in the general population. There is also a higher mortality rate among children and young people having received child welfare services and among their biological parents... Children and young people with a care career seem to be an even more vulnerable group when it comes to welfare policy than revealed in other research. (My translation.)

However, to date there are no studies that can give us a broad and reliable picture of how young people leaving care cope after they leave care, in independent life. We lack what Broad (1998) calls national data on care leavers. Reports from practice indicate that an unspecified number of young people fail to receive support in the transition, although this still needs to be researched.

There are some small-scale, qualitative studies. Veland (1993) found that about two-thirds of young people who left care in one county coped reasonably well. Fourteen years later, Helgeland (2007) reached a similar conclusion for about the same proportion of a population of 30-year-olds formerly connected to a treatment project for young people with behavioural problems. Among the most important findings in my own study was that the young people who left care that I interviewed asked for support from adults and the professional systems they were a part of, and that this apparently was the most significant single factor for how they judged their possibility to cope on their own (Storø 2005). Thanem's (2006) study revealed that conditions for support were connected to the extent to which young people followed workers' rules.

However, none of these studies gives a comprehensive account of the specified group of young people during their transition to independence. They have not been able to use a research design that has allowed general conclusions to be drawn for a wider sample of young people as they leave care. They are however important contributions to developing this field of research in Norway.

During the last few years we have seen a growing interest in leaving care issues, and currently several Norwegian studies are in progress. Elisabeth Fransson and Inger Oterholm are studying how young people construct their ways through care and as a care leaver (EF), and cooperation within the professional field that takes best care of young people in the transition (IO). Also, a group of researchers of *Norges teknisk naturvitenskaplige universitet* (NTNU) are conducting a four-year study on young people leaving care in Trondheim (Norway's third-largest city). They are particularly interested in the measures given by Child Welfare Services, and to what extent these measures fit in with help the young people receive after their care career. Their first report identifies the young people's satisfaction with, but also their critical remarks towards, the services they received (Bratterud *et al.* 2006). Other ongoing studies are focusing on care careers, on homeless young people and on kinship foster care. These studies are to some extent concerned with the transition to independence. The Ministry for Children and Equality is also carrying out research on leaving care issues, such as how these services function throughout the country.

Conclusion

Norway is generally viewed as a social democratic state. The general level of family income means that few Norwegian children live in poverty. The current legal and policy framework has also led to a child welfare system that supports and protects children and young people from maltreatment. Young people leaving care may also receive a number of services to support them. However, legislation that does not specifically instruct Child Welfare Services to deliver leaving care services, as a duty, may leave a number of young people without support during their transition to adult-hood. Statistically, Norway has a well-mapped population, although register data do not give comprehensive information on care leavers. To date, the research field has not taken a substantial interest in this group. Although research is currently in progress, more research is needed to develop a comprehensive picture of the experiences and needs of this vulnerable group of young people.

Key messages for policy and practice

- Young people seem to leave care at 18, 19 or 20 years.
- They need support in the transition to independence.
- When young people leave care, many of them want support and they have specific ideas about what type of support is best.
- Young people with care careers are a vulnerable group when it comes to health and mortality.
- One-third of care leavers seem to be especially vulnerable, even when research is undertaken several years after they left care.

- More research is needed to map the circumstances and experiences of this group of young people, how they cope and what services they need.

Notes

1. If we look at all children in contact with Child Welfare Services during an eight-year period (1990–97), we will see that the dissemination doubles. One of every 20 children received help from Child Welfare Services in this period (Clausen 2000).
2. Adaptation of statistics published in Norwegian at www.ettervern.org.
3. The Norwegian parliament.

References

Bratterud, Å., Binde, R., Horneman, K., Dahlø Husby, I.S. *et al.* (2006) *Ungdom med Barneverntiltak – på vei mot Voksenlivet.* NTNU Arbeidsrapport nr. 18/2006.

Broad, B. (1998) *Young People Leaving Care. Life After the Children Act 1998.* London: Jessica Kingsley Publishers.

Clausen, S.E. (2000) *Barnevern i Norge 1990–1997. En Longitudinell Studie Basert på Registerdata.* Oslo: NIBR.

Clausen, S.E. (2003) 'Plasseringer utenfor hjemmet på 1990 tallet.' In E. Backe-Hansen (ed.) *Barn Utenfor Hjemmet. Plassering i Barnevernets Regi.* Oslo: Gyldendal Akademisk.

Clausen, S.E. (2008) Material in press, presented in the media and confirmed via personal contact with the researcher.

Esping-Andersen, G. (1990) *The Three Worlds of Welfare Capitalism.* New Jersey: Princeton University Press.

Helgeland, I. (2007) *Unge med Alvorlige Atferdsvansker Blir Voksne. Hvordan Kommer de inn i et Positivt Spor? En Oppfølgingsstudie.* Universitetet i Oslo: Det utdanningsvitenskaplige fakultet.

Kristoffersen, L. (2005) *Barnevernbarnas Helse. Uførhet og Dødelighet i Perioden 1990–2002.* Oslo: NIBR.

Statistisk sentralbyrå (Statistics Norway) Accessed 24/02/08 at www.ssb.no

Storø, J. (2004) *Gode Intensjoner, Lite på Papiret. En Undersøkelse om Barneverntjenestenes Arbeid med de Eldste Barnevernbarna.* Accessed 24/02/08 at www.ettervern.org

Storø, J. (2005) *Å gå over Brennende Bruer. En Kvalitativ Studie av Barnevernungdommers Overgang til en Selvstendig Tilværelse.* Oslo: Høgskolen i Oslo.

Thanem, H.A. (2006) *Sist i køa – svik og brutte løfter i barnevernet. En kvalitativ studie av barneverungdoms opplevelser knyttet til overgangen til en selvstendig tilværelse.* Norway: Hovedfagsoppgave i psykologi, NTNU.

Veland, J. (1993) *Hvordan Gikk det med Barnevernets Barn? Resultater fra Barnevernsarbeid i 5 Kommuner i Rogaland.* Stavanger: Senter for Atferdsforskning.

Chapter 12

Romania

Roxana Anghel and Gabriela Dima

Background and key statistics

- Population: over 22 million, of whom 4.4 million are children under 18. In the last decade the country has registered negative population growth.

- Children in out-of-home care: 73,976 in 2006 (153 per 10,000 children).

- Almost 65 per cent of placements are now with foster carers (kinship and professional). Following sustained deinstitutionalisation use of residential placements has decreased from approximately 100,000 in 1990 to approximately 26,000 in 2006 (21,198 in public care and 4907 in the NGO sector).

- Most care is long term and the most common age profiles are 14 to 17 (9000) and 18 to 26 (6500) years.

- Care leaving takes place between 18 and 26 depending on young people's continuing education. Annually approximately 2000 young people leave care, although this is estimated to grow to 5000 in the next four years.

- Care leavers are more numerous in the North East[1] (32%), North West and Centre (each 13%), and Bucharest (8%). Service provision partially reflects the local need with most preparation and career support services located in the North East and South, while supported housing is more developed in the West and North West.

Key sources

- Lazaroiu *et al.* (2005).
- Muga *et al.* (2005).
- National Authority for the Protection of Children's Rights (ANPDC) (2006).
- National Authority for Youth (ANT) (2005).

Introduction

Romania is an Eastern European country bordered by Bulgaria, Hungary, Ukraine, Moldova and the Black Sea. Administratively the country is divided into 41 *judete* (counties) and the capital, which is further divided into six sectors. The country is a parliamentarian democracy. It has been governed by a liberal democrat coalition government since 2004, being previously led by social democrat governments.

In 1990 Romania began the process of recovery from the effects of 40 years of the 'worst totalitarian regime in Central and Eastern Europe' (Bojkov 2004), moving towards the implementation of liberal democracy and free market economic structures. During the 1990s the transition created instability, leading to high unemployment and inflation, corruption and poverty, and at the same time generating a steep decline in social protection (C. Zamfir 1996a).

Since 2000, Romania has begun to recover from this situation, registering consistent annual economic growth (around 6% annually) (National Authority for Youth 2005), stimulated mainly by the negotiations to join the European Union (EU), which came to fruition in January 2007. Following increased foreign investment the unemployment rate has fallen from 11.6 per cent in 1998 to 5.4 per cent in 2007 (National Agency for Employment 2007). Yet a third of the population still lived below the poverty line in 2003 (Lazaroiu *et al.* 2005), and society is perceived by the majority to be polarised between the very poor and very rich (National Authority for Youth 2005). Despite new local employment opportunities, youth has remained severely affected by unemployment. Between 2002 and 2004 just over two-thirds of young people were unable to find work (National Authority for Youth 2005). This generated distrust in government and increased dependency on family support, which remains the main source of income support for 78 per cent of young people, even when married. It also increased interest in economic immigration and more than half of young people wish to leave the country temporarily or for good.

Mirroring this transition, the Romanian child care system, and within it care leaving, have followed a similar pattern of development, moving:

- from a communist, centralised, enclosed and institutionalised model of care, which despite its vast limitations was providing relative security for young people on leaving care through the universal social protection system (pre-1989)

- to a period of profound structural and legislative shifts resulting in disorganisation within the system and fragmented, limited and unregulated after-care provisions (1990–1999)

- finally, to a period of increased development marked by a clearer vision, political will, strong public-voluntary partnership[2] and integrated legislative framework that resulted in increased provisions for young people's after-care social protection (2000–to date).

The Ministry of Labour, Family and Equal Opportunities through its subordinate, the National Authority for the Protection of Children's Rights (ANPDC), manages the protection of children's rights and young people in care. The system has been decentralised since 1997, local Directorates (at county and sector levels) having the main responsibility for children looked after away from home. The system is financed from the local budget, while ANPDC funds priority projects through Programmes of National Interest (PIN), a set of annual programmes focused on the protection of children's rights, based on non-reimbursable funding and open for bidding to NGOs.

Case examples

Ana

Ana is an illegitimate child who was put in public care at birth with two other siblings. Her mother was unemployed, lacked stable accommodation, and cared for five more children. During her time in care Ana moved twice, at three and at seven, as at the time the system was age and gender segregated. In care she was visited once by her mother, during adolescence, shortly after Ana returned from abroad, which made her think her mother came for money. She did not want to maintain contact with her family and the placement centre made no efforts towards that end. She was discharged at 18, qualified as a waitress-cook, lived with various friends, changed jobs twice, and became pregnant.

Mihai

Mihai has been in care for 16 years and left at 19 years of age having qualified as a carpenter. He was not sure whether to continue his education, but the centre was keen to reduce the numbers in care and did not offer him further support. The discharge was sudden and on leaving he received a lump sum and was referred to an NGO for assisted accommodation. This was a shared house where the ten resident care leavers were contributing to some of the household costs. No other support, such as counselling, was offered. He lost three jobs in one year, became unable to pay his bills and was eventually evicted. For a week he shared accommodation with friends and through them he contacted another NGO. This time he received assistance and financial support to rent a flat, career counselling, health checks and regular one-to-one support. Yet in one year this support will end and accommodation will become an issue again.

Romania's welfare regime

During communism, welfare was centralised and universalistic, but underdeveloped. While it provided full employment, free health and education, heavily subsidised foods and rents, relatively high wages and generous child allowance, mismanagement of resources and denial of social problems generated increased poverty and vulnerability of the population (Deacon 1993).

After the fall of communism in 1989, Romania was particularly slow in moving away from the communist economic model, and generally its development lagged behind other transition countries. This was explained by lack of vision and a 'stop-and-go' approach to economic reform affecting economic stability and implicitly welfare development (Sotiropoulos, Neamtu and Stoyanova 2003). This was caused by the impact of the International Monetary Fund and the World Bank favouring a residualist, means-tested social policy, mostly implicit within the economic reforms proposed (C. Zamfir 1996b). Thus in the early 1990s Deacon detected liberal tendencies of welfare policy, anticipating a highly commodified system and increased inequalities (Deacon 1993).

Esping-Andersen (1996, in Fenger 2005) suggests that countries in transition (e.g. from communism) are moving towards one of the three ideal-types of welfare regime (liberal, conservative and social democratic). This is supported by Rys (2001) who sees actual or prospective EU membership as a factor that might determine the Central and Eastern European countries to move towards the European models. Fenger (2005), however, considers that post-communist countries are in the process of developing their own type of welfare. Based on three indicators – characteristics of government programmes, social situation and political participation – he proposes three more types of welfare regime in addition to the Esping-Andersen model: Former USSR; Post-Communist European; and Developing. Because of the high infant mortality rate, and low life expectancy, he places Romania alongside Georgia and Moldova in the 'Developing' model, indicating that the country is still developing toward a mature welfare state.

Legal and policy framework

Young people leaving care have been prioritised in policy making since 2000, recently re-emphasised in the Governing Programme 2005–2008 (Chapter 7, point V). The opportunities and the impetus created by negotiations with the EU, and adherence to international agreements such as the

2000 Millennium Declaration (Lazaroiu *et al.* 2005) or the European Charter for Youth (HG 669/2006), have generated a wealth of youth policy, and the political will to address young people's needs, among them care leavers, being a prioritised group. However, due to lack of communication across institutions, the absence of a centralised database on care leavers, limited resources, adequately trained staff, the development of a structured and holistic approach, and monitoring (HG 669/2006), the real impact at an individual level remains to be seen.

At the beginning of the 1990s, economic instability and cuts in social protection dramatically affected care leavers' chances of social integration. As a result they were unofficially allowed to 'overstay in care', which seemed to be a general 'solution' across the region (UNICEF 1997, p.81). Yet during that decade, as a group, they remained unacknowledged. They were largely ignored by the first childcare reform in 1997, and considered adults who should be able to look after themselves post-care. Meanwhile the legislation provided support through the guaranteed minimum income law, extended child allowance (for over 18s in full-time education), and a minimum wage lump sum at discharge.

Two new laws are particularly relevant to care leavers. First, the Law on Prevention and Eradication of Social Exclusion 2002 prioritises care leavers aged 16 to 35, offering access to health care, significant financial support towards acquiring or renting a house for three years, and a system of employment contracts and incentives to employers meant to stimulate and secure employment for a minimum of two years.

Second, the Law on Promoting and Protecting the Rights of the Child, 2004, closely mirrors the United Nations Convention on the Rights of the Child (UNCRC). The Act emphasises the closure of large institutions; permanent responsibility of families and communities to care, making state intervention complementary; and introduces minimum standards for good practice in public care, following the 2003 EU country report's recommendations. It is also the first childcare law to offer substantial provisions for after care, such as two years of accommodation and employment support after reaching discharge eligibility. While this is generous it remains to be seen whether it will become an exception or the rule, with serious local budget implications. Two of the factors impacting on these provisions of the Act will be the quality of preparation affecting the young people's readiness to leave care, and, being provided on request, the adequacy of information.

As of January 2005, new Services for Developing Independent Living Skills (SDVI), developed with American (USAID/ChildNet) financial and technical input, function as community-integrated services within, or in partnership with, Directorates. The services liaise between young people and resources in the community, and manage the young person's pre-discharge personalised intervention plan put together by a key worker in partnership with the young person, their family and a multi-disciplinary team. However, the capacity of the system to cover the needs of care leavers is affected by the limited ability of the National Agency for Employment (ANOFM) to find employment for care leavers (largely because of their unemployable qualifications,[3] and stigma). In 2003 the Agency organised employment for only half of the targeted 1000 care leavers (Muga *et al.* 2005).

The National Strategy for Social Inclusion of Young People Leaving the Childcare System (HG 669/2006) added new preparation strategies (e.g. module on life and family in school curriculum, higher education access); three-year monitoring; a variety of housing options; access to modern professional training, jobs and GP registration; and a database and research. However, it omits any reference to family involvement.

This is picked up in the new Guide for Independent Living (Mitulescu *et al.* 2005). The document, which refers to the young people as *clients* and *active partners* (p.43), acknowledges the limitations to preparation inherent in a culture of risk prevention,[4] and introduces 'revolutionary' concepts such as: gradual transition, flexible age at discharge, and the possibility to return to care, if initially unsuccessful in integration (p.43). However, some of the language used in this document (pp.18–19) leads us to believe that, while on paper there are many changes mirroring modern (Western) principles of youth work, practice may still be 'contaminated' by defective professional attitudes and views on the nature of desirable rapport with the young people (see also Anghel and Beckett 2007).

Secondary data

Statistical data provided by National Authority for the Protection of Children's Rights (n.d.) give monthly and annual information on the numbers of care leavers and on the support services available to them when continuing education. More data on children in care has been collected since 2004 through the Child Welfare Monitoring and Tracking Information System.

Data on outcomes are limited and fragmented, not yet providing a comprehensive national picture. This may be the result of two factors. First, until recently (as indicated above) there has been no requirement to monitor the post-care progress of young people and, second, insufficient attention has been paid to accountability. Also, the 2006 National Strategy for Social Inclusion of Young People Leaving the Childcare System has not launched improvement targets. Monitoring is also affected by the high mobility of this group, while some want to distance themselves from care.

National data reveal that under half of young people in care have high school or technical qualifications. In 1990/1 10,572 young people in care were registered in higher education (E. Zamfir 1996, p.262), but by 2005 this figure had fallen dramatically to 336 (Muga *et al.* 2005).[5,6] By contrast the number of students in higher education in the general population has increased between 2000/1 and 2004/5 by 22 per cent (Eurochild 2007). A national survey by the Ministry of Labour, Social Solidarity and Family (MLSSF) under the coordination of the Interministerial Group for Young People Leaving Care. (Muga *et al.* 2005) found that most young people did not receive family support, did not find employment, and only half of them had accommodation, mostly temporary. However, there are some acknowledged methodological limitations to data collection,[7] limiting the usefulness of this survey.

Leaving care research

Most studies looking at care and leaving care have used small-scale, qualitative or mixed designs (Balica 2002; Buttu, Alexandrescu and Mihaita 2001; Campean 2004; Marcovici and Dalu 2002; Marginean *et al.* 2004; National Agency for Supporting the Initiative of Young People 2003; Oxford Research International 1999; Subtire 2006). The authors of this chapter also are engaged in doctoral qualitative studies looking at leaving care in Bucharest[8] and one Romanian county.[9]

Looking at the Romanian youth population, a government survey (National Agency for Supporting the Initiative of Young People 2002) found that young people are generally unequipped for the transition to independence. They are highly dependent on families financially and psychologically, which prevents them from becoming autonomous. Qualification levels are polarised with increased numbers of those who have few or no qualifications and those who are highly qualified (Ministerul Educatiei si Cercetarii 2005). Meanwhile young people perceive their environment as full of obstacles, difficult to overcome on their own, and are largely unable to assess risks and find solutions to crises, while society is stimulating inequality, has conflicting rules and a weak sense of community.

Within this wider context of relatively inadequate preparation towards appropriate youth participation in society (Walther *et al.* 2002), Romanian care leavers face added disadvantages. First, separation from family, combined with the length of time in care and the traumatic conditions experienced in care (Stativa 2002), are likely to have a lifelong impact on their emotional development, exposing them to mental health vulnerabilities and difficulties in adjusting to relationships and society's requirements.

Second, young people in care are heavily criticised, mainly by the staff, for growing dependent on care. While the overall perception is that young people 'have it too easy', are demanding, passive and uninvolved in planning for their future (Anghel and Beckett 2007), research has found that more likely causes are the structural inadequacy of the system, including: being isolating and 'all providing'; the poor quality or absence of preparation; the imbalance between rights and responsibilities; the lack of opportunities for a gradual psychological transition; the 'one-plan-fits-all' approach to leaving care; and the pressure of staff who generally expect from young people 'instant adulthood' (Anghel and Beckett 2007; Campean 2004; Hart 1984).

Also, staff are often untrained and unprepared to cope with the challenges faced in working with children and young people, and are often highly dissatisfied with the conditions and pressures of work (Dickens and Serghi 2000) and with their interaction with the young people. This affects the quality of their work, resulting in them often displaying a passive and distant attitude, which makes the young people feel unseen (Anghel and Beckett 2007). To compensate for this, young people seek external sources of preparation, such as NGO programmes, former educators (pre-1997 reform) and alumni peers. Some young people are also able to participate as *assisted* in the halfway after-care programmes of NGOs or the Directorates, an opportunity offered on deserving criteria.[10] Research has found a clear link between living in assisted flats and increased confidence and optimism, including making plans for the future, thinking of entrepreneurship, and not seeing the experience of being in care as a disadvantage (Marginean *et al.* 2004).

Finally, there is evidence that care leavers' social integration is threatened by stigma (Buttu *et al.* 2001; Subtire 2006) and vulnerability to promiscuity and crime (National Authority for Youth 2003, 2005). Although many young people are accommodated in halfway temporary schemes, on leaving these they may still risk homelessness, because of likely low income, instability in employment (Marginean *et al.* 2004), emotional and/or behavioural difficulties, early parenthood or the inability to adjust to community rules.

Despite numerous risk factors, recent research by the authors has also identified a variety of resilience-promoting factors (Gilligan 2001):

- friends in the community and/or family; an attachment person; social network of peers, positive role models

- good education and enrolment on trade courses increasing their employability; plans and hopes to work abroad

- sense of humour, self-worth and self-efficacy; solidarity; ability to learn from mistakes; ambition to overcome their condition; optimism about future; and belief in God.

Conclusion

Romania can be seen as an emerging liberal welfare state. This is reflected in the permissive legal and policy framework, as well as the level of resources, to support young people leaving care. In this context, young people leaving care are assisted with consistent access to accommodation, employment, health care and education, and a sound framework for preparation. But there are also significant gaps in the provision of information, consultation and minimum standards of after-care support. The collection of secondary data is limited, but includes key demographic information prior to leaving care. The following issues are of particular relevance to policy and practice: the balance between rights and responsibilities affecting the quality of preparation for independence; the availability of resources and information to make the access to support opportunities possible; a review of the quality of support offered by NGOs and their outcomes; and the professional quality of the workers. In order to guide the future development of services, there is a need for more research into the medium- and long-term outcomes of care leaving, and how to capitalise on the expertise of care leavers and grassroots professionals.

Key messages for policy and practice

- Preparation for care leaving is largely inadequate or non-existent. Recent research found a perceived imbalance between rights and responsibilities, i.e. heavier on rights, affecting professionals' ability to help and the young people's ability to be proactive.

  Recommendations: adequate framework for professional training; preparation programmes developed with the young people which allow them to learn experientially; value peer 'expertise'; and strengthen young people's informal community networks.

- Although care leavers are prioritised in legislation, a gap between policy and practice is maintained through inappropriate funding and information; slow change of grassroots professional culture; and the provisions being discretionary (offered 'on request', not formulated as 'duties').

  Recommendations: ring-fenced care leaving budget and targeted development of social housing (although already on agenda).

- The public and NGO after-care services vary on quality and standards, and focus on further preparing the young people for independence. In the difficult Romanian social and economic context, on leaving these after-care services young people are likely to be as vulnerable as after discharge from care. A culture of outcomes evaluation would create focus in the field and promote best practice examples leading to improved work with the young people.

- The grassroots are a key problem but also a solution to many difficulties in the system.

  Recommendations: improvement of their professional status and pay and acknowledgement of the pressures inherent in a transitional system are essential to increase their efficiency and job satisfaction.

- Stigma is a threat to young people's survival and integration in the community.

  Recommendation: a national campaign promoting an honest image of the reality of the young people's lives.

- Our knowledge about care leaving in Romania remains limited. National research looking at outcomes (e.g. employment, housing, community participation, family, mental health, etc.) and the dynamic of young people's trajectories from care is needed for a comprehensive and regional picture on the impact of care.

Notes

1. The area with the highest level of poverty in 2000 (Lazaroiu *et al.* 2005), and of unemployment in 2004 (National Agency for Employment 2006).

2. By 2008, the National Authority for the Protection of Children's Rights (ANPDC) intends to contract out 40–45 per cent of the current services to NGOs (www.copii.ro).

3. Most young people in care have technological qualifications being guided by the staff largely based on communist and post-communist parameters of the labour market (focused on industry) no longer relevant in the EU context.

4. For example, care residents are not allowed in the kitchen by the health and safety regulator.

5. In part this reflects a cultural shift away from the prioritisation of education following the 1997 transfer of the administration of care from the Ministries of Education,

Health and Labour to a new governmental authority. Research by Anghel also found that carers feel generally caught in a cycle of passivity regarding the young people's education and preparation for independent life due to the legislation protecting the children's 'moral and physical integrity', which they interpret as forbidding any interference that might cause distress or harm. They complain of lack of methods to replace the old corporal punishments and of an imbalance between the young people's rights and responsibilities.

6. Muga *et al.* advise caution in reading the data presented in their report due to methodological limitations in reporting the data from the field (see note 7).

7. Only half of the counties have returned these data, the questionnaires did not have instructions or explanation of terms, and the care leavers were monitored in the short term. The data possibly therefore do not reflect the actual situation at the time of collection.

8. Longitudinal qualitative study (Dec 2002–March 2004), involving 28 young people (17 followed up after leaving care) and 18 professionals from the statutory and NGO sectors.

9. Psychosocial study (Nov 2005–Feb 2007) involving 34 young people (semi-structured interviews and psychological tests) who left care in one county of Romania and 32 statutory and voluntary professionals (focus groups), aiming towards service development as a collaborative work between service users and service providers.

10. For example, doing well at school or having a non-challenging behaviour.

References

Anghel, R. and Beckett, C. (2007) 'Skateboarding behind the EU lorry: The experience of Romanian professionals struggling to cope with transitions while assisting care leavers.' *European Journal of Social Work 10*, 1, 3–19.

Balica, E. (2002) 'Tinerii din centrele de plasament intre integrare si marginalizare.' *Revista de Asistenta Sociala 6*, 110–113.

Bojkov, V.D. (2004) 'Neither here, nor there: Bulgaria and Romania in current European politics.' *Communist and Post-Communist Studies 37*, 4, 509–522.

Buttu, M., Alexandrescu, E. and Mihaita, E. (2001) *Evaluarea Potentialului de Integrare Socio-Profesionala a Adolecentilor si Tinerilor.* Romania: Feed the Children, and Bucharest: USAID.

Campean, C. (2004) 'Criza dezinstitutionalizarii tinerilor din centrele de plasament.' *Revista de Cercetare si Interventie Sociala 4*, 422–446.

Deacon, B. (1993) 'Developments in Eastern European Social Policy.' In C. Jones (ed.) *New Perspectives on the Welfare State in Europe.* London: Routledge.

Dickens, J. and Serghi, C. (2000) 'Attitudes to childcare reform in Romania: Findings from a survey of Romanian social workers.' *European Journal of Social Work 3*, 3, 247–260.

Esping-Andersen, G. (1996) 'After the golden age? Welfare state dilemmas in a global economy.' In G. Esping-Andersen (ed.) *Welfare States in Transition – National Adaptations in Global Economies.* London: Sage.

Eurochild (2007) *Ending Child Poverty within the EU? A Review of the 2006–2008 National Reports on Strategies for Social Protection and Social Inclusion,* 2nd edition. Accessed 08/10/07 at www.eurochild.org/fileadmin/user_upload/files/NAPs_report_2006_final.pdf

Fenger, H.J.M. (2005) *Welfare Regimes in Central and Eastern Europe – Incorporating Post-communist Countries in a Welfare Regime Typology.* Paper for the NIG 2005 Conference, Nijmegen (permission to quote granted by the author).

Gilligan, R. (2001) *Promoting Resilience.* London: BAAF.

Hart, A. (1984) 'Resources for Transitions from Care.' In *Leaving Care – Where? Conference Report.* London: National Association of Young People in Care.

HG 669/2006 *Privind Aprobarea Strategiei National de Incluziune Sociala a Tinerilor care Parasesc Sistemul de Protectie a Copilului.*

Lazaroiu, S., Abraham, D., Burcea, M., Cartana, C. *et al.* (2005) *National Human Development Report 2003–2005.* Commissioned by the United Nations Development Programme. Accessed 24/02/08 at http://hdr.undp.org/en/reports/nationalreports/europethecis/romania/romania_2005_en.pdf

Marcovici, O. and Dalu, A.M. (2002) *Youth Transitions, Youth Policy and Participation.* Workpackage 2 Report. Bucharest: YOYO Project.

Marginean, I., Popescu, R., Arpinte, D. and Neagu, G. (2004) *Conditii Sociale ale Excluziunii Copilului.* Bucharest: Academia Romana, INCE si ICCV.

Ministerul Educatiei si Cercetarii (2005) *Raport Asupra Starii Sistemului National de Invatamant.* Bucharest: Ministerul Educatiei si Cercetarii.

Mitulescu, S., Parvu, D., Chirila, D. and Ionescu, O. (2005) *Ghid Metodologic Pentru Implementarea Standardelor de Calitate priving Dezvoltarea Deprinderilor de Viata Independenta.* Bucharest: World Learning, ChildNet Programme.

Muga, M., Racoceanu, N., Alexandrescu, A., Polch, A.B. (2005) *Studiu Privind Situatia Tinerilor Care Parasesc Sistemul de Protectie a Copilului.* Bucharest: Institutul National de Cercetare Stiintifica in Domeniul Muncii si Protectie Sociale.

Nation Agency for Employment (ANOFM) (2006) *Situatia Statistica a Somajului la 30 Noiembrie 2006.* Bucharest: National Agency for Employment.

National Agency for Employment (ANOFM) (2007) *Situatia Statistica a Somajului la 31 Ianuarue 2007.* Bucharest: National Agency for Employment.

National Agency for Supporting the Initiative of Young People (ANSIT) (2002) *Starea Tineretului din Romania – Sinteza.* Bucharest: National Agency for Supporting the Initiative of Young People.

National Agency for Supporting the Initiative of Young People (ANSIT) (2003) *Culturi Alternative si Stiluri de Viata ale Tinerilor din Romania.* Bucharest: National Agency for Supporting the Initiative of Young People.

National Agency for Supporting the Initiative of Young People (ANSIT) (2006) *Reducerea Factorilor de Risc la Tineri.* Bucharest: National Agency for Supporting the Initiative of Young People.

National Authority for the Protection of Children's Rights (ANPDC) (2006) *Child Welfare in Romania – The Story of a Reform Process.* Bucharest: National Authority for the Protection of Childrens Rights. Accessed 01/09/07 at www.copii.ro/Files/NAPCR_brochure_200744184931.pdf

National Authority for the Protection of Children's Rights (ANPDC) (n.d.) *Statistics.* Accessed 08/09/2007 at www.copii.ro/content.aspx?id=55

National Authority for Youth (ANT) (2003) *Planul National de Actiune pentru Tineret.* Bucharest: National Authority for Youth.

National Authority for Youth (ANT) (2005) *Planul National de Actiune pentru Tineret 2005–2008.* Bucharest: National Authority for Youth. Accessed 10/07/07 at www.e-tineret.ro/desprenoi.php?id=4

Oxford Research International (1999) *Leaving Institutional Care – Romania.* Florence: Innocenti Research Centre, UNICEF.

Rys, V. (2001) 'Transition countries of Central Europe entering the European Union: Some social protection issues.' *International Social Security Review 54*, 2–3, 177–189.

Sotiropoulos, D.A., Neamtu, I. and Stoyanova, M. (2003) 'The trajectory of post-communist welfare state development: The case of Bulgaria and Romania.' *Social Policy and Administration 37*, 6, 656–673.

Stativa, E. (2002) *Abuzul Asupra Copilului in Institutiile de Protectie Sociala din Romania.* Bucharest: Extreme Group.

Subtire, A.M. (2006) *Perceptia de Sine si Etichetarea Tinerilor Proveniti din Centre de Plasament, Factor de Risc al Comportamentelor Problematice.* Lucrare de diploma, Universitatea 'Babes-Bolyai' Cluj-Napoca (nepublicata).

UNICEF (1997) *Children at Risk in Central and Eastern Europe: Perils and Promises. Regional Monitoring Report No. 4.* Florence: UNICEF International Child Development Centre.

Walther, A., Hejl, G.M., Jensen, T.B. and Hayes, A. (2002) *Youth Transitions, Youth Policy and Participation.* YOYO Research Project Report. Tubingen: IRIS e.V.

Zamfir, C. (1996a) 'Social Policy in Romania in Transition.' In E. Zamfir and C. Zamfir (eds) *Social Policy – Romania in the European Context.* Bucharest: Editura Alternative.

Zamfir, C. (1996b) 'Social Policy in Eastern Europe in Transition.' In E. Zamfir and C. Zamfir (eds) *Social Policy – Romania in the European Context.* Bucharest: Editura Alternative.

Zamfir, E. (1996) 'The Policy of Child Protection in Romania.' In E. Zamfir and C. Zamfir (eds) *Social Policy – Romania in the European Context.* Bucharest: Editura Alternative.

Chapter 13

Spain

Jorge F. Del Valle

Background and key statistics

- Spain is home to around 44 million people, 7.6 million (17%) of whom are aged under 18.

- In 2004, more than 30,000 children were looked after in Spain (a rate of 40 per 10,000 population).

- The most common placement type for looked after children in Spain is kinship care (accounting for 46% of all placements) closely followed by residential care (accounting for 45%).

- Even though the Spanish legal framework prioritises the use of foster care, only 8 per cent of placements are with non-relative foster carers.

- Spain is one of the countries where normative transitions to adulthood take place at the latest age. It is not until aged 30 that half this population have left the parental home.

- There are not specific data about care leavers in Spain and very few pieces of research on this topic.

Key sources

- Del Valle and Bravo (2203).
- Instituto de la Juventud (INJUVE) (2004).

- Ministerio de Trabajo y Asuntos Sociales (2005).

Introduction

During the Franco era, which effectively lasted from the end of the Spanish Civil War (1936–1939) until the Constitution in 1978, three years after Franco's death, child social assistance was based on the charity model. It was usually provided by the Catholic Church and based in large residential institutions. In the 1970s, child care in Spain still consisted of an extensive network of large institutions for orphans, abandoned children and children in poverty. Institutionalisation was the only response for children in need of care, whether as a consequence of maltreatment, families with large numbers of children, parental alcohol abuse, prostitution, or other factors.

The development of the personal social services system in Spain over the last two decades would have been very difficult without political decentralisation which created the 'State of the Autonomous Communities'. Spain was divided into 17 Autonomous Communities, some of them with a strong tradition of autonomy, such as Catalonia or the Basque Country, and all with their own parliament and government, as well as responsibility for administering the main services (education, health, social services and so on). During the 1980s, Autonomous Communities began drafting their own social services laws, with support from central government in respect of both financial and technical aspects, so that there was some degree of harmony across the different communities.

During the last 20 years, a child care system has been developed in Spain on the general social services model of the welfare state, in an effort to supplant the old charitable and institutionalising model from the dictatorship era. Bearing this in mind, it is understandable how the principal concerns up to now have been broader structural child care issues, and that specific aspects, such as leaving care processes, have received very little attention. Only recently has interest and concern been expressed in relation to young people leaving care, and this has been more so from residential workers and managers (observing the urgent need for transition services and support resources for those who must leave at age 18) than politicians. Demand from residential workers for social and independent skills training programmes has greatly increased, and some programmes have been implemented, such as Umbrella (Del Valle and García) or Personal Welfare (López *et al.* 2006).

Spain has over 44 million inhabitants, of whom 7.6 million (17%) are aged under 18. According to national statistics, in 2004 more than 30,000 child protection files were opened (Ministerio de Trabajo y Asuntos Sociales 2005), though these figures are almost certainly approximate and conservative. The results of a descriptive study (Del Valle and Bravo 2003) on the situation of children in out-of-home care is shown in Table 13.1. As can be seen, the commonest situation is kinship and residential care, in similar proportions, with a small representation of non-relative foster care.

Table 13.1: Distribution of cases in out-of-home care in Spain, December 2002

	Frequency	Percentage
Kinship care	14,670	46.8
Non-relative foster care	2487	7.9
Residential care	14,211	45.3
Total	**31,368**	**100**

There are no national statistics on the profiles of child care cases in Spain, since each Autonomous Community keeps its own records, and only a few publish them.

Case examples

Isabel

Isabel is 19 years old and was admitted to a children's home because of her continual behavioural problems that her parents were incapable of controlling: she does not attend school, she goes out at night without permission, she hangs around with friends who take drugs, and she is aggressive towards her parents. Her parents were granted support from a family intervention programme and Isabel receives therapeutic support.

Pedro

Pedro is 19 years old. From the age of six he lived with his grandparents because his drug-dependent mother was sent to prison. His grandparents were granted kinship care with financial support. Pedro's mother has since died, and he decided to live independently. Pedro is now working in a temporary job and receiving a special allowance for care leavers to pay for a rented flat which he shares with other young people.

Spain's welfare regime

Spain has made great progress in social services, from the charitable model, still prevalent in the 1980s, to the welfare state model that guarantees social benefits as citizens' rights and the responsibility of government. During the Franco era, social services were focused on poverty, and the main resources were large institutions run by religious orders for orphans and other children in poverty.

One of the most important milestones in this evolution was the social security reform of 1986, which extended health services to all citizens. Until that time, social security benefits were only for those in work. Those living in poverty or unable to pay were attended to by charitable medical services run by municipalities. The main paradigm of the new system of social services in Spain was decentralisation. The model was based on giving the Autonomous Communities responsibility for managing a wide range of services, with municipalities in charge of managing community and local services.

In terms of Esping-Andersen's typology (1990), the current Spanish welfare regime can be distinguished both from liberal regimes, in which the services depend mainly on the market, and from social democratic regimes, in which the state is the main provider of services. As an example, health services in Spain are based on the social democratic model, guaranteeing universal health care for all citizens, but at the same time there is a comprehensive private network of health care services available for those with sufficient economic resources. Likewise, education is free of charge throughout the compulsory school phase (age 5–16), but there is also a substantial private market covering the same age range.

With regard to social services, despite the developments outlined in the introduction, the main provider of support for the elderly, children and young people is still the family itself, though there is also a significant network of private services, especially for the elderly and the disabled. Nevertheless, the new Law of Dependent People (the details of which are still under discussion in Parliament) will introduce major measures of state support (through the Autonomous Communities) for a wide range of social services covering these groups.

Thus, the welfare regime in Spain could be considered within the southern European or Mediterranean model, along with those of Italy, Portugal and Greece. As regards the relative importance of state, the market and family as social service providers, Spanish society still depends significantly on the family structure, as was shown with respect to young people. Another striking statistic, this time from the child care context, is that kinship care represents 85 per cent of foster care in Spain, and nearly 50 per cent of all out-of-home care. However, in recent years, large-scale state programmes and new laws, such as the Law for Protecting Women from Gender Violence (2004) or the Law of Dependency for the Elderly and Disabled (2006), have increased the participation of the state in welfare provision in a substantial way, even in terms of the national budget.

Legal and policy framework

Following the introduction of the 1978 Constitution, great efforts were made to create a new system of social services aimed at replacing the old system, which was based on the 19th-century charity approach. These new social services systems were designed around the newly-established responsibilities of the Autonomous Communities. As discussed above, all Autonomous Communities had responsibility for drawing up their own social service legislation between 1982 and 1991. Given that there are two levels of administrative organisation (Municipalities and Autonomous Communities) in Spain, there are two separate levels of social services. These are:

1. Community social services: run by Municipalities and based on the community model. The types of services offered to children

and families include prevention programmes and the identification of risk situations, family support programmes and social integration programmes aimed at individuals who are socially excluded.

2. Specialised social services: responsibility for these services lies with the Autonomous Community administration. Specialised services in the field of child protection include:

   ○ residential child care: both for welfare and judicial reasons

   ○ foster care and adoption services

   ○ coordination and support for community programmes.

The municipal and regional levels (Autonomous Communities) have complementary roles in terms of social services. In the field of child protection, the main responsibilities of the municipalities lie in the areas of prevention, early detection and family intervention. On the other hand, regional social services are responsible for child protection files, legal decisions, and specific programmes such as residential child care, family foster care and adoption.

The recent development of the legal framework with respect to child care provision can be summarised as follows:

- *Foster Care and Adoption Law, 1987.* This law reformed the civil code in Spain, facilitating foster care and adoption. This same law also established new responsibilities and a new model in child care.

- *The Constitutional Child Protection Law, 1996.* This law constitutes the main legislative framework for child protection, enhancing all aspects of children's rights and treating children as citizens. It also established different types of foster care and introduced an important concept into child care practice: considering the interests of the child as paramount in all decisions taken with regard to his/her welfare.

In addition to the above, each Autonomous Community has developed its own social services laws and its own child protection laws.

Despite the fact that this legal and administrative framework presents significant improvements with respect to the previous charitable model, the needs of young people leaving care were not included as a priority in the design of child care services. There are no explicit references to care leavers in the main legislation, and only very general comments about the importance of continued support services for them. Currently, many Autonomous Communities are really concerned about this topic, and are in fact developing a number of services, such as special allowances, help with accommodation costs, priority for entering adult social integration programmes, systems for case follow-up, and so on. So far, the main intervention measure has consisted of connecting care leavers to adult social services, but without specific support. One valuable exception was the implementation of mentoring programmes for care leavers in some Autonomous Communities, but this is not a generalised practice.

Finally, it is worth bearing in mind that leaving care in Spain is only a visible problem with regard to residential care, and not to foster care, due to the direct experience of residential workers, who observe the severe difficulties many care leavers encounter after they leave care.

Secondary data

There is some general data on young people's needs and transitions to adulthood. The latest report on Spanish youth (Instituto de la Juventud 2004) shows that young people aged 15–29 numbered around nine million, representing 21.4 per cent of the Spanish population. It is important to point out, however, that the distribution of ages in this range is not homogeneous: the number of 29-year-olds is double that of 15-year-olds, due to a sharp decline in birth rate. This report specifically explores the question of the transition to independence in young people. According to the data, 71 per cent of those in this age range still live at home with their parents, making Spain one of the countries in which the transition to independent life for young people is the most extended. In fact, it is not until the age of 30 that half of this population leave the parental home, while this percentage is attained by young people at the age of 23–24 in other countries, such as the United Kingdom, Germany or Luxembourg.

However, other Mediterranean countries, such as Italy or Greece, show similar patterns of transition to independence.

The conclusions of this report on youth in Spain show that the traditional continuum education–training–job–independence has now been broken. Instead of this linear process of transition, young people experience various transitions in many different ways, including getting a job, unemployment, re-training, getting a new, temporary job, and so on. Instead of the highly structured and homogeneous process of transition that formerly occurred, nowadays a large range of individual transitions are possible, depending on a complex combination of variables. Different factors such as stability of employment, incomes, couple relationships, family type or relationship with parents determine the different kinds of situations and transitions.

As a main conclusion, we can say that families in Spain are becoming the main provider of support and 'services' for young people at this critical period, when society does not facilitate the process of becoming independent as it did in the past. Families have become a protected and supportive space in Spanish culture, addressing the needs of young people with regard to transition, in the absence of relevant social service resources. This situation is in stark contrast to that of young people in Nordic countries, with their well-developed welfare state, or even to that of those covered by the Central European model.

If this is the transition situation for young people in the general population, then care leavers are likely to have many more difficulties during this process, since they lack supportive families, and once they reach adulthood (age 18) they can no longer receive child care services. In this socio-political context care leaver transitions have become a major challenge, and are gradually being brought onto the political agenda.

As detailed above, one of the most notable characteristics of the Spanish social service system, including child care, is that the responsibility for managing these services lies with the Autonomous Communities. Thus, each Autonomous Community manages its own statistics and database on child care, but in the majority of cases they do not publish them in any formal way, so that national and even regional statistics are scarce and difficult to find, not only on child care but also on other social services.

Consequently, the possibilities of consulting databases – even with secondary data – for gathering information or indicators about leaving care in Spain are extremely limited.

Leaving care research

As regards the specific issue of young people leaving care, very little research has been carried out in the Spanish context. Panchón *et al.* (1999) at the University of Barcelona carried out a study about the needs of young people in residential care, in order to identify specific needs in relation to transition. The research describes this group (16–18 years old), assessing their special needs with respect to labour-market integration. The results of the study indicate the need for programmes to support young people on reaching age 18, and for after-care programmes to continue working with this age group.

Del Valle, Alvarez-Baz and Fernanz (1999) carried out a study exploring the current situation of young people discharged from residential care. A sample of 270 cases of young people discharged from care (aged 19 to 29) was studied, analysing the young people's socio-economic conditions, health, employment situation, family relations, social integration, problems of substance abuse or delinquency, and so on. This research showed that most of the young people were in a good situation, and only 13 per

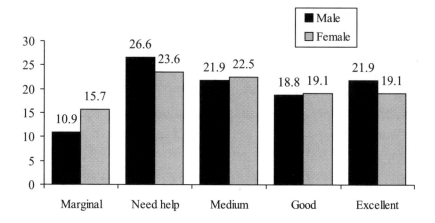

Figure 13.1: Social integration level in residential care leavers

cent had problems with drugs or delinquency. Figure 13.1 shows percentages for the level of social integration achieved by the young people in the sample. This level was calculated by taking into account a number of criteria, such as housing, job, health or social network.

The study concludes that there are very few variables related to these levels. Significant correlations were only found with changes of children's home (the more the changes, the poorer the result) and a history of behavioural problems at the children's home. However, a highly significant finding was a significant correlation between age at the start of follow-up and the level of social integration: those aged 25 to 29 showed much greater integration, and the cases of marginalisation were found mainly in the youngest age group (16–21). This study was replicated in the Autonomous Community of Castilla y León (Arias and Del Valle 2002) obtaining similar results.

Following up cases of young people who had been in residential care was used in another pair of studies in Spain (Vives and Rodríguez 2003). In the first study, researchers interviewed a sample of 100 people who had lived in a particular children's home in the Basque Country at some time in their life. The sample included people aged from 20 to 69, and the conclusions showed that, although the level of education attained was quite low, labour-market integration was fairly high. In the second study, the Spanish children's charity organisation Aldeas Infantiles SOS carried out a follow-up study of minors who attended their programmes (Delgado 2005), which presents a highly comprehensive descriptive picture, though it remains unpublished.

In another study, yet to be published (Del Valle, Lopo and Fernanz in press), a sample of 143 young people who reached the age of 18 while in kinship care was followed up when they were aged between 18 and 30 (mean 23). Also in progress is a study commissioned by the Spanish Ministry of Work and Social Affairs (Del Valle, López and Bravo in press), due for completion in 2007, on the results of foster care in Spain, including follow-up of care leavers and their level of social integration.

Conclusion

Spain could be located within the southern European or Mediterranean model of welfare states. Families play an important supportive role in Spanish culture, addressing the needs of young people making the transition to adulthood, in the absence of relevant social service resources. Despite the recent and innovative legal and policy framework, there are no explicit references to care leavers in the main child welfare legislation, and only very general comments about the importance of continued support services for them. However, concern about leaving care and the need for support programmes for care leavers is increasingly recognised. As a result, some programmes for social or independent living skills are being implemented in residential care.

There are no national statistics on the profiles of children in public care or care leavers in Spain, since each Autonomous Community keeps its own records, and only a few publish them. Moreover, there is no secondary data about care leavers. Very little research has been carried out in Spain about leaving care, and only with regard to residential care. Results indicate the need for programmes to support young people on reaching age 18, and for after-care programmes.

Key messages for policy and practice

- More attention must be devoted to child care statistics and databases, to improve on the current lack of national and secondary data.

- Although leaving care from residential placements is recognised in Spain, leaving care from other placement types, such as foster and kinship care, should also be included on the policy agenda.

- Lack of stability in child care placements is a key factor related to poor outcomes in adulthood transitions.

- One in four young people leaving residential care depend on social services support after they have been discharged. The quality of this support is a key issue for social integration as adults.

- The type of assistance given to young people leaving care must be detailed in regulations and standards of practice in child care.

- More research is required to evaluate care leavers' needs and paths of transition.

References

Arias, B. and Del Valle, J.F. (2002) *Integración Social de Jóvenes que han Estado en Acogimiento Residencial.* Valladolid: Informe de investigación no publicado.

Del Valle, J.F. and Bravo, A. (2003) *La Situación del Acogimiento Familiar en España.* Madrid: Ministerio de Trabajo y Asuntos Sociales.

Del Valle, J.F. and García, J.L. (2006) *Programa Umbrella. Habilidades para la vida.* Oviedo: ASACI.

Del Valle, J.F., Alvarez-Baz, E. and Fernanz, A. (1999) *Y Después... qué? Estudio y Seguimiento de Casos que Fueron Acogidos en Residencias de Protección de Menores en el Principado de Asturias.* Oviedo: Servicio de Publicaciones del Principado de Asturias.

Del Valle, J.F., López, M. and Bravo, A. (in press) *Evaluación de Resultados en Acogimiento Familiar en España.* Madrid: Ministerio de Trabajo y Asuntos Sociales.

Del Valle, J.F., Lopo, D. and Fernanz, A. (in press) *Evaluación de Seguimiento en Menores Acogidos en Familia Extensa.* Oviedo: Universidad de Oviedo.

Delgado, C. (2005) *Estudio de Seguimiento de Egresados en Aldeas SOS.* Madrid: Informe no publicado.

Esping-Andersen, G. (1990) *The Three Worlds of Welfare Capitalism.* New Jersey: Princeton University Press.

Instituto de la Juventud (INJUVE) (2004) *Informe Juventud en España.* Madrid: Instituto de la Juventud.

López, F., Carpintero, E., Del Campo, A., Lázaro, S. and Soriano, S. (2006) *El Bienestar Personal y Social y la Prevención del Malestar y la Violencia.* Madrid: Pirámide.

Ministerio de Trabajo y Asuntos Sociales (2005) *Boletín Estadístico de Protección a la Infancia 06.* Madrid: MTAS.

Panchón, C., Del Valle, J.F., Vizcarro, C., Antón, V. and Martín, C. (1999) *Situación de Menores de 16 a 18 Años En Centros De Protección.* Barcelona: Dulac.

Vives, J.A. and Rodríguez, C. (2003) *Hogar Saltillo: 50 Años De Vida Familiar.* Valencia: Martín Impresores.

Chapter 14

Sweden

Ingrid Höjer

Background and key statistics

- Sweden has 9.1 million inhabitants. About one-fifth, 1.9 million, are under 18 years of age, and 2.3 million are under 20 years of age. A total of 25 per cent of all Swedish children under the age of 18 have their origins in other countries.

- About 20,300 children and young people (0–20 years of age) were placed in residential care or foster care at some time during 2005.

- The most common placement type for looked after children and young people is foster care. A total of 74 per cent are placed in foster care; the other 26 per cent in public or private residential care.

- Out-of-home care is most common for children and young people between 13 and 17 years of age. A total of 45 per cent of children in care are between 13 and 17 years of age.

- In 2005, the median length of time in care was 4.5 months for children and young people placed voluntarily and 16.8 months for those placed by mandatory means.

- In 2005, 4198 young people aged 15–21 left care in Sweden.

Key sources

- Socialstyrelsen (National Board of Health and Welfare) (2006).
- Statistics Sweden (2006).

Introduction

In Sweden the Social Democratic Party has dominated the political scene since the 1930s. However, in the last election in September 2006, an alliance of the non-socialist parties managed to gain power. Traditionally, Sweden has been a country with strong centralist and nationally homogeneous traditions, where compromise, coalition and negotiation have been significant features. This has had a positive influence on the development of the modern welfare state and social policy reforms in Sweden (Salonen 2001). Over the last decades Sweden has experienced extensive immigration, and immigrants now represent more than 12 per cent of the total population (Swedish Integration Board 2006).

Out-of-home care

Table 14.1 shows types of placement for children and young people in care.

Table 14.1: Type of placement for children and young people in care, 1 November 2005

	Type of placement					
	Foster home	Public residential home	Private residential home	Home for special supervision	Other type of placement	Total
Percentage of children and young people in care	74%	4%	15%	4%	3%	100%

When it comes to the number of young people leaving care, the figures are derived from the statistics collected by the municipalities, and may vary in

Table 14.2: Number of young people (15–20 years of age) who left out-of-home placements, and their situation after they had left care

	Total	Returned to parents	Independent living	New placement (voluntary)	New placement (mandatory)	Still in foster care with foster carers as custodians	Adopted by foster carers	Other type of situation
Type of law *SoL (SSA) (Voluntary)*								
Age 15–17	1687	1200	65	0	242	37	2	141
18 or more	1640	397	723	0	47	4	3	466
LvU (CYPA) (Mandatory)								
Age 15–17	266	120	8	98	16	3	0	21
18 or more	605	122	103	282	3	1	0	94

accuracy. Table 14.2 shows the number of young people (15–20 years of age) reported to have left out-of-home placements, and their situation after they had left care.

Few young people ($n = 65$) under the age of 18 move from care to independent living. When young people under 18 leave care, they either return to their parents, or enter a new placement. Most young people stay in care until they have completed their upper secondary school education. This means that most young people who leave foster care and institutional care are about 19 years old. A few will have reached the age of 20 before they have finished upper secondary school and are ready to make the transition from care to independent living.

Case examples

Hedda

Hedda was admitted to foster care when she was four years old, following severe neglect and her parents' alcohol abuse. She and a younger brother moved in to a foster family where they both stayed until she was 15. At that time the placement broke down due to behavioural difficulties and conflicts with the foster parents, and Hedda was placed in another foster family. The first years in this new foster family were turbulent, but eventually Hedda became attached to the foster carers, especially to the foster father. When Hedda was 19 years old, the foster care placement was formally ended. Hedda's biological mother died when she was six years old due to her alcohol abuse, and Hedda has little contact with her father, who still has alcohol problems. Hedda gets no support from social services, her father or from relatives. All the support she receives is given voluntarily by the foster carers. When interviewed at 20, Hedda was living with her boyfriend, attending full-time adult education in order to complete her senior secondary school exams, and working part time. Hedda says she needs help to organise her budget and her everyday life. She has regular contact with her foster carers, who provide both practical and emotional support. The foster carers themselves are prepared to give support to Hedda, but also state that this is not always easy, as Hedda needs constant reassurance of their loyalty and affection.

Niclas

Niclas first came into residential care when he was 15 years old. He had an extensive record of violence and criminality. His mother has alcohol problems, and his father was homeless due to alcohol abuse and social problems. His parents are separated. Niclas was placed in two residential homes, followed by a placement in a foster home. All placements broke down because of Niclas' violent behaviour and criminality. When interviewed at 20 he was staying in a transitional apartment, provided by a third residential home. The care order had been changed from mandatory to voluntary. He has kept in touch with his mother, father, siblings and other relatives. Information from the residential staff indicates a great improvement in Niclas' behaviour and his ability to relate to peers and to staff. After leaving care, Niclas will have regular contact with a centre for young people organised by the social services in his municipality once or twice a month for six months. Support from the residential home will also continue for six more months after the placement ends. When these six months have passed, Niclas will be on his own. Niclas is worried about his budget, and about having periods of depression, which he has experienced several times. Nevertheless, when interviewed he was working with a relative, planning to complete his secondary school exam, and was positive about his future life.

Sweden's welfare regime

According to Esping-Andersen's (1990, 1999) categorisation of welfare regimes in Europe, Sweden, along with other Nordic countries, is defined as a social democratic welfare regime. This implies an institutional welfare state with universal, and not selective, means-tested benefits, equal distribution of social resources, social insurances based on citizenship, de-commodification and a generous family welfare policy.

In Sweden, the core components of the welfare state were not put in place until the 1960s and 1970s. Social expenditure of the state increased at the beginning of the 1980s, and has been fairly stable since then, representing about one-third of the annual GDP (Salonen 2001).

The Swedish welfare regime implies a high degree of state intervention, based on high taxes and public expenditure. There is public legitimacy for such a high level of social expenditure. Swedish citizens generally have established confidence in state interventions, and expect the state to provide institutionalised solutions, for example care for children and the elderly. According to surveys, there is more public support for universal than for targeted programmes (Salonen 2001). In the Swedish Welfare system, the principle of universal rights of security and service is more or less guaranteed in childhood and old age. However, for the period where people are supposed to be part of the labour force, benefits connected to the welfare system are performance related (Salonen 2001). This means that citizens who, for various reasons, are excluded from the labour market are also excluded from the general benefits of the institutional welfare state.

Sweden used to be a homogeneous society, but this has changed over the last decades. Today about 18 per cent of the Swedish population have their family origins in other countries, either because they were born outside of Sweden, or because one or both of their parents are of non-Swedish origin. This change has had a substantial impact on the social structure of society. Swedish social policy has not succeeded in including all people with an immigrant background in the welfare system.

During the 1990s general living conditions went through some major changes. There was an increase in the proportion of the population who experienced difficulties and adversities in their life. Unemployment and a change of policy in favour of short-term employment created more insecurity in the labour market, and the number of people who were in need of long-term financial assistance thus increased. People born outside Sweden and young people had considerable difficulties establishing themselves in the labour market. This is still the prevalent situation, although the current economic situation in Sweden is more stable now than it was in the 1990s. Apparently, some of the structural changes in Swedish society over the last decades have proved to be too hard a challenge for the welfare system (DS 2002).

Legal and policy framework

Sweden has three democratic levels of government: the Parliament at national level; county councils at regional level; and municipalities at local level. There are 21 county councils and 290 municipalities. County councils and municipalities have their own decision-making powers. They are run by elected bodies, known as municipal and county council assemblies. These assemblies consist of politicians who are directly elected in general elections every four years. In the municipalities, social welfare committees, formed by directly elected politicians, govern social services. Thus, the work performed by social workers in the municipalities is politically controlled at a local level, and is thereby also dependent on the views of the political majority in each municipality. At state level, social services are supervised by the National Board of Health and Welfare. At a regional level the work of the social welfare committees is supervised by the County Administrative Board, which can be said to extend the reach of the state in the 21 counties.

Sweden has a family services orientation rather than a child protection orientation, and there is a high level of legitimacy for state intervention (Andersson 1999). There is no 'Children's Act', as in many other countries. The work performed by the social services is regulated by two Acts: the Social Services Act (SSA), which is a 'frame law' and regulates different areas of social support on a voluntary basis; and the Care of Young People Act (CYPA), which regulates taking children and young people into care without the parents' or child's consent.

In Sweden, foster care (rather than residential care) is the preferred placement choice. Swedish authorities have explicitly announced that residential care should only be used for emergency placements, or for children and young people with severe problems. In the Swedish child welfare system there is no permanency planning. Usually there are no time limits to placements. Children stay in care as long as this is deemed as the best alternative. Adoption without the parents' consent does not exist, and children in care are not 'freed for adoption'.[1] Biological parents still retain 'custody' of their children, even though their children are in care. The law explicitly emphasises that contact with birth parents and other relatives should be maintained when children are placed in out-of-home care.

Youth justice is included in Swedish child welfare, and therefore criminal and drug abusing youths make up a substantial proportion of children in care. For several decades special residential care has been used for this group. These 'homes for special supervision' have facilities for incarcerating youth. There are 30 residential units of this kind, and since 1994 they have been monitored by a national government agency. Local authorities apply for placements and are obliged to pay for the care (Hessle and Vinnerljung 2000).

For children and young people placed in out-of-home care under the Social Services Act, there are no specific regulations for how, or when, a placement should be ended. A voluntary placement is regarded as a way to assist children and their parents, and placements end when the young person is 18, or when the circumstances have changed and the child or young person can return home.

When a child or young person is placed under the Care of Young People Act, the social welfare committee can decide when to end the placement. According to the law, the social welfare committee is obliged to thoroughly prepare for the reunification with birth parents. If the young person is placed in care due to care deficits, abuse or other problems in the home, the placement should be ended at the latest at the age of 18. If a young person is placed because of his or her own behaviour (for example drug abuse and/or criminal activities), the placement should end at the latest at the age of 21.

The law gives no specific advice on how a placement in care should be ended, or what support should be given to the young person after he or she has left care. There is a praxis for the social welfare committees to give financial support until the young person has finished all three years of secondary school, but this is not regulated by law.

Secondary data

The National Board of Health and Welfare collects statistics from all the 290 municipalities in Sweden concerning children and young people placed in out-of-home care. All data are presented in the 'Registry of Children and Young Persons Subjected to Child Welfare'. The accuracy for such statistical reports varies considerably from municipality to municipality (these figures can be marred by a number of mistakes, which has to be taken into account when data are presented). The extent of incorrect data is for the most part unknown, due to data being reported at an aggregated level (Socialstyrelsen 2006).

In Sweden, national registers cover the entire population. The data collected in these registers are based on the individually unique ten-digit personal identification number that follows every Swedish resident from birth to death. This type of data also makes it possible to follow members of the same family. Ethical and legal issues do not present a problem in these studies as registers are de-personalised and individuals only appear as coded numbers.

Leaving care research

At the Centre for Epidemiology and the Institute for Evidence-Based Social Work Practice, in the National Board of Health and Welfare, researchers have used data concerning several cohorts of young people from these national registers, together with data from the 'Registry of Children and Young Persons Subjected to Child Welfare'. They have also made use of the opportunity to link data over generations, and connected data about the situation for young care leavers to data about their parents, such as socio-economic situation, education and health. Their work has resulted in extensive information about the current situation for young people who have had experiences of out-of-home care. The outcomes from registers of former care leavers have also been compared with cohorts of young people from adverse circumstances with no experiences of out-of-home care. These data give a good coverage of several outcomes for care leavers, and have greatly contributed to the knowledge of the situation for care leavers in Sweden. Results from this research show a bleak picture of former care leavers' situations. Young people who have been placed in out-of-home care showed elevated risk of higher mortality, mental health problems, suicide attempts, poor educational attainment and teenage pregnancy (Franzén and Vinnerljung 2006; Vinnerljung, Hjern and Lindblad 2006; Vinnerljung, Öman and Gunnarsson 2005).

The research detailed above emanates from the analysis of extensive register studies. As such it provides vital and important quantitative information about former care leavers. However, the voices of care leavers themselves are not heard. Qualitative research in the area of leaving care is almost non-existent. A report on a pilot study on 16 care leavers, their birth parents, foster carers, institutional staff and social workers is currently in progress (Höjer and Sjöblom forthcoming).

Conclusion

In the UK, as in many other countries, there has been an awareness of the problems faced by young people leaving care, which has resulted in a development of numerous leaving care services (Wade and Dixon 2006). This is not the situation in Sweden, where special programmes designed to support young people leaving care are almost non-existent. So far, little attention has been given to interventions from social services directed towards this group, and the law gives no advice on these matters.

The lack of specific measures towards young people leaving care presents a problem in the area of research on this group. For example, in the UK quite a lot of studies have used samples from specialist leaving care programmes and leaving care teams (see for example Biehal and Wade 1996; Broad 1999; Stein 2006). In Sweden it is more complicated to identify care leavers and engage them in research projects. Many social service units may only have a few care leavers over a year, and therefore may not be motivated to participate in research projects (Höjer and Sjöblom forthcoming).

Results from the Swedish register study, presented above, provide evidence that the institutional welfare system, despite its many advantages, does not succeed in helping young care leavers in the transition from care to independent living. More research is needed in this area, to find out what positive and negative factors might influence the transitional phase.

Key messages for policy and practice

- The welfare state has not succeeded in including young people with a care background. Evidence from research clearly shows that this group face great difficulties when they leave care. They are excluded both from the labour market and the educational system, to a much higher degree than their peers.

- Social services need to change their policy, and direct more attention towards this group. Special programmes are needed, for supplying practical, financial and emotional support to young care leavers.

- More research is needed on young care leavers' own experiences, and their perspectives on the transitional phase from care to independent living.

Note

1.   Childless couples who want to adopt turn to international adoptions.

References

Andersson, G. (1999) 'Children in residential and foster care – a Swedish example.' *International Journal of Social Welfare 8*, 253–266.

Biehal, N. and Wade, J. (1996) 'Looking back, looking forward: Care leavers, families and change.' *Children and Youth Services Review 18*, 4–5, 425–445.

Broad, B. (1999) 'Young people leaving care: Moving towards "joined up" solutions.' *Children and Society 13*, 81–93.

DS (2002) *Welfare in Sweden: The Balance Sheet for the 1990s.* Stockholm: Ministry of Health and Social Affairs.

Esping-Andersen, G. (1990) *The Three Worlds of Welfare Capitalism.* New Jersey: Princeton University Press.

Esping-Andersen, G. (1999) *Social Foundations of Post-industrial Economics.* Oxford: Oxford University Press.

Franzén, E. and Vinnerljung, B. (2006) 'Foster children as young adults: Many motherless, fatherless or orphaned – a Swedish national cohort study.' *Child and Family Social Work 11*, 254–263.

Hessle, S. and Vinnerljung, B. (2000) *Child Welfare in Sweden – An Overview. Stockholm Studies in Social Work, 15.* Stockholm: Stockholm University, Department of Social Work.

Höjer, I. and Sjöblom, Y. (forthcoming) 'Young people leaving care in Sweden.' Submitted article not yet published.

Salonen, T. (2001) 'Sweden: Between Model and Reality.' In P. Alcock and G. Craig (eds) *International Social Policy.* Basingstoke: Palgrave Macmillan.

Socialstyrelsen (National Board of Health and Welfare) (2006) *Socialtjänst 2006:9. Statistik.* Stockholm: Socialstyrelsen.

Statistics Sweden (2006) *Barn och deras Familjer 2005. [Children and their Families.]* Demografiska Rapporter. Stockholm: Statistiska Centralbyrån [Statistics Sweden].

Stein, M. (2006) 'Research review: Young people leaving care.' *Child and Family Social Work 11*, 273–279.

Swedish Integration Board (2006) *Pocket Facts – Statistics on Integration.* Stockholm: Swedish Integration Board.

Vinnerljung, B., Hjern, A. and Lindblad, F. (2006) 'Suicide attempts and severe psychiatric morbidity among former child welfare clients – a national cohort study.' *Journal of Child and Psychiatry 47*, 7, 723–733.

Vinnerljung, B., Öman, M. and Gunnarsson, T. (2005) 'Educational attainments of former child welfare clients – a Swedish national cohort study.' *International Journal of Social Welfare 14*, 265–276.

Wade, J. and Dixon, J. (2006) 'Making a home, finding a job: Investigating early housing and employment outcomes for young people leaving care.' *Child and Family Social Work 11*, 199–208.

Chapter 15

Switzerland

Thomas Gabriel and Renate Stohler

Background and key statistics

- Switzerland is home to around 7.46 million people; approximately 1.63 million are under the age of 19.

- No national data are available on the total childcare population, care leavers or children in need. At the national level there are also no data available on placement types, lengths of stay in care or on the age profile of looked after children.

- Available statistics at the canton level show that the rates of looked after children differ enormously. The rate of children looked after (per 10,000 of the population aged 0–19) is 139 in Neuenburg, whereas the rate in Obwalden is about 12.

- The proportion of males to females is two-thirds to one-third. The proportion of looked after children who are not of Swiss origin is approximately 17 per cent in Baselland and 49 per cent in Tessin.

- There are no data on the age that young people leave care. The proportion of young adolescents in care also differs when inter-cantonal comparisons are undertaken. In Baselstadt only 1.9 per cent of young people in care are over 18 years old; in Wallis 24.6 per cent of young people in care are over 17 years old.

- There are no national data about the proportions of children and young people living in foster care and residential care.

Key sources

- Bundesamt für Statistik (2006).
- Piller (2002).

Introduction

Since 1848, Switzerland has been organised as a federal state which consists of 26 cantons. The most important elements of the state organisation is a strong federalism and the polarity of its federal and centralistic structures. There is a complex distribution of power and competences between the confederation (central government) and the 26 cantons (Kantone). The confederation has exclusive rights to legislate in the following five areas: customs, railways, transportation, currency and postal services. In seven additional areas, although the confederation legislates, implementation is carried out by cantonal regulations, which may differ from canton to canton. Labour legislation and education, civil and penal codes, among others, belong to these seven fields. The penal code for juveniles has 26 cantonal regulations on juvenile jurisdiction and therefore the same number of ways in which adolescents are assigned to juvenile correction institutions, or to residential care facilities, which are both part of the child care sector. Finally, there are three additional fields where the cantons have exclusive rights to legislate; among these are welfare and child care laws. This structure explains the fact that in Switzerland there is neither a specific ministry for education, nor one for social welfare. Consequently, there are no centrally collected data available about the whole child care sector (see Gottesmann 1991; Riklin 1983).

Case examples

Elisabeth

(CIVIL CODE)

Elisabeth is 11 years old. She has been abused by Fred, her mother's current partner. After telling her teacher, professionals intervene. Family and medical diagnoses are made. The assessment concludes that the physical, emotional and intellectual development of Elisabeth is in danger. She is placed in a residential home. After the therapeutic treatment of her mother, the *Vormundschaftsbehörde* (guardianship authority) decides that Elisabeth should live at home. She is now 13 years old. Fred left the family after spending 12 months in jail.

Simon

(PENAL CODE)

Fourteen-year-old Simon is highly aggressive in school and gets excluded. He is taught at home by the 'Flying Teachers'. After several delinquent acts, including theft and armed robbery, he is admitted to a secure observation unit for five months. The court decides to place him in a *Therapieheim* (therapeutic home). He stays there for six years, until he has finished school, which includes vocational training as a butcher. Aged 21, he lives in his own flat. After losing his job, he uses the opportunity to receive financial support from the work department and afterwards from the social department. After being out of work for three years Simon participates in a programme which aims at re-integrating people into the labour market. Although the programme succeeds, his social and personal problems are still unresolved. Aged 27, after two attempts to commit suicide, Simon lives in a psychiatric unit.

Switzerland's welfare regime

The three main types of welfare regime identified by Esping-Andersen only partly match the situation in Switzerland (Esping-Andersen 1990, pp.69–77). A distinction has to be drawn between a weak liberal welfare regime (focusing on citizenship but with very low guarantees and/or social rights, respectively) and a strong liberal welfare regime (Opielka

2004, 2005), which includes more social rights, like Switzerland. Although different studies have identified Switzerland as a liberal welfare state, the expenditure on social assistance since 1990 has been steadily increasing, and costs for social security are currently equivalent to the European average.

The Swiss welfare state is characterised by a strong emphasis on inclusive social rights in some policy areas, especially in retirement insurance and in health insurance. By contrast, in other areas, such as family or labour-market policy, there is – corresponding to the liberal paradigm – very little social assistance. According to Opielka, Swiss social policy can be identified as a 'weak guaranteeism' (Opielka 2005, p.3). Also, as a result of the federal structure, there is strong empirical evidence for significant inter-cantonal variation in welfare state policies.

Legal and policy framework

On a federal level, protection provision for children and young people is included in the federal constitution and the civil and penal codes. In addition, there are legal regulations concerning children and youths on a cantonal basis which must not contradict federal law (von Sturm zu Vehlingen 1999, p.240).

According to the federal constitution, children and youths are, as a basic principle, eligible for protection of their physical well-being and for the advancement of their development (federal constitution art. 11, art. 41, art. 62, art. 67). Furthermore, according to the Swiss civil code, parents have the right and the responsibility to care for their children. Consistent with this, and with the welfare of the child constituting the central principle (civil code art. 301,1), parents have to raise the child according to their circumstances and to support and protect their physical, intellectual and moral development (civil code art. 302,1). If the welfare of the child is at risk, and/or if the parents neglect their responsibilities, there are three ways into out-of-home placement: (1) child protection by civil law; (2) penal child and youth protection; and (3) voluntary child and youth protection (von Sturm zu Vehlingen 1999, p.264). On a federal level, child protection by civil law, and measures of the penal child and youth protection, are uniformly regulated.

However, there are broad inter-cantonal variations in the way the legal framework is put into practice. This is caused by different administrative structures and historical developments within the 26 cantons (Tuggener 1975, p.236). In Switzerland, a variety of different residential care settings for children and youths (Tanner 2000) exist, according to cantons or linguistic regions (Piller 2004, p.55). There is no legal framework concerning 'leaving care' on a federal level. In addition to the development of young people, and the circumstances of their families, attaining the age of majority (18 years) may have an impact. Cantonal child care codes regulate that young people can live in residential homes until they reach 21, but the end of their first vocational training is a deadline for the placement (see Interkantonale Vereinbarung für soziale Einrichtungen, art. 2). Young people, placed by penal code in a juvenile correction institution or a therapeutical home (both parts of child care), can stay in care until they reach their 25th birthday (ibid). Young adults unable to live independently have the right to be supported and guided by federal law (federal constitution art. 12).

Secondary data

Due to federal state organisation, as discussed above, there is neither a specific ministry for education nor one for social welfare in Switzerland. Consequently, there are no data available at any central office about the whole child care sector (see Gottesmann 1991). Various initiatives for the establishment of federal statistics of institutions have consistently failed because of a lack of consensus (UNICEF Schweiz 1999, p.72). For this reason, national administrative data on child care do not exist. However, this does not mean that there are no statistics about Swiss institutions. Data do exist, at least for some cantons, but each set provides information only for a distinct and limited region, and only for certain types of existing institutions in these regions (Piller 2002).

Leaving care research

In Switzerland, there has been little research carried out on child care and the outcomes of residential and foster care, although the need for it was referred to in the mid-1970s (Kuntsch and Nett 2002, p.427). There is also very little research on the social integration of former clients of the youth welfare service. In 1951, the first study was published in Switzerland based on data from male juvenile delinquents. It investigated the causes and effect of early and persistent criminal behaviour (Boehlen 1983, p.6). However, until well into the 1970s, just five studies followed, all concerned with juvenile delinquents (ibid). Since the beginning of the 1980s, a small number of studies have been carried out and the main findings are summarised below.

First, the only longitudinal study to date (over ten years) about the effects of residential care on young offenders was conducted. Data were collected on a total of 273 especially 'difficult to educate' (Tanner 1992, p.53) juvenile delinquents, who had been placed either in a *Therapieheim* (therapeutic home) or in a *Anstalt für Nacherziehung* (correctional education setting). As part of the study, a total of 135 young men and women were interviewed, and information was obtained from the authorities, after they had left the institutions for one to three years (ibid, p.84). At the time of the follow-up examination, 34 per cent of the former female clients from the French-speaking region and 27 per cent from the German-speaking region were socially integrated; that is, since they had been released they had not committed any offences that would have resulted in some sort of imprisonment (ibid, p.90). The results for the former male clients clearly turned out lower: 15 per cent for young men from the French-speaking region and 16 per cent for young men from the German-speaking region. Furthermore, 12 per cent of the young men from the French-speaking region and 17 per cent of the young men from the German-speaking region were in penal or correctional facilities at the time of follow-up (ibid, p.90). The figures for women were significantly lower (0% in the French-speaking region and 1.6% in the German-speaking region). Further differences between the French- and the German-speaking regions originate mainly from women calling upon social or therapeutic assistance having been released from the institutions. The proportion of women who, at the time of the evaluation, were calling upon assistance was about four times higher in the French-speaking region than in the German-speaking part (ibid, p.91).

The fact that the former clients from the French-speaking part of Switzerland receive more intensive assistance during the process of integration than their counterparts from the German-speaking part is taken as evidence of differences in the area of residential child care between the linguistic regions (ibid). An analysis of the institutions has shown that there are 'different residential-care cultures' (ibid, p.54) for the different linguistic parts of Switzerland. For example, smaller homes were much more prominent in the French-speaking part than they were in the German-speaking part.

Another significant result of the follow-up study was the mortality rate among former male clients. At the time of the study, 11.7 per cent of the German-speaking former clients had died compared to 9.3 per cent of their French-speaking counterparts (ibid, p.90). In his results, Tanner identifies that the process of social integration, for a considerable number of former clients, was quite problematic. He suggested that post-care assistance should be provided in such a way 'that the transfer into independence does not become an excessive demand' (ibid, p.97).

In a more recent small-scale ($n = 37$), non-representative study, former clients that had been institutionalised as a result of mental health and penal problems in a residential care facility (with emphasis on vocational training) were questioned about their job-related and social situation one to ten years after leaving the institution (Stohler 2005). Just over two-thirds (68.5%) of the former clients had completed professional training, and 30 per cent of those interviewed had a permanent work place in the first sector of the labour market (ibid, p.62). The study also showed that 32 per cent of all former clients were working in protected work, or only partially integrated into the work force, since they were employed only temporarily (ibid, p.61). Another 30 per cent of the women and men interviewed were not employed and not integrated in the workforce, respectively (ibid). It is crucial to note, however, that the gross income of all the employed former clients was clearly below the Swiss average and, in some cases, close to the officially defined poverty level (ibid, p.59).

In respect of social relationships, the evaluation has shown that over half (59%) of those interviewed were living alone (ibid, p.67). A very small proportion were in a permanent relationship and only one person had a child (ibid, p.15). The analysis of the social networks of those interviewed suggests that about one-third of the women and men can be defined as socially isolated (ibid, p.94). Employed persons interact with other people significantly more than former clients that are not employed (ibid). Furthermore, the study also showed a high mortality rate of 6 per cent for the sample.

These two studies do not allow precise predictions of the social situation and/or exclusion, respectively, of former clients of the care system. The results of Tanner's (1992) study, as well as the follow-up examination conducted by Stohler (2005), identify that the integration process, or the transition to independence for former youth welfare system clients, is quite problematic. However, only if the course of life of former clients is studied more systematically can the frequently quoted experience-based rule, which says that a third of all clients are going to prove themselves well, a third fairly well (existing on the fringe) and a third not at all (Tanner 1992, p.93), after leaving an institution, be asserted empirically.

Although there are no comprehensive data, there is some evidence available in Switzerland that clients of the welfare system experience disadvantages in many areas. For example, juveniles who are placed in residential institutions are considered to constitute a risk group when it comes to job-related integration (Piller 2004, p.2). Institutions are obligated to make academic or operational training possible for juveniles and some facilities offer training and teaching internally (ibid, p.4). There are hardly any data available concerning the acquired skills or the whereabouts of the young women and men, although the work-related training has always been of central importance in the history of residential care (ibid, p.2–3). A representative evaluation of 114 judiciary institutions,[1] which was conducted for the first time in 2004, has shown that juveniles who live in welfare homes attend school types that offer low educational attainment (ibid, p.39), which in turn leads to them being disadvantaged concerning the labour and apprenticeship market (ibid, p.56). There is a need for further research concerning the accomplishment of transition into apprenticeship/training, or into a working life, as well as the job-related whereabouts of former clients of the youth welfare system. Studies about the 'leaving care process', or about the biographies of children and youths who were placed in a residential home or a foster family, do not exist.

Conclusion

Switzerland can be seen as a liberal welfare state in transformation. This is reflected in the increase in expenditure on social security, as well as in the strong emphasis on inclusive social rights in some policy areas (health insurance, retirement insurance). On the other hand, there is little assistance in some areas, for example support for families. In general young adults unable to live independently have the right to be supported by social welfare or other programmes which aim to integrate young people by getting them into work. However, there are no special programmes to support young people leaving care, except the opportunity to stay in care until vocational training has been completed. Generally, therapeutic help, or social work support, is used more frequently by female care leavers and in the French-speaking part of Switzerland (Tanner 1999, p.100). Because of the federal state organisation there are only limited secondary data available, and where information is available it tends not to be comparable with that collected in other cantons (Piller 2002). In Switzerland, there is a lack of analysis of the complex dynamics of successful and unsuccessful integration processes for juveniles at risk.

On the basis of the existing knowledge, we can assume the risk of social exclusion for young people leaving care is high: poor education, low levels of attainment and qualification, difficulties in finding housing and employment (especially for ethnic minority groups), a low take-up of medical services and a high level of youth and adult offending and imprisonment. Young people who lack social networks before they enter the care system and while living in care have a higher risk of social exclusion. In addition, the general influences of education and vocational training, as well as gender differences, have to be considered. Young male persistent offenders, especially from ethnic minority groups, have a higher risk of social exclusion, as do those young people who only receive short-term vocational training without any therapeutic support from the child care system. The impact of gender on offending in the after care process is clearly documented by research findings.

About 85 per cent of males failed to integrate socially after one intervention, compared to 66 per cent of females. In the long run, 12 (French-speaking part) to 16 per cent (German-speaking part) of males returned to a care institution or went to jail (compared with 0% (French-speaking part) to 1.6 per cent (German-speaking part) of the female population) (Tanner 1999). Besides delinquency, the lack of economic as well as social resources and professional support seems to influence the careers of young care leavers. After care programmes are more frequently used in the French-speaking part of Switzerland. This seems to be one reason why delinquency, social exclusion and mortality rates after care are higher in the German-speaking part of Switzerland. Finally, thinking about transitions to adulthood, the high mortality of about 10 per cent of young male care leavers in Switzerland has to be kept in mind as a risk that needs to be explored through further research.

Key messages for policy and practice

- Although there is only limited research on the child care system, there is strong evidence that young people in care, especially young offenders, are at high risk of being excluded from society (low education, poverty, high mortality rate).

- More research about the impact of the care system on the life-course of children and youth is necessary (especially longitudinal studies).

- Political and practical measures to promote successful integration for this vulnerable group will require a strong evidence base.

- The differences between the French- and the German-speaking parts of Switzerland reflect different child care cultures with different effects on young care leavers. Further comparisons would be of interest.

- Data on child care are needed at a national level for research and political purposes.

Note

1. Judiciary institutions are defined as 'approved' residential facilities that fulfil specific standards as requested by the Federal Justice Office and are partially financed through the federal budget (Piller 2004, p.4).

References

Boehlen, M. (1983) *Das Jugendheim als Faktor der Sozialen Integration*. Bern/Stuttgart: Verlag Paul Haupt.

Bundesamt für Statistik (2006) *Statistik des Jährlichen Bevölkerungsstandes (ESPOP) und der Natürlichen Bevölkerungsbewegung (BEVNAT) 2005*. Neuchâtel: Bundesverfassung der Schweizerischen Eidgenossenschaft vom 18. April 1999 (Stand am 8. August 2006).

Esping-Andersen, G. (1990) *The Three Worlds of Welfare Capitalism*. New Jersey: Princeton University Press.

Gottesmann, M. (1991) *Residential Child Care. An International Reader*. London: Interkantonale Vereinbarung für Soziale Einrichtungen (IVSE) vom 13. Dezember 2002.

Kuntsch, E.N. and Nett, J.C. (2002) 'Zur Situation der Stationären Erziehungseinrichtungen in der Schweiz. Eine Bedarfsanalyse Wissenschaftlicher Begleitforschung.' *Vierteljahresschrift für Heilpädagogik und ihre Nachbargebiete (VHN) 71*. Jahrgang, Luzern, S.426–S439.

Opielka, M. (2004) 'Die Grundeinkommensversicherung. Schweizer Erfahrungen, Deutsche Perspektiven?' *Sozialer Fortschritt 5*, 114–126.

Opielka, M. (2005) 'Der "Weiche Garantismus" der Schweiz. Teilhaberechte in der Sozialpolitik.' *NFP 51 Bulletin Nr. 2*, December 2005, 1–6.

Piller, E.M. (2002) *Ausmass und Entwicklung von Fremdplatzierungen in der Schweiz. Eine Bestandesaufnahme der Anzahl Kinder und Jugendlichen in Stationären Einrichtungen*. Brugg: Fachhochschule Aargau.

Piller, E.M. (2004) *Berufliche Ausbildung von Jugendlichen in der Stationären Jugendhilfe der Schweiz: Eine Bestandesaufnahme*. Brugg: Fachhochschule Aargau/Departement Soziale Arbeit.

Riklin, A. (ed.) (1983) *Handbuch Politisches System der Schweiz, Band 1*. Bern/Stuttgart: Haupt.

Stohler, R. (2005) *Nachuntersuchung Lernstatt Känguruh*. Accessed 19/02/08 at www.paed.uniz.ch/psp/download/Lernstatt_schlussbericht.pdf.

Tanner, H. (1992) 'Effekte des Massnahmenvollzuges bei besonders erziehungsschwierigen Jugendlichen in der Schweiz. Ueberblick über Ergebnisse der Längsschnittuntersuchung.' *Kriminologisches Bulletin 18*, Jahrgang, Heft Nr. 1–2, S.53–S158.

Tanner, H. (1999) 'Pflegekinderwesen und Heimerziehung in der Schweiz.' In H. Colla, T. Gabriel, S. Millham, S. Müller-Teusler and M. Winkler (eds) *Handbuch Heimerziehung und Pflegekinderwesen in Europa*. Neuwied: Luchterhand.

Tanner, H. (2000) 'Jugend(hilfe) in Bewegung.' In H. Moser and H.U. Grunder (eds) *Jahrhundert des Kindes: Eine Bilanz.* Zürich: Verlag Pestalozzianum.

Tuggener, H. (1975) 'Warum und wozu Forschung in der Heimerziehung?' *Vierteljahresschrift für Heilpädagogik und ihre Nachbargebiete 44*, Jahrgang, Heft 3, S.236–S.248.

UNICEF Schweiz (1999) *Kinder und Jugendluche in der Schweiz: Bericht zu ihrer Situation.* Zürich: Schweizerisches Komitee für UNICEF.

von Sturm zu Vehlingen, C. (1999) *Rechtliche Rahmenbedingungen für sozialpädagogische Entscheidungen nach dem Recht der Jugendhilfe in England, Schweden, der Schweiz und Deutschland.* St. Gallen/Lachen: Dike Verlag AG.

Chapter 16

United Kingdom

Jim Wade and Emily R. Munro

Background and key statistics

- The UK is home to around 60.2 million people, approximately one in five of whom are children aged under 16 years.

- In 2005–2006, a total of 80,015 were looked after – 60,300 in England; 12,750 in Scotland; 4529 in Wales; and 2436 in Northern Ireland.

- England and Northern Ireland have similar rates of looked after children per 10,000 population (55 and 56 children per 10,000 respectively). The rate in Wales is 70 and is highest in Scotland at 120 children per 10,000 population.

- The most common placement type for looked after children in England, Wales and Northern Ireland is foster care (accounting for around 70% of all placements). Fifty-six per cent of all placements in Scotland are at home with parents or with friends/relatives.

- Care leavers tend to move to independent living at a much earlier age than their peers.

- In 2005–2006, around 10,075 young people aged 16–18 and over left care in the UK – 8100 in England; 1393 in Scotland; 382 in Wales; and approximately 200 in Northern Ireland.

Key sources

- Department for Education and Skills (2006).
- Department for Health, Social Services and Public Safety (DHSSPS), Northern Ireland (2006).
- Mooney *et al.* (2006).
- National Assembly for Wales (2006).
- Northern Ireland Statistics and Research Agency.
- Office for National Statistics (2006).
- Scottish Executive (2006).

Introduction

Countries are facing new challenges as they seek to respond to globalisation, ideological shifts in the political economy of welfare, technological advances and changes in the world of work (Hudson and Lowe 2004). Recently, in liberal welfare states such as the UK, emphasis has been placed upon a 'social investment state', including investment in children as citizen-workers-of-the-future (Williams 2004; see also Dobrowolsky 2002; Fawcett, Featherstone and Goddard 2003; Lister 2003). While emphasis is placed upon *all* children, specific groups, including looked after children and those leaving public care are targeted for additional support because they do not have a 'responsible' parent and because they are at risk of low educational attainment and social exclusion (Fawcett *et al.* 2003; Williams 2004).

During 2005–2006, around 10,075 young people aged 16–18 years and over left care in the UK (Department for Education and Skills 2006; National Assembly for Wales 2006; Scottish Executive 2006). This chapter outlines the UK's position in welfare regime typologies and provides a brief overview of the legal and policy frameworks in place to support and promote young people's transitions from public care to independence. Following this, secondary data and research findings on leaving care are discussed and outcomes considered.

Case examples

Matt

Matt was admitted to care when he was eight years old, following physical and emotional abuse. He was placed with foster carers and a care order was granted. Attempts at rehabilitation failed and a care plan for long-term fostering was agreed. His foster placement broke down as the foster carers could not cope with Matt's emotional and behavioural difficulties. He is currently in a residential unit where he is likely to remain until he moves into supported accommodation.

Amanda

Amanda left foster care when she was 16 years old and moved into a council house with her baby. Before she moved, a Pathway Plan was developed to identify the resources and support she would need to ease her transition to independence. Amanda found living independently more difficult than she had expected but initially she was reluctant to accept the support that was available from social services. Professionals were concerned about her lifestyle, the company she was keeping and the parenting her son was receiving. Intensive support was provided by her leaving care worker, social worker and health visitor to help her develop her parenting capacity and improve her coping skills. A year on she is positive about the future and social workers are no longer concerned about her child's welfare.

The United Kingdom's welfare regime

In Esping-Andersen's (1990) welfare regime typology[1] the UK is identified as a 'liberal welfare state' in which the principles of 'less eligibility' and 'self-help' are evident as is the importance of promoting the market (Esping-Andersen 1999). 'Entitlement rules are strict and often associated with stigma; and benefits are typically modest' (Esping-Andersen 1990, p.26). However, positions in the typology are not necessarily static.

> Had we made our comparisons in the immediate post-war decades we almost certainly would have put Britain and Scandinavia in the same

cluster: both built on universal flat benefit programmes, national health care, and a vocal political commitment to full employment. (Esping-Andersen 1999, p.87)

Vogel's (2002) analysis of European welfare regimes and the transition to adulthood places the UK in a 'central European cluster' ('mixed welfare regimes') which is located in an intermediate position concerning welfare mix as well as distributive outcome (p.278). Once again, the UK does not fit comfortably within the typology as it joins the southern cluster in relation to high levels of income inequality and poverty. Wider internal and external pressures are also influential in countries' approaches to welfare provision.

Legal and policy framework

During the 1980s major changes were taking place in the structure of youth transitions, including a concomitant decline in youth labour markets and in affordable housing for young people. Care leavers were particularly vulnerable to unemployment and homelessness and one strategy adopted by the statutory and voluntary sectors to tackle the particular problems faced by this group was the gradual development of specialist leaving care schemes (Coles 1995; Jones 2002; Stein 2004; Wade and Dixon 2006).

At this time, reforms to child welfare legislation were being debated across the UK. Legislation implemented in each constituent country placed new duties on local authorities to 'advise, assist and befriend' looked after children and to promote their welfare when they ceased to be looked after (Children Act 1989,[2] s.24; Children (Northern Ireland) Order 1995,[3] s.35; Children (Scotland) Act 1995, s.29[4]). Although ongoing developments took place in leaving care services during the 1990s, the overly 'permissive' nature of the Acts meant that large variations continued to exist in the support and financial assistance provided to care leavers across different regions (Biehal *et al.* 1995; Broad 1998; Department of Health 1997; Department of Health and Social Services 1999).

As part of a strategy to tackle this pattern of inconsistency, constituent countries in the UK implemented a range of initiatives intended to improve outcomes for care leavers. In England, for example, the Quality Protects initiative, introduced in 1998, linked central government funding to specific service objectives, including targets for improvements in housing, education and training and personal support for care leavers (Department of Health 1998).[5] Additionally, further targeted legislation was passed to strengthen provisions to support care leavers.

The Children (Leaving Care) Act 2000, Children (Leaving Care) Act (Northern Ireland) 2002 and Regulation of Care (Scotland) Act 2001

In England and Wales plans were announced to tighten the duties of local authorities with respect to young people leaving care (Department of Health 1999). Similar developments took place in Northern Ireland (see the Proposal for the Children Leaving Care Bill). The purpose of both the Children (Leaving Care) Act 2000 (in England and Wales) and the Children (Leaving Care) Act (Northern Ireland) 2002 were to delay transitions from care, improve the preparation, planning and consistency of support for young people, and strengthen arrangements for financial assistance. The Acts included new duties to assess and meet needs, provide personal advisers and develop pathway planning for those eligible to receive services up to the age of 21 (or beyond if continuing in education).

The general provisions of the Children (Leaving Care) Act 2000 apply to England and Wales. The transfer of financial support for qualifying 16- and 17-year-olds to local authorities was also applicable to Scotland and Northern Ireland. In Scotland a decision was taken to delay implementation to allow authorities to develop information systems to identify those young people eligible for through care and after care services. In 2004, the Regulation of Care (Scotland) Act 2001 was also implemented (see Section 73(1)). This strengthened the duties placed on local authorities under the Children (Scotland) Act 1995 (under Section 29).

Overall, early research evidence indicates that the new legislative frameworks have prompted a further expansion of leaving care services and led to some improvements in the planning, consistency and equity of these services (Broad 2003; Dixon *et al.* 2006; Hai and Williams 2004).

Secondary data

The exploitation of large-scale datasets to develop knowledge on how care leavers fare in adulthood has been limited in the UK. Data protection and human rights legislation have tended to preclude access to general administrative records that might facilitate longitudinal or comparative work on leaving care. In addition, prior to the implementation of the Quality Protects Initative in 1998, there were no official government statistics on outcomes for care leavers. This has subsequently changed and all local authorities now have to submit descriptive data, on an annual basis, about qualifications on leaving care and housing, economic activity and social work contact at age 19 for all care leavers.[6] While these data would allow for connections to be made between outcomes and key aspects of young people's care careers, they have not generally been used in this way.

Secondary data on care leavers is also provided by youth cohort studies, although the information on the care careers of young people is highly variable. Cohort data relevant to leaving care include the National Child Development Study (NCDS), which has provided regular surveys of a cohort born within one week in 1958 ($n = 17,773$), and the British Cohort Study (BCS70), which has followed up a similar cohort born in 1970 ($n = 17,200$). These surveys were combined for the latest sweep of data collection in 1999–2000 at ages 41–42 and 29–30 respectively.[7]

Cheung and Heath's (1994) analysis of NCDS data revealed that adults who had spent time in care had lower educational attainment, higher levels of unemployment and, where they were employed, were more likely to be in semi-skilled or unskilled employment than those who had never been in care. This remained true even when they controlled for social disadvantage (Cheung and Heath 1994). Buchanan (1999) used NCDS data to explore whether people who had experience of care were at greater risk of psychological problems and of lower levels of life satisfaction at age 33 when compared to those coming from other family settings (including disadvantaged backgrounds). One in five adults with a care background had psychological problems. Positive life satisfaction was associated with having qualifications, a job and a partner (especially for females).

Leaving care research

From the late 1970s, small-scale exploratory studies highlighted the diversity of experience that exists among young people leaving care, but also drew attention to the difficulties many encountered, including risks of further movement and disruption, of unemployment and homelessness and of involvement in the criminal justice system (Godek 1976; Kahan 1979; Lupton 1985; Morgan-Klein 1985; Prison Reform Trust 1991; Randall 1989; Stein and Carey 1986; Triseliotis 1980). Exploratory studies continue to document the experiences of care leavers, open up new areas of investigation and identify gaps in service provision for particular groups, including work on the physical, mental and emotional health of young people leaving care (Broad 1999, 2005), on disabled young people (Priestley, Rabiee and Harris 2003; Rabiee, Priestley and Knowles 2001) and on those from minority ethnic backgrounds (Barn, Andrew and Mantovani 2005; First Key 1987), including unaccompanied asylum seeking children (Broad and Robbins 2005; Wade, Mitchell and Baylis 2005). Research since 1990 has mapped out more systematically the patterns and outcomes associated with leaving care, made connections with young people's past experiences and made comparisons with their peers in the wider population.

Transitions and social exclusion

Research has demonstrated the high risk of social exclusion faced by young people leaving care. Care leavers assume adult responsibilities at a much younger age than their peers (Biehal *et al.* 1995; Dixon and Stein 2005; Garnett 1992; Jones 1995; Pinkerton and McCrea 1999). Youth transitions have generally become more extended and families have an increasing role in supporting children into adulthood (Jones 2002). However, the main elements of transition tend to be compressed for care leavers, who often have to learn to manage a home and start a career or their own family shortly after leaving care (Biehal *et al.* 1995; Stein 2004). This is often in a context where they are unable to rely on consistent support from their families (Biehal and Wade 1996; Sinclair *et al.* 2005).

While some young people therefore go on to fare quite well as young adults, others do not. Care leavers have far fewer educational qualifications than their peers and much lower rates of participation in post-16 further and higher education (Biehal *et al.* 1995; Broad 1998; Jackson, Ajayi and Quigley 2003; Pinkerton and McCrea 1999). They are more likely than their peers to experience unemployment, homelessness, mental health problems (Biehal *et al.* 1995; Broad 1998, 1999; Dixon and Stein 2005) and early parenthood (Chase and Knight 2006; Corlyon and McGuire 1997). While this evidence suggests that care leavers are often ill-equipped to negotiate their way in increasingly competitive youth labour and housing markets, there is also some evidence of a long-lasting legacy from care into adulthood (Cheung and Heath 1994).

Characteristics, care and after care

Some young people face additional difficulties on leaving care, resulting from their characteristics or from aspects of their care experience. Studies reveal a high incidence of emotional and behavioural disturbance among young people referred to social services and a higher incidence of psychiatric disorders among looked after children (Broad 2005; McCann *et al.* 1996; Sinclair *et al.* 1995). Young people with mental health or emotional and behavioural problems also appear to be a high-risk group for poor overall outcomes on leaving care (Sinclair *et al.* 2005; Wade and Dixon 2006). In certain respects this is also the case for disabled young people, especially where they fail to meet the threshold for adult services and attempt independent living. There is evidence of limited planning and consultation leading to abrupt or delayed transitions and, where they do move to independence, of insufficient support to enable some to manage their homes successfully (Priestley *et al.* 2003; Rabiee *et al.* 2001; Wade and Dixon 2006).

Research on care leavers from minority ethnic backgrounds has alerted us to additional risks that can arise when young people lose contact with their families and communities and through the impact of racism and discrimination. However, recent work also stresses the commonalities in key aspects of the experience of all care leavers and the need to disaggregate carefully the experiences of young people from different ethnic backgrounds (Barn *et al.* 2005; First Key 1987). There is also evidence that many local authorities had, at least until recently, largely abrogated its leaving care responsibilities to many unaccompanied asylum seeking children by not supporting them within the looked after system or, where they were eligible to receive leaving care services, by not providing them at the same level as for citizen young people (Hai and Williams 2004; Wade *et al.* 2005).

Studies have also begun to elaborate more systematically the connections between aspects of young people's experience of care and their lives after leaving. There is a growing consensus about the importance of stability and continuity in relationships for looked after children and about the challenges of providing it (Jackson 2002; Stein 2004). There is evidence that those who tend to fare well educationally tend to be female, to have been looked after longer, more commonly in stable foster settings, and to have been offered active support and encouragement to succeed from foster carers, birth families and social workers (Biehal *et al.* 1995; Jackson *et al.* 2003; Robbins 2001). Settled care careers and continuity in schooling have been found to be important factors for the small number of care leavers who go on to higher education (Jackson *et al.* 2003). Stability after leaving care, settled housing, strong life skills, the absence of significant troubles (substance misuse or offending) and targeted careers support have been associated with more positive early employment career outcomes for young people some 12–15 months after leaving care. In contrast, leaving care early (before the age of 18) may increase the risk of later unemployment (Dixon *et al.* 2006; Wade and Dixon 2006).

Some damaging features of young people's early experiences (such as emotional or behavioural disturbance) may bear heavily on young people's progress after leaving care. However, research by Sinclair *et al.* (2005) on young people leaving foster care found that a strong attachment to a birth parent, foster carer, partner or partner's family was associated with a positive outcome. Wade and Dixon (2006) also found that how young people fared in their homes and employment careers was, in large part, shaped by events in their lives *after* leaving care. Young people do not follow pre-determined pathways. They experience life in an inter-connected way and positive events in one sphere of life can have positive effects on others and on young people's overall sense of well-being. In this respect, recent work applying the literature on resilience to leaving care is likely to prove helpful (Stein 2005). These findings also offer encouragement, since they imply that there is also considerable scope for intervention by leaving care services to help young people shape their lives after leaving care.

Leaving care services

Research on the outcomes and effectiveness of leaving care services is at a relatively early stage. However, completed research suggests that they can make a significant contribution to the outcomes attained by young people leaving care (Biehal *et al.* 1995; Dixon and Stein 2005; Dixon *et al.* 2006; Wade and Dixon 2006). Leaving care services have been shown to be effective in developing housing resources and helping young people to settle, even those who have experienced past instability and homelessness, in providing financial support to young people and in helping young people to strengthen their life skills. Specialist services may also help young people to form new links and social relationships through group work, guidance on social skills and links with leisure provision. However, they have in the past been less effective in helping young people into education or employment, in meeting young people's mental and emotional health needs and in brokering young people's relationships with their families – an important area that has received insufficient attention from schemes (Marsh and Peel 1999; Wade 2006).

Studies on the early impact of recent leaving care legislation reveal that the additional duties given to local authorities have led to some improvements in assessment and pathway planning, in the consistency of after care contact with personal advisers and in approaches to multi-agency working with housing, education, employment and health professionals (Broad 2003; Dixon *et al.* 2006; Hai and Williams 2004). These are welcome developments that are likely to strengthen the consistency and equity of services. However, concerns remain about the resources that are available for leaving care work, the lack of specialist resources to assist young people with more complex needs and the pattern of uneven development in service provision across local authorities that continues to persist.

Conclusion

At present, we know much more about the problems or risks faced by young people leaving care (about what does not work well) than we do about the forms of support that may be effective in helping them to negotiate a successful transition to adulthood. The consistency of these findings over time (and from different countries) makes them persuasive. More recent work has attempted to disentangle features of young people's experience in the looked after system that may be protective or create risks and to relate these to the progress young people make after leaving. Although at an early stage, there have also been efforts to evaluate the contribution made by specialist leaving care services. In general terms, the findings are not surprising. Young people tend to fare better if they are offered stability, opportunities for new attachments, continuity in their relationships with family, carers and friends, where education is prioritised as part of care planning, and where they are well supported on leaving care. However, we are also more aware that young people are not set on pathways predetermined by their past experiences, that there is considerable scope at the leaving care stage to provide young people with turning points and fresh opportunities for change. We also know that leaving care schemes are quite successful at providing these and that the new legislative environment is broadly helpful to their endeavours.

However, there is much we do not yet know. There is a need to take forward more systematic and comparative analyses of services to understand what forms of support appear most helpful to particular groups of young people in different contexts. There is a need for more longitudinal work, perhaps drawing on existing large-scale datasets and new ethnographic research, to understand more about pathways and outcomes in later adulthood and how these may compare to those of other adults from socially disadvantaged backgrounds. There is also a need for focused work on particular groups of care leavers, such as those with mental health problems, disabilities or other more complex needs, whose particular experiences and service needs have been insufficiently researched in the past. Finally, we need to develop comparative work across countries to understand what is common or different in the experiences of care leavers in different socio-economic landscapes.

Key messages for policy and practice

- Research conducted over time (and across countries) has consistently highlighted the poor life chances of young people leaving care. Compared to their non-care peers, they are at greater risk of social exclusion in early adulthood.

- Some groups with more complex needs are at particular risk of poor outcomes on leaving care, including young people with mental health or emotional or behavioural difficulties, disabled young people and young offenders or substance misusers. Mechanisms need to be found to address their support needs more effectively.

- How young people fare after leaving care, however, does not appear to be predetermined by their past experiences. Events after leaving are also influential and offer considerable scope for fresh turning points to be provided at this stage.

- Research has highlighted the valuable contribution made by specialist leaving care services, especially in regard to housing, financial support, life skills and in reducing risks of social isolation. Improvements are also being made in education, employment and health services for care leavers.

- Specific UK legislation targeting care leavers appears to be leading to improvements in assessment, planning, consistency of aftercare contact and in multi-agency working. However, regional disparities in resources and services continue to persist and need to be addressed.

Notes

1. Use of welfare regimes as a comparative tool has been questioned (see among others, Arts and Gelissen 2002; Bambra 2005, 2006; Castles and Mitchell 1993; Scruggs and Allan 2006).

2. See Hendrick (2003) and Daguerre (2000).

3. See Kelly and Pinkerton (1996).

4. See McGhee and Francis (2003).

5. For further information on wider policies in Wales, Scotland and Northern Ireland see Williams (2003), Cohen (2003) and Pinkerton (2003).

6. Data for England are available at: www.dfes.gov.uk/rsgateway/DB/VOL; for Scotland at: www.scotland.gov.uk/Topics/Statistics/Browse/Children/PubChildrenLookedAfter; for Wales at: www.dataunitwales.gov.uk/eng/Data.asp?cat=123; and for Northern Ireland at: www.dhsspsni.gov.uk/index/stats_research.

7. Further information on the NCDS and BCS70 is available at: www. esds.ac.uk/longitudinal. The newer Millennium Cohort Study ($n = 19,000$), following up babies born between September 2000 and August 2001, may also offer potential for comparative analysis on looked after children.

References

Arts, W. and Gelissen, J. (2002) 'Three worlds of welfare or more?' *Journal of European Social Policy 12*, 2, 137–158.

Bambra, C. (2005) 'Worlds of welfare and the health care discrepancy.' *Social Policy and Society 4*, 1, 31–41.

Bambra, C. (2006) 'Decommodification and worlds of welfare revisited.' *Journal of European Social Policy 16*, 1, 73–80.

Barn, R., Andrew, L. and Mantovani, N. (2005) *Life After Care: A Study of Young People from Different Ethnic Groups.* York: Joseph Rowntree Foundation.

Biehal, N. and Wade, J. (1996) 'Looking back, looking forward: Care leavers, families and change.' *Children and Youth Services Review 18*, 4/5, 425–446.

Biehal, N., Clayden, J., Stein, M. and Wade, J. (1995) *Moving On: Young People and Leaving Care Schemes.* London: HMSO.

Broad, B. (1998) *Young People Leaving Care: Life After the Children Act 1989.* London: Jessica Kingsley Publishers.

Broad, B. (1999) 'Improving the health of children and young people leaving care.' *Adoption and Fostering 23*, 1, 40–48.

Broad, B. (2003) *After the Act: Implementing the Children (Leaving Care) Act 2000.* Monograph, Number 3. Leicester: Children and Families Research Unit, De Montfort University.

Broad, B. (2005) *Improving the Health and Wellbeing of Young People Leaving Care.* Lyme Regis: Russell House Publishing.

Broad, B. and Robbins, I. (2005) 'The wellbeing of unaccompanied asylum seekers leaving care.' *Diversity in Health and Social Care 2*, 271–277.

Buchanan, A. (1999) 'Are care leavers significantly dissatisfied and depressed in adult life?' *Adoption and Fostering 23*, 4, 35–40.

Castles, F. and Mitchell, D. (1993) 'Three Worlds of Welfare Capitalism or Four?' In F. Castles (ed.) *Families of Nations*. Brookfields, VT: Dartmouth.

Chase, E. and Knight, A. (2006) 'Is Early Parenthood Such a Bad Thing?' In E. Chase, A. Simon and S. Jackson (eds) *In Care and After: A Positive Perspective*. London: Routledge.

Cheung, S.Y. and Heath, A. (1994) 'After care: The education and occupation of adults who have been in care.' *Oxford Review of Education 20*, 3, 361–374.

Children Act (1989). London: HMSO.

Children (Leaving Care) Act (2000). London: The Stationery Office.

Children (Leaving Care) Act (Northern Ireland) (2002). London: The Stationery Office.

Children (Northern Ireland) Order (1995). London: The Stationery Office.

Children (Scotland) Act (1995). London: The Stationery Office.

Cohen, B. (2003) 'Scotland's children and the new parliament.' *Children and Society 17*, 236–246.

Coles, B. (1995) *Youth and Social Policy*. London: UCL Press.

Corlyon, J. and McGuire, C. (1997) *Young Parents in Public Care: Pregnancy and Parenthood Amongst Young People Looked After by Local Authorities*. London: National Children's Bureau.

Daguerre, A. (2000) 'Policy networks in England and France: The case of child care policy 1980–1989.' *Journal of European Public Policy 7*, 2, 244–260.

Department for Education and Skills (2006) *Children Looked After in England (including Adoptions and Care Leavers) 2005–6*. London: DfES.

Department of Health (1997) *'When Leaving Home is also Leaving Care': An Inspection of Services for Young People Leaving Care*. London: Social Services Inspectorate, Department of Health.

Department of Health (1998) *Modernising Health and Social Services: National Priorities Guidance 1999/2000–2001/2*. London: Department of Health.

Department of Health (1999) *Me, Survive, Out There? New Arrangements for Young People Living in and Leaving Care*. London: Department of Health.

Department of Health and Social Services (1999) *Children Order Report 1999*. London: The Stationery Office.

Department for Health, Social Services and Public Safety (DHSSPS) (2006) *Statistics and Research*. Northern Ireland: DHSSPS. Accessed 04/10/07 at www.dhsspsni.gov.uk/index/stats_research/family_practitioner.htm

Dixon, J. and Stein, M. (2005) *Leaving Care: Throughcare and Aftercare in Scotland*. London: Jessica Kingsley Publishers.

Dixon, J., Wade, J., Byford, S., Weatherly, H. and Lee, J. (2006) *Young People Leaving Care: A Study of Costs and Outcomes. Report to the Department for Education and Skills*. York: Social Work Research and Development Unit, University of York.

Dobrowolsky, A. (2002) 'Rhetoric versus reality: The figure of the child and New Labour's strategic "social investment state".' *Studies in Political Economy*, Autumn, 43–73.

Esping-Andersen, G. (1990) *The Three Worlds of Welfare Capitalism*. New Jersey: Princeton University Press.

Esping-Andersen, G. (1999) *Social Foundations of Post-industrial Economies*. Oxford: Oxford University Press.

Fawcett, B., Featherstone, B. and Goddard, J. (2003) 'From the Womb to the Workplace: Child Welfare under New Labour.' Paper presented to the *Annual Conference of the Social Policy Association*, 15 July. Middlesbrough: University of Teesside.

First Key (1987) *A Study of Young Black People Leaving Care*. Leeds: First Key.

Garnett, L. (1992) *Leaving Care and After*. London: National Children's Bureau.

Godek, S. (1976) *Leaving Care.* Barkingside: Barnardo's.

Hai, N. and Williams, A. (2004) *Implementing the Children Leaving Care Act 2000: The Experience of Eight London Boroughs.* London: National Children's Bureau.

Hendrick, H. (2003) *Child Welfare: Historical Dimensions, Contemporary Debates.* Bristol: Policy Press.

Hudson, J. and Lowe, S. (2004) *Understanding the Policy Process: Analysing Welfare Policy and Practice.* Bristol: Policy Press.

Jackson, S. (2002) 'Promoting Stability and Continuity in Care Away from Home.' In D. McNeish, T. Newman and R. Roberts (eds) *What Works for Children?* Buckingham: Open University Press.

Jackson, S., Ajayi, S. and Quigley, M. (2003) *By Degrees: The First Year from Care to University.* London: The Frank Buttle Trust.

Jones, G. (1995) *Leaving Home.* Buckingham: Open University Press.

Jones, G. (2002) *The Youth Divide: Diverging Paths to Adulthood.* York: Joseph Rowntree Foundation.

Kahan, B. (1979) *Growing Up in Care.* Oxford: Blackwell.

Kelly, G. and Pinkerton, J. (1996) 'The Children (Northern Ireland) Order 1995 – Prospects for Progress?' In M. Hill and J. Aldgate (eds) *Child Welfare Services.* London: Jessica Kingsley Publishers.

Lister, R. (2003) 'Investing in the citizen-workers of the future: Transformations in citizenship and the state under New Labour.' *Social Policy and Administration 37,* 5, 427–443.

Lupton, C. (1985) *Moving Out.* Portsmouth: Portsmouth Polytechnic.

Marsh, P. and Peel, M. (1999) *Leaving Care in Partnership: Family Involvement with Care Leavers.* London: The Stationery Office.

McCann, J., James, A., Wilson, S. and Dunn, G. (1996) 'Prevalence of psychiatric disorders in young people in the care system.' *British Medical Journal 313,* 14 December, 1529–1530.

McGhee, J. and Francis, J. (2003) 'Protecting children in Scotland: Examining the impact of the Children (Scotland) Act 1995.' *Child and Family Social Work 8,* 2, 133–142.

Mooney, E., Fitzpatrick, M., Orr, J. and Hewitt, R. (2006) *Children Order Statistical Bulletin 2006.* Northern Ireland Statistics and Research Agency and Department of Health, Social Services and Public Safety.

Morgan-Klein, B. (1985) *Where Am I Going to Stay?* Edinburgh: Scottish Council for Single Homeless.

National Assembly for Wales (2006) *Children Looked After 2005–06.* Cardiff: National Assembly for Wales.

Northern Ireland Statistics and Research Agency (NISRA). Accessed 04/10/07 at www.nisra.gov.uk/statistics/keystatistics.html

Office for National Statistics (2006) *Mid-year Population Estimates: Office for National Statistics, General Register.*

Pinkerton, J. (2003) 'From parity to subsidiarity? Children's policy in Northern Ireland under New Labour: The case of children welfare.' *Children and Society 17,* 254–260.

Pinkerton, J. and McCrea, R. (1999) *Meeting the Challenge? Young People Leaving Care in Northern Ireland.* Aldershot: Ashgate.

Priestley, M., Rabiee, P. and Harris, J. (2003) 'Young disabled people and the "new arrangements" for leaving care in England and Wales.' *Children and Youth Services Review 25,* 863–890.

Prison Reform Trust (1991) *The Identikit Prisoner.* London: Prison Reform Trust.

Rabiee, P., Priestley, M. and Knowles, J. (2001) *Whatever Next? Young Disabled People Leaving Care.* York: York Publishing Services.

Randall, G. (1989) *Homeless and Hungry.* London: Centrepoint.

Regulation of Care (Scotland) Act (2001). London: The Stationery Office.

Robbins, D. (2001) *Transforming Children's Services: An Evaluation of Local Responses to the Quality Protects Programme, Year 3.* London: Department of Health.

Scottish Executive (2006) *Looked After Children 2005–06.* Edinburgh: Scottish Executive.

Scruggs, L. and Allan, J. (2006) 'Welfare-state decommodification in 18 OECD countries: A replication and revision.' *Journal of European Social Policy 16*, 1, 55–72.

Sinclair, R., Garnett, L. and Berridge, D. (1995) *Social Work and Assessment with Adolescents.* London: NCB.

Sinclair, I., Baker, C., Wilson, K. and Gibbs, I. (2005) *Foster Children: Where They Go and How They Get On.* London: Jessica Kingsley Publishers.

Stein, M. (2004) *What Works for Young People Leaving Care?* Barkingside: Barnardo's.

Stein, M. (2005) *Resilience and Young People Leaving Care: Overcoming the Odds.* York: Joseph Rowntree Foundation.

Stein, M. and Carey, K. (1986) *Leaving Care.* Oxford: Blackwell.

Triseliotis, J. (1980) 'Growing Up in Foster Care.' In J. Triseliotis (ed.) *New Developments in Foster Care and Adoption.* London: Routledge and Keegan Paul.

Vogel, J. (2002) 'European welfare regimes and the transition to adulthood: A comparative and longitudinal perspective.' *Social Indicators Research 59*, 275–299.

Wade, J. (2006) 'The ties that bind: Support from birth families and substitute families for young people leaving care.' *British Journal of Social Work*, Advanced Access: doi: 10.1093/bjsw/bcl342

Wade, J. and Dixon, J. (2006) 'Making a home, finding a job: Investigating early housing and employment outcomes for young people leaving care.' *Child and Family Social Work 11*, 199–208.

Wade, J., Mitchell, F. and Baylis, G. (2005) *Unaccompanied Asylum Seeking Children: The Response of Social Work Services.* London: BAAF.

Williams, C. (2003) 'The impact of Labour on policies for children and young people in Wales.' *Children and Society 17*, 247–253.

Williams, F. (2004) 'What matters is who works: Why every child matters to New Labour. Commentary on the DfES Green Paper "Every Child Matters".' *Critical Social Policy 24*, 3, 406–427.

Chapter 17

United States

Mark E. Courtney

Background and key statistics

- The US is home to about 300 million people, approximately 80 million of whom are under 20 years old.

- In 2004, approximately 517,000 children lived in out-of-home care in the US.

- About six children and adolescents per thousand in the US live in out-of-home care.

- Almost half of all children in out-of-home care live with non-relative foster parents, about one-quarter live in relative or "kinship" foster care, and about one-fifth live in group care with the remainder living in a variety of other settings.

- In the vast majority of states young people are discharged from care at the age of majority (18), rendering them on their own at a younger age than is typical in the US.

- About 25,000 young people per year exit out-of-home care in the US through legal "emancipation," usually due to reaching the age of majority or graduating from secondary school.

Key sources

- Courtney and Hughes-Heuring (2005).

- US Department of Health and Human Services, Administration on Children, Youth and Families (2006).
- US General Accountability Office (2004).

Introduction

Although the US social safety net is in many ways less comprehensive than that found in other post-industrial democracies, former foster youth receive considerable attention in US social policy directed at the transition to adulthood. Below I briefly describe the social policy context in which young people in the US make the transition to adulthood from foster care. I provide an introduction to the US child welfare system, basic demographic information about children in care, and an overview of policies intended to support foster youth in transition. I describe currently available and anticipated sources of data on the care histories and young adult outcomes of foster youth. Lastly, I briefly summarize the literature on the young adult outcomes of former foster youth.

Case examples

Paul

Paul (17) entered care when he was ten years old due to his single mother's substance abuse problem that seriously interfered with her parenting. He was placed in the court-ordered supervision of the state child welfare agency under the state's child maltreatment statute. Paul's mother did not comply with the court-ordered treatment plan and her parental rights were terminated, making the juvenile court Paul's legal parent. Paul has lived in three different foster homes since entering care, including once with his maternal grandmother who ultimately decided that she could no longer care for Paul due to her chronic health problems. He has been living in the same foster home for the last three years with a foster mother and father not related to him. State support for his care will end at age 18, but Paul's foster parents say that they will allow him to stay with them, at least for a while.

Jasmine

Jasmine (17) entered care when she was 16 because of sexual abuse by her step-father. Efforts to reunify the family failed and Jasmine does not want to be adopted, so her case plan is preparation for independent living. Jasmine has emotional problems stemming from her abuse and has lived in group care since being removed from home. She sees the group home psychologist for individual cognitive-behavioral psychotherapy on a weekly basis. Her group home provides weekly group meetings that focus on preparing foster youth for adulthood by teaching them life skills. Jasmine has also been involved in a mentoring program that pairs foster youth with adult mentors who have committed to providing advice and support to youth as they make the transition to adulthood. She will exit state care on her 18th birthday but plans to move into an apartment supervised by a voluntary-sector transitional living program that receives funding from the state child welfare agency. The program will provide her housing for up to 18 months and help her to continue her education and find employment. The state Jasmine lives in provides Medicaid (government health care for low-income people) to former foster youth through age 21, so Jasmine will continue to be eligible for health and mental health services for a few years after leaving care.

The United States' welfare regime

The US welfare state has been characterized as "liberal" by Esping-Andersen (1990). Two factors must be taken into account in examining public policy in the US as it pertains to young people making the transition to adulthood from foster care. First, the US has a relatively residual and decentralized welfare state in comparison to most post-industrial democracies. For example, there is no entitlement to cash assistance for low-income adults in the US; available assistance is limited to low-income parents with children, is tied to efforts to gain and maintain employment, and is time limited (Gallagher *et al.* 1998; Greenberg 2004). Similarly, in-kind food assistance through the Food Stamp Program is generally available only to low-income families with children, with only very limited assistance for single childless adults. There is no federal entitlement to housing assistance in the US and available programs meet the needs of only a small percentage of persons who cannot afford housing. There is no guarantee of financial support for students attending either public or private institutions of higher education in the US and federal grant support for low-income students has declined, increasing the debt load of low-income college graduates (Maag and Fitzpatrick 2004). Lastly, health care in the US is financed by a patchwork of private insurance and government-supported programs, leaving 31 per cent of adults between 19 and 29 without health insurance (Collins *et al.* 2006).

Decentralization is an important characteristic of US social policy; the 50 states exercise considerable autonomy in how they operate federally supported programs and in state-level per-capita expenditures on social, educational, and health programs. In addition, many states delegate the responsibility for delivering services to counties and local government. As a result of this decentralization, the US social safety net for young adults varies considerably between and within states.

A second important aspect of the US context is that it is normative for young adults in the US to rely heavily on their families for support during the transition to adulthood (Settersten, Furstenberg and Rumbaut 2005). For example, in 2001 approximately 63 percent of men between 18 and 24 years old and 51 percent of women in that age range lived with one or both of their parents (US Census Bureau 2001). Young adults in the US also rely heavily on their parents for material assistance during the transition to adulthood; parents provide roughly $38,000 for food, housing, education, or direct cash assistance from 18–34 (Schoeni and Ross 2004).

Put simply, US social policy assumes that young people will either be self-sufficient or will be able to rely on their families during the transition to adulthood. Whether this assumption makes sense for young adults in general is a question that has received considerable attention lately in the US (Settersten *et al.* 2005), with some observers pointing out that "vulnerable populations" facing the transition to adulthood (e.g. foster youth) are particularly ill-served by current policy (Osgood *et al.* 2005).

Legal and policy framework

States operate their foster care programs under the legal framework provided by Titles IV-E and IV-B of the Social Security Act. Juvenile and family courts supervise the care of children by state and local public child welfare agencies. Children enter out-of-home care when a court determines that they should be removed from their home in order to protect them from abuse or neglect. Child welfare agencies are required to make "reasonable efforts" to prevent placement of children in out-of-home care, usually in the form of social services for their families. When the child welfare agency and court deem these efforts unsuccessful and the child enters out-of-home care, the court must approve a "permanency plan" for the child. Most commonly, the initial plan is for the child to return to the care of parents or other family members. Once again, the court generally requires the child welfare agency to make reasonable efforts to preserve the child's family of origin, in this case by providing services intended to help reunite the child with the family. In many cases, however, children and youth cannot return to the care of their families. When this happens, the child welfare agency and the court attempt to find another permanent home for the child through adoption or legal guardianship.

There were an estimated 81.5 million US residents under 20 years of age in 2004 (US Census Bureau 2006). Approximately 517,000 children lived in out-of-home care on September 30, 2004, the most recent year for which national estimates are available (US Department of Health and Human Services, Administration on Children, Youth and Families 2006); about six children and adolescents per thousand in the US live in out-of-home care. Fifty-two percent of these children were Black and/or Hispanic, 53 percent were male, and their median age was 10.9 years. About 5 percent (24,492) were between 18 and 21 years old. Almost half (46%) of these children lived with non-relative foster parents, 24 percent lived in relative or "kinship" foster care, 19 percent lived in group homes or other children's institutions, 4 percent in a pre-adoptive home, 4 percent were living at home during a trial home visit, 2 percent had run away from care but were still under child welfare agency legal custody, and 1 percent were living in supervised independent living settings. Although children living in kinship foster care remain in the day-to-day care of their extended families, the public child welfare agency has authority over these placements under the same laws used to supervise non-relative foster care.

The vast majority of children in out-of-home care will exit care to what are considered "permanent" placements; of the estimated 283,000 children who left out-of-home care in the US during 2004, 88 percent went to live with family, were adopted, or were placed in the home of a legal guardian (US Department of Health and Human Services, Administration on Children, Youth and Families 2006). A few (2%) were transferred to another public agency such as a probation or mental health department and a few (2%) ran away and were discharged from care. Eight percent, or 23,121, remained in care until they were legally "emancipated" to "independent living," usually due to reaching the age of majority or upon graduation from high school. In practice, few states allow youth to remain in care much past their 18th birthday (Bussey *et al.* 2000).

In the 1980s, child welfare advocates pushed for funding to help foster youth prepare for adulthood. In 1986, the Independent Living Initiative (Public Law 99-272) provided federal funds to states to help adolescents develop skills needed for independent living. The law gave states great flexibility in terms of what kinds of services they could provide to eligible youth who were at least 16 and no more than 21 years old. Basic services outlined in the law included outreach programs to attract youth, training in daily living skills, education and employment assistance, counseling, case management, and written transitional independent living plans. These funds could not, however, be used for room and board.

The Foster Care Independence Act (FCIA) of 1999 amended Title IV-E to give states more funding and greater flexibility in providing support for youths making the transition to independent living. The FCIA doubles federal independent living services funding to $140 million per year, allows states to use up to 30 percent of these funds for room and board, enables states to assist young adults 18–21 years old who have left foster care, and permits states to extend federally supported health care to former foster children up to age 21. An amendment to the law authorizes Congress to appropriate up to $60 million per year for education and training vouchers of up to $5000 per year for youth up to 23 years old, though appropriations have never reached this level. The FCIA requires the Department of Health and Human Services (HHS) to develop a set of outcome measures to assess state performance in managing independent living programs and states will be required to collect data on these outcomes. HHS proposed regulations in 2006 to implement these aspects of the FCIA through a National Youth in Transition Database (NYTD).

The term "independent living services" describes a wide range of approaches to meeting the needs of youth who child welfare authorities expect to age out of foster care or have already done so. No neat categorization adequately captures the range of these services and there are no reliable national data on their scope. In general, agencies delivering these services tend to provide multiple services, serve broad and sometimes ill-defined populations, and may focus on multiple outcomes. One typology of independent living services categorizes them into life skills training, mentoring programs, transitional housing, health and behavioral health services, educational services, and employment services (Courtney and Terao 2002). Although these categories largely capture the range of independent living services, they can obscure certain common elements of the programs that deliver such services, such as case management and a "youth development" philosophy. A survey of programs by Sheehy *et al.* (2000) found that many provide a wide range of services. Thus, it is important to keep in mind that independent living services are generally delivered in the context of more comprehensive social service programs.

In addition, categorization of services does not provide information about state and local *policies* intended to support independent living. For example, some jurisdictions allow youth to remain in foster care past age 18, other states have waived tuition for foster youth who attend state colleges or universities, and at least one state (Illinois) has created a wage subsidy for youth under 21 who have aged out of foster care. Such policies might ultimately have more influence than independent living services on adult outcomes for former foster youth.

The range of services funded by the FCIA should not lead the reader to believe that these services are available to all foster youth and former foster youth; 40 states responding to a survey regarding provision of independent living services reported serving about 56,000 youth in 2003, or approximately 44 percent of youth in foster care who were eligible for services in those states (US General Accountability Office 2004). Moreover, service availability varies widely between states and even between counties within states (Sheehy *et al.* 2000; US General Accountability Office 2004).

Secondary data

The US is in a comparatively good position with respect to the availability of data on the transition to adulthood for foster youth. States operate data systems intended to track the placement history of children in state-supervised out-of-home care and make regular reports to the federally operated Adoption and Foster Care Analysis and Reporting System (AFCARS). The nature of the data contained in these databases varies considerably between states, though federal reporting requirements have established some consistency. AFCARS requirements ask for basic demographic information on children in out-of-home care and the details of their care histories (e.g. reasons for removal from home, number and types of placements, and reasons for discharge from care).

Federal, state, and local governments in the US collect data for the purposes of administering a variety of government programs. Under certain circumstances, these data can be used to examine the experiences of care leavers both before and after they leave care. Some examples of these kinds of data include: data on health and mental health problems and the utilization of health and mental/behavioral health services from government-funded health care programs; utilization of public assistance programs (e.g. cash or in-kind subsidies for food, housing, or other basic necessities); involvement with criminal justice programs; enrollment and performance in educational institutions; earnings and income; and births and deaths. Administrative data in the US have already been used to study earnings (Dworsky and Courtney 2000; Goerge *et al.* 2002) and public assistance utilization (Dworsky and Courtney 2000) of large samples of care leavers in the US.

As noted above, the federal government plans to implement the NYTD, which would require states to track through age 21 a random sample of all youth in out-of-home care in the state at age 17. The proposed data collection would cover youth characteristics, outcomes (financial self-sufficiency, experience with homelessness, educational attainment, positive connections with adults, high-risk behavior, and access to health insurance), and services received.

Leaving care research

Interest in understanding how former foster youth fare in adulthood led to a number of studies over the years. This research literature is limited in a number of ways, which calls for caution in interpretation (Courtney and Hughes-Heuring 2005). Nevertheless, the findings of these studies suggest that the transition to adulthood for foster youth in the US is difficult, to say the least. On average, they have had poor educational experiences, leading them to bring to the transition very limited human capital upon which to build a career or economic assets (Barth 1990; Cook Fleischman and Grimes 1991; Courtney *et al.* 2001, 2005; Festinger 1983; Frost and Jurich 1983; Jones and Moses 1984; Pecora *et al.* 2005; Zimmerman 1982). They often suffer from mental health problems that can negatively affect other outcome domains and these problems are less likely to be treated once they leave care (Barth 1990; Cook 1992; Cook *et al.* 1991; Courtney *et al.* 2005; Fanshel, Finch and Grundy 1990; Festinger 1983; Jones and Moses 1984; McDonald *et al.* 1996; Pecora *et al.* 2005; Robins 1966; Zimmerman 1982). They often become involved in crime and with the justice and corrections systems after aging out of foster care (Barth 1990; Courtney *et al.* 2001, 2005; Fanshel *et al.* 1990; Frost and Jurich 1983; Jones and Moses 1984; McCord, McCord and Thurber 1960; Zimmerman 1982). Their employment prospects are bleak and few of them escape poverty during the transition (Barth 1990; Cook *et al.* 1991; Courtney *et al.* 2001, 2005; Dworsky and Courtney 2000; Festinger 1993; Goerge *et al.* 2002; Jones and Moses 1984; Pecora *et al.* 2005; Pettiford 1981; Zimmerman 1982). Many former foster youth experience homelessness and housing instability after leaving care (Cook *et al.* 1991; Courtney *et al.* 2001, 2005; Fanshel *et al.* 1990; Jones and Moses 1984; Mangine *et al.* 1990; Pecora *et al.* 2005; Sosin, Coulson and

Grossman 1988; Sosin, Piliavin and Westerfelt 1990; Susser *et al.* 1991). Former foster youth have higher rates of out-of-wedlock parenting than their peers (Cook *et al.* 1991; Courtney *et al.* 2005; Festinger 1983; Meier 1965). Interestingly, in spite of court-ordered separation from their families, often for many years, most former foster youth can rely on their families to some extent during the transition to adulthood, though this is not always without risk (Barth 1990; Cook *et al.* 1991; Courtney *et al.* 2001, 2005; Festinger 1983; Frost and Jurich 1983; Harari 1980; Jones and Moses 1984; Zimmerman 1982).

Conclusion

The US can be described as a liberal welfare state with decentralized administration of most government services, including child welfare services. Secondary data exist regarding a range of adult outcomes for foster youth, have been used for research purposes, and a national data system to track adult outcomes is in the works. Available research suggests that the transition to adulthood for foster youth in the US is often difficult. Fortunately, in the past 20 years US policy has evolved to focus on this population. As a result, states are now providing a wider range of services intended to assist young people leaving care. A coalition of US foundations has also recently formed, reflecting philanthropic interest in the population (Youth Transition Funders Group 2006).

Nevertheless, policy and practice need to evolve to address the challenges that foster youth often bring to the transition to adulthood. Practitioners should redouble efforts to ameliorate the challenges faced by many foster youth in transition (e.g. educational deficits; behavioral and emotional problems) and prevent critical events that can disrupt the transition to adulthood (e.g. unplanned parenting; involvement with the criminal justice system). Practitioners also need to place a much greater emphasis on assisting foster youth in establishing and maintaining supportive relations into adulthood with members of their extended families. Too often current practice reflects the erroneous assumption that these young people either do not have families or that their families cannot be a source of support. Practice also needs to better address the needs of parenting foster youth.

Policy should clearly support provision of services well past age 18. A wide range of public institutions (e.g. education, workforce development, and public housing) will need to place a priority on supporting former foster youth if outcomes are to improve. In particular, national policy should better support continuity of access to health and mental health services into adulthood for this population. In order for US foster youth to experience successful transitions to adulthood, the public and all relevant public institutions must embrace the collective responsibility for continuing to parent these children of the state into adulthood.

Key messages for policy and practice

- Practitioners should redouble efforts to ameliorate the challenges faced by many foster youth as they approach the transition to adulthood and prevent events that can disrupt an otherwise successful transition.

- Policy should clearly support provision of services well past age 18.

- A wide range of public institutions will need to place a priority on supporting former foster youth if their outcomes are to improve.

- In particular, national policy should better support continuity of access to health and mental health services into adulthood for this population.

- Practitioners need to place a much greater emphasis on assisting foster youth in establishing and maintaining supportive relations into adulthood with members of their extended families.

- Policies and practices need to acknowledge the fact that many foster youth in transition have children of their own.

References

Barth, R. (1990) 'On their own: The experiences of youth after foster care.' *Child and Adolescent Social Work 7*, 419–440.

Bussey, M., Feagans, L., Arnold, L., Wulczyn, F. *et al.* (2000) *Transition for Foster Care: A State-by-State Data Base Analysis.* Seattle, WA: Casey Family Programs.

Collins, S.R., Schoen, C., Kriss, J.L., Doty, M.M. and Mahato, B. (2006) *Rite of Passage? Why Young Adults Become Uninsured and How New Policies Can Help.* New York: The Commonwealth Fund.

Cook, R., Fleischman, E. and Grimes, V. (1991) *A National Evaluation of Title IV-E Foster Care Independent Living Programs for Youth in Foster Care: Phase 2, Final Report Volume 1.* Rockville, MD: Westat, Inc.

Cook, S.K. (1992) *Long Term Consequences of Foster Care for Adult Well-Being.* Ph.D. dissertation. Lincoln: University of Nebraska.

Courtney, M.E. and Hughes-Heuring, D. (2005) 'The Transition to Adulthood for Youth 'Aging Out' of the Foster Care System.' In W. Osgood, C. Flanagan, E.M. Foster and G. Ruth (eds) *On Your Own Without a Net: The Transition to Adulthood for Vulnerable Populations.* Chicago: University of Chicago Press.

Courtney, M.E. and Terao, S. (2002) *Classification of Independent Living Services* (unpublished report). Chicago: Chapin Hall Center for Children, University of Chicago.

Courtney, M.E., Dworsky, A., Ruth, G., Keller, T., Havlicek, J. and Bost, N. (2005) *Midwest Evaluation of the Adult Functioning of Former Foster Youth: Outcomes at Age 19.* Chicago: Chapin Hall Center for Children, University of Chicago.

Courtney, M.E., Piliavin, I., Grogan-Kaylor, A. and Nesmith, A. (2001) 'Foster youth transitions to adulthood: A longitudinal view of youth leaving care.' *Child Welfare 6*, 685–717.

Dworsky, A. and Courtney, M.E. (2000) *Self-Sufficiency of Former Foster Youth in Wisconsin: Analysis of Unemployment Insurance Wage Data and Public Assistance Data.* Madison, WI: IRP. Accessed 25/08/07 at http://aspe.hhs.gov/hsp/fosteryouthWI00

Esping-Andersen, G. (1990) *The Three Worlds of Welfare Capitalism.* New Jersey: Princeton University Press.

Fanshel, D., Finch, S.J. and Grundy, J.F. (1990) *Foster Children in Life Course Perspective.* New York: Columbia University.

Festinger, T. (1983) *No One Ever Asked Us: A Postscript to Foster Care.* New York: Columbia University.

Frost, S. and Jurich, A.P. (1983) *Follow-up Study of Children Residing in the Villages* (unpublished report). Topeka, KS: The Villages.

Gallagher, L.J., Gallagher, M., Perese, K., Schreiber, S. and Watson, K. (1998) *One Year After Federal Welfare Reform: A Description of State Temporary Assistance for Needy Families (TANF) Decisions as of October 1997.* Washington, DC: The Urban Institute.

Goerge, R., Bilaver, L., Joo Lee, B., Needell, B., Brookhart, A. and Jackman, W. (2002) *Employment Outcomes for Youth Aging out of Foster Care.* Chicago: Chapin Hall Center for Children, University of Chicago. Accessed 25/08/07 at http://aspe.os.dhhs.gov/hsp/fostercare- agingout02

Greenberg, M. (2004). 'Welfare reform, phase two: Doing less with less. *The American Prospect 15*, 9, September. Accessed 30/08/06 at: www.prospect.org/web/page.ww?section= rootandname=ViewPrintandarticleId=8358

Harari, T. (1980) *Teenagers Exiting from Family Foster Care: A Retrospective Look* (Ph.D. dissertation). Berkeley: University of California.

Jones, M.A. and Moses, B. (1984) *West Virginia's Former Foster Children: Their Experiences in Care and their Lives as Young Adults.* New York: CWLA.

Maag, E.M. and Fitzpatrick, K. (2004) *Federal Financial Aid for Higher Education: Programs and Prospects.* Washington, DC: The Urban Institute.

Mangine, S., Royse, D., Wiehe, V. and Nietzel, M. (1990) 'Homelessness among adults raised as foster children: A survey of drop-in center users.' *Psychological Reports 67*, 739–745.

McCord, J., McCord, W. and Thurber, E. (1960) The effects of foster home placement in the prevention of adult antisocial behavior. *Social Service Review 34*, 415–419.

McDonald, T.P., Allen, R.I., Westerfelt, A. and Piliavin, I. (1996) *Assessing the Long-Term Effects of Foster Care: A Research Synthesis.* Washington, DC: CWLA.

Meier, E.G. (1965) 'Current circumstances of former foster children.' *Child Welfare 44*, 196–206.

Osgood, D.W., Foster, E.M., Flanagan, C. and Ruth, G.R. (eds) (2005) *On Your Own Without a Net: The Transition to Adulthood for Vulnerable Populations.* Chicago: University of Chicago Press.

Pecora, P.J., Kessler, R.C., Williams, J., Downs, A.C. *et al.* (2005) *Improving Family Foster Care: Findings from the Northwest Alumni Study.* Seattle, Washington: Casey Family Programs.

Pettiford, P. (1981) *Foster Care and Welfare Dependency: A Research Note.* New York: Human Resources Administration, Office of Policy and Program Development.

Robins, L.N. (1966) *Deviant Children Grown Up: A Sociological and Psychiatric Study of Sociopathic Personality.* Baltimore: Williams and Wilkins.

Schoeni, R. and Ross, K. (2004) *Family Support during the Transition to Adulthood.* Network on Transitions to Adulthood Policy Brief 12. Philadelphia, PA: University of Pennsylvania, Department of Sociology.

Settersten, R., Furstenberg, F.F. and Rumbaut, R.G. (eds) (2005) *On the Frontier of Adulthood: Theory, Research, and Public Policy.* Chicago: University of Chicago Press.

Sheehy, A., Oldham, E., Zanghi, M., Ansell, D., Correia, P. and Copeland, R. (2000) *Promising Practices: Supporting Transition of Youth Served by the Foster Care System.* Portland, ME: Edmund S. Muskie Institute of Public Affairs.

Sosin, M., Coulson, P. and Grossman, S. (1988) *Homelessness in Chicago: Poverty and Pathology, Social Institutions, and Social Change.* Chicago: University of Chicago, Social Service Administration.

Sosin, M., Piliavin, I. and Westerfelt, H. (1990) 'Toward a longitudinal analysis of homelessness.' *Journal of Social Issues 46*, 4, 157–174.

Susser, E., Lin, S., Conover, S. and Streuning, E. (1991) 'Childhood antecedents of homelessness in psychiatric patients.' *American Journal of Psychiatry 148*, 1026–1030.

US Census Bureau (2001) *Survey of Income and Program Participation, 2001, Wave 2.* Accessed 30/08/06 at www.census.gov/population/socdemo/child/sipp2001/tab04.xls

US Census Bureau (2006) *Table 1: Annual Estimates of the Population by Sex and Five-Year Age Groups for the United States: April 1, 2000 to July 1, 2005 (NC-EST2005-01).* Accessed 01/03/07 at: www.census.gov/popest/national/asrh/NC-EST2005/NC-EST2005-01.xls

US Department of Health and Human Services, Administration on Children, Youth and Families. (2006) *The AFCARS Report: Preliminary FY 2004 Estimates as of June 2006.* Accessed 30/08/06: www.acf.hhs.gov/programs/cb/stats_research/afcars/tar/report11.htm

US General Accountability Office (2004) *HHS Actions Could Improve Coordination of Services and Monitoring of States Independent Living Programs.* Report no. GAO-05-25. Washington, DC: US General Accountability Office.

Youth Transition Funders Group (2006) *Safe Passage: How Philanthropy is Working Together to Help All of America's Youth Connect by Age 25.* Chicago: Youth Transition Funders Group.

Zimmerman, R.B. (1982) 'Foster care in retrospect.' *Tulane Studies in Social Welfare 14.* New Orleans: Tulane University.

Part II

Thematic Issues

Chapter 18

States of Care Leaving

Towards International Exchange as a Global Resource

John Pinkerton

Introduction

Within a British context there has never been greater concern to ensure that young people leaving state care do so equipped to deal with the challenges of making the transition from youth to adulthood. That concern has both encouraged and been fuelled by a growing understanding of the complexity of care leavings – in particular the recognition that it is a process and one that takes shape according to the specific social and emotional circumstances of the individual care leaver. Progress in understanding has been made through drawing on a range of sources. Young people and the practitioners who work closely with them have made their own voices heard. Qualitative and quantitative research studies have been undertaken. Administrative data has been gathered and reviewed. Limited work has even been done on providing an historical account of developments in the field. However, one other source of understanding that has not yet been used to any significant extent is that of international comparison. The purpose of this chapter is to suggest why it is worth undertaking international comparison, how it can be approached and what issues comparative work needs to address at this stage in its contribution to understanding care leavings. It sets out some of the challenges involved, and outlines a conceptual model for approaching these in a way that links the global to the national and local. Further, it suggests that through considering work already done on describing different types of welfare regime it is possible to chart a way forward in the comparative study of young people making the transition from state care.

Why international comparison?

The reason for needing to develop an international perspective on leaving care is deceptively simple – globalisation. The features of contemporary living most closely associated with the notion of globalisation are an ever quickening pace of change, the influence of information technology and ever more porous national boundaries open to all sorts of cross-national economic, political and cultural influences. These features are perhaps most vividly seen in the lives of young people. 'Youth culture is often viewed as the cutting edge of an increasingly liquid modernity within which mobility and communication are crucial resources' (Henderson *et al.* 2007, p.103). The mobile phone is as ubiquitous on the roads of South Africa's townships as it is in the streets of British suburbs and indeed in the hands of care leavers in both those countries.

Along with the sense of opening possibilities that goes with globalisation, as stressed by its enthusiastic supporters, goes an increasing sense of insecurity, as is pointed out by those who oppose it with equal vigour. All young people today making their transition to adulthood have to 'negotiate a set of risks which were largely unknown to their parents' and contend with a pace of change that creates 'increased uncertainty [that] can be seen as a source of stress and vulnerability' (Furlong and Cartmel 1997, p.1). The 'compressed and accelerated transitions' (Stein 2004, p.53) that research across the UK has consistently shown to be the experience of care leavers is a variation of the uneven and fragmented transitions that now characterise this stage of the life cycle: 'Uneven, because different groups of young people have very different experiences of the transition to adulthood. Fragmented, because the different markers of adulthood are increasingly uncoupled from each other' (Thompson *et al.* 2004, p.14).

For all young people, including care leavers, 'motivation to participate (to stay on board) is secured largely by the strength of certainty about the destinations that are likely to be reached. Today's globalised world carries little certainty' (Williamson 2005, p.23). Research in the UK and elsewhere (Pinkerton 2002) has consistently shown that such uncertainty about the future is compounded by the experience of care leaving. Young people making their transition to adulthood from state care are vulnerable in every area of their lives: accommodation, physical health, early parenthood, education, occupational training, life skills, social networks, relationships and identity. This vulnerability is an expression of the particular experiences these young people have had as their care careers unfolded but it also reflects the wider features and changes that globalisation is driving in the areas which define the context of the transition from youth to adulthood – family life, education, training, employment, income support and housing.

It is also the pace and direction of change driven by globalisation which is prompting many governments to review the form and function of state welfare provision. Terms such as the 'investment state' and 'developmental state' are gaining influence. Such changes in state provision constrain or enable those who are working alongside care leavers to optimise their life chances. As has been pointed out for social workers, who in the UK continue to play a key role in care leaving, '[we] are all now operating in – or struggling with – conditions affected by globalization' (Lyons 2006, p.378). Along with the boundaries of nation states, the internal welfare regimes and the professional practices within them are being challenged by cross-national economics, politics and culture. There is a need for social workers and others engaging professionally with care leavers to recognise that they are part of an increasingly mobile global workforce. With that goes a responsibility, to make sense of, and respond to, the commonalities and differences in developments in the type of state services that they are a part of and how that influences their practice. Such active engagement with globalisation is necessary to help ensure that the changes that it is driving work for and not against young people making the transition from state care.

The United Nations Convention on the Rights of the Child (UNCRC) is the most advanced and overarching expression of a global agenda for children and young people. It provides an essential framework for thinking about the international dimension of care leaving. Although it is formally restricted to children, understood as those under the age of 18, the UNCRC is relevant to young people leaving care. There is now a clear understanding that care leaving is a process of transition bridging a period from youth to adulthood. That is, approximately between the ages of 15 and 21 years old, which makes the UNCRC directly applicable for almost half that time. In addition it is increasingly accepted that it is appropriate to continue to use the UNCRC to consider the rights and service provision for young people with additional needs to their peers. Care leavers are one such group.

The Committee that monitors the implementation of the UNCRC periodically sets aside a day for general discussion of a specific issue. In 2005 it held such a day on 'children without parental care'. One of the limited number of themes highlighted in the record of that day was the 'Transition period'. Reflecting its discussion the Committee recommended:

> that States parties and other stakeholders facilitate and enhance the child's transition from institutional care to independent living providing a child with an external contact person, promoting contacts with the biological parents, teaching children how to live on their own and manage their own households, providing overlapping half-way houses during a transition period etc...and standardise the out-of-home care and the transition from the out-of-home care back to the family or into society. (Committee on the Rights of the Child 2006, p.9)

While the terminology has a rather outdated ring to it, certainly within a UK context, it is a clear assertion of leaving care as a global issue and of the aspiration for a global standard in handling it.

While globalisation may be the obvious driver behind adding an international perspective to how care leaving is understood, it is also important to be mindful of the contested and complex nature of the phenomena that the concept of globalisation seeks to capture. There are considerable differences in how globalisation is defined (Lyons, Manion and Calseton 2006). It may have become part of the everyday vocabulary of culture, politics and economics but there is no consensus as to what implications it has for understanding the past, making sense of the present or charting the future (Calomiris 2002; Khan and Dominneli 2000; Mann 2001; Midgley 2000; Yeates 2001). Part of the problem is the intellectual challenge of providing a unifying perspective on the complex range of phenomena that globalisation is trying to address. Not only is it trying to encompass economic, demographic, cultural, social, psychological and political international trends, but it is trying to do so while many aspects of these phenomena themselves remain imprecisely described and understood. In addition there are deep value-based political divisions over whether globalisation, or to be exact its present form, promotes or impedes human well-being (Midgley 2004). Accordingly it is best to adopt a cautious and provisional view of how the concept can help understand welfare in general, and support for care leavers, in particular. 'Globalization should be viewed in a more conditional way so that assessments of its impact take account of the divergent ways in which international changes have affected human well-being' (Midgley 2004, p.24).

A means to approach international comparison

A cautious approach to viewing care leavings through the lens of globalisation is also advisable because of the very real difficulties there are in undertaking international comparison. It involves a complex and demanding process of knowledge management. Information from two or more countries has to be gathered, evaluated for comparability and analysed for similarities and differences. Despite the huge amount of information ever more easily accessed through the internet (though the extent of the continuing 'digital divide' should not be underestimated) many people, particularly English speakers, continue to be limited to only one language. Also while information may be accessible, it may not be reliable or comparable across jurisdictions. Material may prove too specific to a single country; both in terms of general social, economic and political context and in terms of how services to care leavers are organised. It is very striking in reading the national accounts provided in this book that, while at the individual level the challenges facing the young people described in the case studies share many characteristics, at state level the amounts and types of information about care leavers and the provision made for them is much less similar across the countries.

Setting aside the obvious cultural and geographical differences between, for example, Jordan, France and the US, in terms of sheer scale, can state provision for young people leaving care in a jurisdiction with a population of around five and a half million, Jordan, sensibly be compared to one with a population of over 60 million, France, or one with a population of over 300 million, the US? For one thing, as a number of the chapters in this book show, larger countries are more likely to have very influential federal structures that introduce an additional level of comparison to consider. A further complication is the impact of supra-national regional structures such as the European Union.

To deal with the demanding process of knowledge management required for integrating national descriptions within an international framework there are a number of strategies. Payne, in his discussion of the impact of globalisation on social work, suggests three (2006, pp.179–80). The first he terms 'holistic strategies'. These pursue an all encompassing framework concerned to define a global practice and identify the worldwide processes that drive it. This approach assumes that it is possible to understand globalisation and the associated global processes and phenomena using a number of key ideas. These ideas provide the conceptual currency for international exchange. In the field of leaving care such ideas might include, in addition to globalisation, those of citizenship, social capital, youth transition, social exclusion, care career, risk and resilience. Actually using those terms to describe and understand the transition from state care as a global phenomenon is no easy challenge. Not only is there the complex data identification, management and analysis required to meaningfully link national material together through the use of the global concepts but there is also as yet an absence of theoretical agreement about what the key concepts are and how they configure in explanations of care leaving. There continues to be an absence of concern with such issues in the leaving care field (Stein 2006).

A second less ambitious approach Payne identifies as 'partialising and comparative strategies'. Here the goal is to better understand a particular phenomenon thought to exist in a number of national contexts by 'confronting the differences between them, rather than asserting their wholeness' (Payne 2006, p.179). From this perspective globalisation means understanding commonalities and differences in how the needs of care leavers are understood and how they are met by different states. The starting question has to be whether within a particular country there actually are young people making the transition to adulthood from state care. Once that is established it is then a matter of identifying sources of national information and using them to gather together more or less comparable data on various dimensions of the issue. The national chapters in this book can be seen as an example of this approach. In each country material on care leavings has been gathered to cover the political, legal, policy and practice dimensions. With that done it is possible to start identifying what lessons there may be to exchange between countries in order to improve legislation, policy and practice.

The sort of questions that are relevant at the level of the state are: How important is it to use the UNCRC as the starting point for developing services as in Jordan and Romania? Is it critical to have legislation that specifically addresses the needs of care leavers, as in the case of the US and Norway? Is direct financial support for individual young people a key provision as in France? Can the state direct practice centrally as attempted in the UK or is decentralisation necessary to allow grounded local provision as in Sweden? Answering such questions requires attention to the feasibility of transposing and adapting learning from one country to another. Through focusing on detailed description of existing needs and services the partialising and comparative approach may pragmatically side step some of the theoretical issues waiting to be addressed but it still has the conceptual and methodological difficulties of identifying and marshalling diverse sets of data for comparison.

Although holistic strategies are more ambitious than the partialising and comparative, both approaches provide the means for cross-national transfer of knowledge and information which can provide the basis for global benchmarking. Such benchmarking is probably the best way in which the global standards aspired to by the UN Committee could be developed in line with the UNCRC. By contrast to the other two approaches the third identified by Payne, which he terms 'discourse strategies', is much less instrumental. 'In this approach, we do not seek wholeness through one perspective. Instead, we value the discourse between perspectives as constructing a whole while exploring and valuing difference' (Payne 2006, p.180). This requires a much looser, though no less information rich, exploration through dialogue around the various perspectives on an issue that exists in different countries. The aim is to provide a mutually enhanced understanding of the meanings that surround an issue in a way that generally promotes a global sensibility. That enriched perspective will help those engaged in the dialogue with the critical review and creative development of their own services in ways that make sense to them irrespective of what others may take from the exchange. Such exchanges can be expected to reveal as much about the differing assumptions that underlie national cultures, politics and economics as about the needs and services particular to care leavers. For example, to reflect on the implications of adolescent male circumcision in the culture of some care leavers in South Africa is to raise questions about access and estrangement from rites of passage particular to one or other side of the sectarian divide in Northern Ireland and vice versa. Both South African and Northern Ireland parties to such an exchange deepen their understanding of care leaving as a transition from life spaces defined primarily by the state to those defined primarily by civil society.

Modelling across state comparisons

What approach is adopted to international comparison will in part reflect what is of interest to those directly involved in it and agreed as the purpose of any particular international project but it also has to reflect what is feasible given existing resources – resources both in terms of the national leaving care systems that exist within different countries and the resources that are available to undertake comparative work. It also needs to be noted that strategies falling into Payne's groups are not necessarily mutually exclusive. Indeed they can usefully be combined using a model of international comparison based on Houston and Campbell's (2001) work. They suggest that there are three nested domains that need to be considered when undertaking international comparison. Each domain has within it the three dimensions of culture, politics and economics:

> The macro domain refers to large scale international social processes directly affecting nation states and indirectly effecting local...practices within them... The mezzo domain can be viewed as the site where relationships between the nation-state, welfare regimes and social professions are played out... Whilst the macro and mezzo domains tend to focus more on the role of wider social structures and institutional prerogatives, the micro domain alludes to the specific activity of everyday... practice. (Houston and Campbell 2001, p.68)

Using the idea of nested domains Figure 18.1 presents two countries, the two inner sets of concentric circles, within a global context, the other ring.

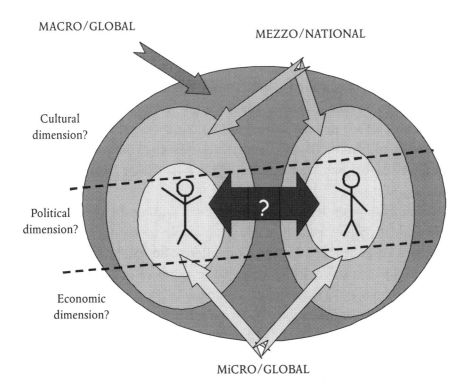

Figure 18.1: Three-domains model for international comparison

It places the young person making the transition from state care, the stick figure, at the centre of the model. That figure is located within a local/micro context. That context is made up of a wide range of relationships and circumstances, formal and informal, positive and negative, specific to a locality. In considering that local context it is helpful to reflect on the three dimensions – the economic, the political and the cultural. Does the local labour market provide opportunities for young people? Is there an active care leavers organisation in the area? What range and types of neighbourhood youth groupings exist? Information on that micro context needs to be collected separately for Country A and Country B through, for example, case studies and practice-focused research as done in some of the national chapters in this book. That description of the micro context has to be set, as shown in Figure 18.1, within a national/mezzo context. The information needed to flesh out the national domain has to be collected separately by country covering the three dimensions. As done for the national chapters in this book, mezzo-level information is sourced from relevant national laws, statutory guidance and regulations, government statistics and academic research. The description of the mezzo and the micro domains and the relationship between them then needs to be situated within the cultural, political and economic dimensions of a global/macro domain. By definition that domain requires a single set of information addressing international institutions, such as the World Bank, documents, such as the UNCRC, and processes, such as the trans-national transfer of capital and labour (Axford and Ross 2005; Deacon 2007; Pollock 2007).

If information on leaving care was gathered using the two-country framework in Figure 18.1 it would be possible to say this aspect of Country A's experience looks similar to/different from Country B's experience in this or that regard and at what level, micro or mezzo. So for instance Mendes and Moslehuddin's Australia/UK comparison (2004) is primarily focused at the national/mezzo level. It stresses similarity in the identified needs of the young people while drawing attention to the absence of national policy in Australia compared to the clear central policy direction in the UK. Using the three-domain model it would be possible to go beyond that observation to explore whether that difference resulted from the nature of state welfare in each of the two countries (mezzo level), from different degrees of impact on the countries by the UNCRC (macro level) or as a result of practice developments within each of them (micro level) – or, as is most likely, some combination of all three.

Where more than two countries are being compared the question arises as to whether some sets of countries look more like each other than other sets of countries. This is an important question for international comparison in determining existing and possible future patterns of convergence and divergence between countries. As noted earlier, the management of change driven by globalisation is a core concern behind international comparison. The process of exchange between countries driven by globalisation may be leading to a single internationally valid understanding of leaving care both in terms of needs and what works in meeting those needs.

There has been considerable work done within social policy on sorting out countries according to typologies of welfare regimes (Abrahamson 1999). Esping-Andersen (1990), author of the seminal work in this area, defined the welfare state regime as 'the institutional arrangements, rules and understandings that guide and shape concurrent social policy decisions, expenditure developments, problem definitions, and even the respond and demand structure of citizens and welfare consumers' (Esping-Andersen quoted by Abrahamson 1999, p.401). From that broad perspective he considered the defining characteristics of existing welfare states and concluded that they tended to cluster around three basic types of welfare regime: conservative, liberal and social democrat. The positioning of a country within one or other of these clusters is judged according to how dominant two characteristics are within its welfare regime. One of these is the extent of decommodification which is reflected in whether services are provided as of right and make it possible to sustain a livelihood without participation in the market. The other is the degree to which the state reduces social stratification and promotes social solidarity. Social democratic welfare regimes score high on decommodification and social solidarity with the purpose of state support for the common good.

Liberal welfare regimes have low levels of decommodification and high social stratification with the purpose of freeing the market and allowing individuals to optimise their potential. Conservative welfare regimes have medium levels of decommodification and social solidarity as state provision is used to maintain traditional structures of power and authority both between the state and civil society and within civil society. The categories are theoretical constructs and so states should not be shoehorned into them but rather referenced against them. Of the countries covered in the descriptive chapters in this book, Norway would be positioned within the social democratic cluster of welfare regimes, the US within the liberal and Germany within the conservative one.

Esping-Andersen's typology offers a useful starting place for asking questions about what international patterns may exist in the leaving care field. It is particularly helpful for 'partialising and comparative strategies'. For example, from the description of the models it might be predicted that liberal regimes will pay particular attention to preparation for independent living whereas conservative regimes will be more concerned to ensure family reunification and social democratic regimes will be prepared to provide extensive state after care support. Those predictions could be used in analysing material gathered from Australia and Canada, Spain and Israel and Norway and Sweden as pairs of countries representing liberal, conservative and social democratic welfare regimes respectively. It is worth stressing again that the purpose is not to squeeze complex national experiences into the three categories but provide a means of sorting through and reflecting on that complexity.

It is also important to note that Esping-Andersen's model has not been without criticism. It can be viewed as very Eurocentric in its focus. Even though countries outside of Europe such as the US, Canada, Australia and Israel have been categorised using the three-regime typology, it can be argued that this was done by incorporating them into the model's very European terms rather than giving real expression to their own national and possibly regional characteristics. Indeed it has been suggested that the typology fails on that account even within Europe where it fails to capture the distinctive features of the Mediterranean countries. To take into account the full global range of welfare states it has been suggested there are distinctive Antipodean regimes (discussed in Arts and Gelissen 2002), Southeast Asian, post-communist regimes (both discussed in Abrahamson

1999) and development regimes (Gough *et al.* 2004). Data collected on leaving state care in these regions might throw interesting light on how distinctive these suggested welfare regimes actually are.

The most fundamental criticism of the three-regime typology, and the various refinements and alternatives that have been suggested to it, is that they are all limited to a very traditional productionist/dependency view of welfare which is focused on redistribution of cash benefits from those with employment to those without. This fails to incorporate the insights of a gendered and child-centred social policy which reframes social care as a particular form of labour (generally female), a moral obligation and responsibility and 'an activity with costs, both financial and emotional, which extend across public/private boundaries' (Daly and Lewis 2000, p.285).

From that more informed perspective the distribution of resources can be understood in a way that recognises the mutual benefits of the interdependence of material production and social reproduction. Attention is drawn to the social care infrastructure and to the shifting balance between the family, community, state and market within it and how that is driven by power relations based on class, age, gender, race and disability that are constantly being contested. That perspective resonates well with what is now known about the central importance for care leavings of the processes and dynamics of interdependence, both within and between formal and informal social care networks.

Trying to characterise welfare regimes and their handling of youth transitions from state care from this perspective would encourage, for example, exchanges over the role of the extended family in care leavings. Exploring the experience of a conservative welfare regime, such as Spain, based on a subsidiarity principle that assumes a proactive role for the family independent of the state, could help throw light on why in the liberal regime of the UK family continues to be so underestimated as a resource by the state (Marsh and Peel 1999).

Getting a focus for international exchanges on youth transitions from state care

From the discussion above it should be clear that international comparison is now firmly on the leaving care agenda due to globalisation and needs to be addressed. But it should be equally clear that doing so will be a difficult and time-consuming challenge. The absence of work of this type to date should caution against underestimating the opportunity costs attached to getting involved in international exchanges. The challenges are both intellectual and logistical. To address them there is a need to have a systemic way of thinking about leaving care globally that allows for the various subsystems to be identified, described and exchanged. The three-domain model presented in Figure 18.1 (p.247) allows for that and any one of the domains can provide a starting point for gathering and exchanging information. Wherever a start is made the other two domains will inevitably have to be addressed too. What is important is that there are clear questions to be asked which are appropriate to the domains and their interlinking.

This book has taken the mezzo domain as its focus. Basic descriptions of a range of countries have been gathered along the four dimensions of politics, law, policy and practice. However, that is just a start, not only because more countries need to be added to the set here which is so clearly skewed towards Europe and North America but also because comparison really only becomes useful when specific questions are asked. How influential is the UNCRC in giving direction to national systems? Is there a link between the nature of the welfare regime and the approach to care leavings? Are the needs of young people leaving state care essentially the same irrespective of their country? Are there globalising processes driving a convergence of national law, policy, service design and practice? Only very tentative answers are possible to such questions at this time. Generally asking a question gets answered with another question. There is a long way to go before there is anything close to an adequately informed and coherent picture of how different states, or clusters of states, are dealing with leaving care.

At present it is not possible to do more than speculate on the core question of whether and in what way the concept of globalisation helps in understanding and explaining state provision and its role in determining the outcomes achieved by care leavers. Without an informed view on that it is hard to know whether the explanation of poor employment outcomes lies in the global dominance of neo-liberal economics and the impact that has had on local labour markets. It is in turn hard to judge whether there is a useful role for international institutions like UNICEF and the World Bank in encouraging national governments to ensure their responses to economic restructuring pays attention to care leavers as an identifiable vulnerable group to whom there is a state responsibility. However, driving forward comparative work from its present very formative stage requires more than just swapping information in a loosely managed fashion. It requires a project around which those interested could focus.

A project that might serve that purpose well given many of the points made in this chapter, not least about the contested nature of globalisation and of the different forms of welfare regime, would be an exploration of youth transitions from state care and the meaning of citizenship, both where it exists and where it is denied to non-nationals. The aim would not only be to identify different approaches taken within different welfare regimes and whether these 'natural experiments' suggest that certain approaches get better results in relation to particular goals but also what is the purpose of state engagement that lies behind the approaches and their goals.

Taking forward any of those questions first requires recognition that there is a global responsibility by those involved in whatever way within the leaving care field to make an effort to engage in cross-national exchange. The potential benefits for everyone involved, policy makers, operational managers, practitioners, researchers and especially the young people themselves and their families, would seem to justify the effort. Recognising and understanding the characteristics and processes of change through globalisation is essential if it is to be engaged with in the interests of care leavers to make sure they are not socially excluded further than they already are. Ensuring the well-being and realising the potential of young people making the transition from state care will increasingly depend on sharing understanding of any national advances so that international exchange becomes part of a global resource for care leavers.

References

Abrahamson, P. (1999) 'The welfare modelling business.' *Social Policy and Administration 33*, 4, 394–415.

Arts, W. and Gelissen, J. (2002) 'Three worlds of welfare or more?' *Journal of European Social Policy 12*, 2, 137–158.

Axford, N. and Ross, G. (2005) *The Influence of International Governmental Organisations on Nation State Child Welfare Policy.* Dartington Social Research: unpublished paper.

Calomiris, C. (2002) *A Globalist Manifesto for Public Policy.* London: The Institute of Economic Affairs.

Committee on the Rights of the Child (2006) 'Committee on the Rights of the Child 40th Session, Geneva, 12–30 September 2005.' *Day of General Discussion: Children Without Parental Care.* CRC/C/153. Accessed 08/01/08 at www.docsohchr.org/english/bodies/crc/docs/discussion/recommendations2005.doc

Daly, M. and Lewis, J. (2000) 'The concept of social care and the analysis of contemporary welfare states.' *British Journal of Sociology 51*, 2, 281–298.

Deacon, B. (2007) *Global Social Policy and Governance.* London: Sage.

Esping-Andersen, G. (1990) *The Three Worlds of Welfare Capitalism.* New Jersey: Princeton University Press.

Furlong, A. and Cartmel, F. (1997) *Young People and Social Change.* Buckingham: Open University Press.

Gough, I., Wood, G., Barrientos, A., Bevan, P., Davis, P. and Room, G. (2004) *Insecurity and Welfare Regimes in Asia, Africa and Latin America.* Cambridge: Cambridge University Press.

Henderson, S., Holland, J., McGrellis, S., Sharpe, S. and Thompson, R. (2007) *Inventing Childhoods: A Biographical Approach to Youth Transitions.* London: Sage.

Houston, S. and Campbell, J. (2001) 'Using critical social theory to develop a conceptual framework for comparative social work.' *International Social Welfare 10*, 66–73.

Khan, P. and Dominneli, L. (2000) 'The impact of globalization on social work in the UK.' *European Journal of Social Work 3*, 2, 95–108.

Lyons, K. (2006) 'Globalization and social work: International and local implications.' *British Journal of Social Work 36*, 365–380.

Lyons, K., Manion, H.K. and Calseton, M. (2006) *International Social Work: Global Conditions and Local Practice.* Basingstoke: Palgrave Macmillan.

Mann, M. (2001) 'Globalization and September 11.' *New Left Review 12*, Second Series, 51–72.

Marsh, P. and Peel, M. (1999) *Leaving Care in Partnership: Family Involvement with Care Leavers.* London: HMSO.

Mendes, P. and Moslehuddin, B. (2004) 'Graduating from the child welfare system: A comparison of the UK and Australian leaving care debates.' *International Journal of Social Welfare 13*, 4. 332–339.

Midgley, J. (2000) 'Globalization, Capitalism and Social Welfare: A Social Development Perspective.' In B. Rowe (ed.) *Social Work and Globalization.* Ontario: Canadian Association of Social Workers.

Midgley, J. (2004) 'The Complexities of Globalisation: Challenges to Social Work.' In N.T. Tan and A. Rowlands (eds) *Social Work Around the World III: Globalization, Social Welfare and Social Work.* Berne: International Federation of Social Workers.

Payne, M. (2006) *What is Professional Social Work?* Bristol: BASW/The Policy Press.

Pinkerton, J. (2002) 'Developing an International Perspective on Leaving Care.' In A. Wheal (ed.) *The RHP Companion to Leaving Care.* Dorset: Russell House Publishing.

Pollock, D. (2007) 'Social workers and the United Nations: Effective advocacy strategies.' *International Social Work 50,* 1, 113–119.

Stein, M. (2004) *What Works for Young People Leaving Care.* Essex: Barnardo's.

Stein, M. (2006) 'Young people aging out of care: The poverty of theory.' *Children and Youth Services Review 28,* 422–434.

Thompson, R., Flynn, R., Roche, J. and Tucker, S. (2004) *Youth in Society: Contemporary Theory, Policy and Practice* (2nd edition). London: Sage.

Williamson, H. (2005) 'Young People and Social Inclusion – An Overview of Policy and Practice.' In M. Barry (ed.) *Youth Policy and Social Inclusion: Critical Debates with Young People.* London: Routledge.

Yeates, N. (2001) *Globalization and Social Policy.* London: Sage.

Chapter 19

Legal and Policy Frameworks

Harriet Ward

Introduction

The transition from adolescence to adulthood is marked by a number of different processes: the move from education to employment, from the family home to independent living; from the single state to cohabitation or marriage; and from childlessness to parenthood (see Biehal and Wade 1996; Vogel 2002). Of course adulthood can be satisfactorily achieved without passing through all these stages, but nevertheless, taken together, they form the key components of the move from the final phase of childhood and its dependence upon parents to the point at which the young person takes his or her independent place in adult society.

There is evidence that, over the last 20 years or so, normative transitions to adulthood have become increasingly protracted in most developed societies. More young people are staying longer in education and taking longer to move out of the family home; they are also both marrying and having their first children several years later than their parents' generation (Alcock 2001). Such extended transitions are a response to a complex combination of socio-economic factors, including a decline in manufacturing and low-skilled employment, a shortage of low cost housing, changes in sexual mores and young women's increased participation in the labour market.

The balance of responsibilities

Alcock (2001, p.3) demonstrates how 'the mix of welfare provision between the state, the individual, the family and other sectors of provider agencies varies from country to country'. Vogel (2002) argues that the welfare mix (the institutional configuration of labour market, welfare state and family) represents a functional division of responsibility for welfare delivery. In his view:

> We should designate the major role to the labour market. Malfunctioning of the labour market will exhaust the welfare state as well as the family. Welfare state and family are two alternative correctives; 'efficient' labour markets (jobs, earnings) will relieve the welfare state as well as the family. In reverse, the generous welfare state requires an efficient labour market and promotes emancipation from the family. (p.277)

The extent to which populations of young people succeed in negotiating the transition reflects the efficiency of these three institutions in supporting their establishment in adult society.

This chapter explores how, within these constructs, differences in the perceived balance of responsibilities between the individual, the state and the family may impact on the legislation and policies affecting care leavers in the countries illustrated. The previous chapter proposes a three-domain model for international comparison and argues that any one of the domains (macro: global; mezzo: national; or micro: local) can provide a starting point for gathering and exchanging information. This chapter adds an additional dimension to this model, suggesting that at the mezzo and the micro levels, differences in legislation, policy and consequent service development might be explored with reference to differences in this perceived balance of responsibilities.

Over the last few decades, much of Europe and the developed world has seen a retraction of the welfare state, with the result that the response to changing socio-economic factors has largely been the development of policies for young people that rely on increased levels of support from parents (see Jones and Bell 2000). However, 'a combination of factors, such as increased longevity, the declining value of pensions, unemployment and increased divorce rates…put much greater stress on family resources'

(Morrow and Richards 1996), making it less likely that extended family support will be available to young people throughout the process of a lengthy transition. Indeed, a review of the literature (Jones and Bell 2000) found that the assumption by policy makers that parents or carers will always support young people by providing a home and financial assistance is not backed up by research evidence. The result is that many young people are thrown on their own resources, and those who do not have adequate coping skills experience particularly problematic transitions. The chapter from Sweden suggests that this may be a particular issue in those countries where a strong welfare state may have weakened the perceived responsibilities of the extended family, as these have now been difficult to re-establish following a reduction in welfare provision.

Within such a context it is particularly important to consider how the public responsibilities of the state align with the private responsibilities of the family to support young people throughout the process of transition. Within the population of young people whose families are unable to provide extended support through a lengthy transition to adulthood, those who have spent a large part of their lives in public care stand out as a group that reflects the extent to which the state succeeds in providing compensatory support. For these young people the state has, to a varying extent, taken on the role of a corporate parent, and it is important to know how far and in what circumstances it can succeed (see Bullock *et al.* 2006). There are inevitable limitations in the extent to which this role can be executed, for in the provision of public care the two institutions that act as correctives to malfunctions in the labour market, the welfare state and the family, are finely balanced against one another: if public care is seen to be too generous, then public money is regarded as being unwisely used to encourage dependency; if too parsimonious, then the duties of the corporate parent are not being fulfilled.

Young people whose parents are unable to provide financial assistance or accommodation may find themselves moving through the processes of transition more rapidly and at a much earlier age than their peers. There is some evidence that this may be the case for many young people from families with profiles of vulnerability: for instance step-children (Morrow and Richards 1996) and young carers (Becker and Dearden 2000). However, there is an established body of evidence that demonstrates that young people who leave public care are particularly likely to experience compressed and accelerated transitions and that these reflect the limitations of the state as a corporate parent (see Kufeldt and Stein 2005; Stein 2004). As several of the chapters in this book demonstrate, in many societies the state withdraws support for care leavers at an age when their peers might expect to receive continuing help from their families for several more years to come; in those societies where support is extended, it may be withdrawn abruptly, without adequate preparation for independence. The abrupt or premature withdrawal of support means that care leavers also tend to be faced with the task of negotiating many of the processes of transition simultaneously, rather than sequentially; for instance they may move from education to employment (or unemployment) at the same time as they move from a foster home into independent living.

The risks inherent in negotiating such compressed, accelerated and abrupt transitions may render care leavers vulnerable to increasing social exclusion, characterised by a number of poor coping indicators, such as lack of educational qualifications, unemployment, homelessness, broken relationships and single, premature parenthood (Bynner *et al.* 2002; Pinkerton and Macrae 1999; Stein 2004). Those young people who have few expectations for the future may regard themselves as having little stake in mainstream society and turn increasingly to risk-taking behaviours such as substance abuse and crime (Pinkerton 2006). All of these factors entail not only a high financial cost to the state (see Raman, Inder and Forbes 2005) but also an extensive emotional cost to the young people themselves.

This chapter therefore explores some of the key differences in legal and policy frameworks and service delivery within the 16 countries that are likely to indicate ways in which the state fulfils the role of the corporate parent by supporting successful transitions from adolescence to adulthood of care leavers. Many of these reflect differences in the perceived balance of responsibilities between the individual, the state and the family during the time of transition. The chapter draws on the data from the international chapters (2–17) and also uses some of the data from questionnaires completed by representatives from each country in preparation for the first meeting of the working party.

However, such differences cannot be properly explored without first examining the different factors that need to be taken into account in making *any* comparisons of the experiences of care leavers in different societies. Any attempt to explore how differences in legal and policy frameworks are likely to affect the experiences of care leavers in the countries illustrated in this book needs first to clarify two terms: what we mean by 'public care', and what we mean by a 'care leaver'.

What does public care encompass?

Although international comparisons are now recognised as an important component of policy development (see HM Treasury 2006), attempts to identify key messages by exploring child welfare policies and their implementation across different societies are bedevilled by semantic and conceptual differences. Even such apparently simple concepts as what we mean by a 'child' can differ substantially over time and place. In the 16 jurisdictions illustrated in this book, the age at which childhood officially ends ranges from 17 to 20; thus even attempts to compare the proportion of dependent children in each society are problematic.

Child welfare legislation

All 16 countries illustrated in this book have introduced child welfare legislation, formalising the relationship between the state and parents when children do not receive adequate care and protection within their homes. The term most commonly used for the provision offered by the state when children cannot remain with their parents is 'public care', but even this is problematic, being subject to change over time and to different implications in different societies. Differences in the terminology are likely to relate to different views of the appropriate balance of the relationship between children in public care, their parents and the state, also reflected in the legislation, and to differences in the perceived purposes of care.

In some countries, children and young people who are committed to care by the state are not expected to return to their families: in Canada, for instance, there is no expectation of contact between these children and young people (crown wards) and their parents (Thomas 2003). In other countries, care has been seen more as one element in a range of services, offered by the state to support parents in difficulties. This is the case in France, for instance, where the vast majority of children and young people in care follow an administrative route, in which care is one of a number of services provided on a voluntary basis in partnership with parents. It was also one underlying objective of the Children Act 1989, introduced in England and Wales in 1991, and later used as the basis for developing legislation by a number of countries in Eastern Europe as well as others in the UK. This Act aimed both to reinforce parental responsibilities, making it clear that these were enduring, and at the same time introduce the concept that the state should work in partnership with parents to promote the well-being of children. The expectation was that, unless there were clear contra-indications, the vast majority of children in public care would remain in contact with their parents and eventually return to them. Under this legislation, only those children and young people who are committed to the care of local authorities under legal orders are formally placed 'in care'; those who are voluntarily placed, at the request or with the agreement of parents, are 'accommodated' by the local authority, while both groups are described as 'looked after children'.

Almost all countries are now signatories to the United Nations Convention on the Rights of the Child (UNCRC). The UNCRC specifies a comprehensive set of legal standards for safeguarding and promoting the well-being of the world's children, and introduces a number of explicit principles to support the development of legislation and services for children and young people. These include, among others, the principles that the best interests of the child should be a primary consideration (Article 3); that, unless a competent authority determines that it is in their best interests, children should not be separated from their parents against their will (Article 9); that if separated they have a right to maintain personal relationships and direct contact with both parents (Article 9); and that in matters affecting them children should have a right to express their views freely and that these should be given due weight, according to their age and maturity (Article 12). Almost universally agreed principles such as these

have provided a framework for the development of recent child welfare legislation throughout the world. Those countries such as Romania, Jordan and Israel, which are in the process of constructing new child welfare systems, are explicitly using the UNCRC as a basis for developing their legislation and policy. Other countries which have not made such far-reaching changes have nevertheless based new policy developments on the principles of the UNCRC (see Chapter 10).

As the chapter from the Netherlands shows, the UNCRC has been particularly influential in introducing the concept of children's rights into the development of policy in this area. It has also been influential in shaping policy development towards an outcomes perspective. The Millennium Development Goals (1990–2003) (United Nations 1990) identify specific targets for all signatories to aim towards, linked to the principles and standards introduced by the UNCRC. A primary objective is to ensure that 'all children get the best possible start in life' and all have 'ample opportunity to develop their individual capacities in a safe and supportive environment' (United Nations 2002, p.4).

These two concepts, that children and young people have the right to express their views and have them taken into account, and that they should have opportunities to develop to their full capacity, are in contradiction to many of the preconceptions behind policies for children in public care in much of the developed world prior to the introduction of the UNCRC in 1989. They make it possible to conceptualise that, rather than simply providing children with food and accommodation, public care should help them fulfil their potential – a break away from both the communist ideologies of Eastern Europe and the 'less eligibility' principle that has dogged the provision of care in English-speaking countries. They also make it imperative to consult with children and young people in care about plans for their future and other matters that affect their well-being – again a huge step forwards in societies where they had traditionally been seen as passive recipients of services rather than active participants in their own development. Finally, the Millennium Development Goals specify aspirations for *all* children; in doing so, they ignore and consequently weaken the conceptual boundaries which have tended to consider children in care in isolation, as a group apart, and thereby hampered much policy development concerning their well-being.

The growing interest in developing legislation and policy to support care leavers through the transition to adulthood can be traced partly to the stress on children's rights and achieving potential to be found in the UNCRC. However, the current concerns also reflect hard economic evidence concerning the costs of failing to support young people, a particular factor in developing policy in countries such as the US, Australia and the UK, where concerns about the negative consequences of encouraging dependency on the state have led in the past to an early withdrawal of support for care leavers. The poor coping indicators that are over-represented in care leavers – unemployment, teenage pregnancy, mental health problems and criminality – can entail long-term costs to the public purse and greater dependency on the state over the lifespan than would be incurred by legislation and policies to provide support for a longer transitional period (see Knapp, Scott and Davies 1999; Raman *et al.* 2005; Romeo, Byford and Knapp 2005). Far better (and cheaper) to attempt to reduce some of these negative and costly indicators by extending the support available to prevent their becoming entrenched.

Needs and numbers

As Thoburn (2007) has demonstrated, an exploration of the administrative data on children in public care, now collected and published by many states, needs to take careful account of differences in how care is defined before meaningful comparisons can be made. Does care solely refer to those children committed to the care of the state under legal orders? If so, then the figures for several countries, for instance France, Germany and the UK, would need considerable adjustment, as they include children and young people accommodated with the agreement of parents. Should care be restricted to placements away from home? If so, the figures for the UK and the US would need adjusting, as 10 per cent of children and young people in care in England and 4 per cent of those in the US are placed at home with their families, although on a trial basis and subject to legal orders that allow the state to remove them should their circumstances prove unsatisfactory.

In some countries there are sharp divisions between children and young people who are placed away from home for child welfare reasons and those who follow a youth justice route and are separated from their families by the courts following criminal convictions. Over the last 15 years or so, youth justice policy in England has increasingly diverged from child welfare policy, with the former focusing on reducing the risks of offending behaviour and mitigating the effects of crime, and the latter aiming to promote children's well-being and encourage the development of potential, a divergence that has brought criticism from the UNCRC (2002). National statistics on children in care in England do not include young offenders in youth justice provision, or indeed several thousand children and young people who are not officially in care, but are placed by education (now children's services) departments in boarding schools for children with special educational needs or by health authorities in mental or physical health provision.

However, not only is it often chance that determines which route many of these children will follow; in other countries child welfare is often more widely interpreted and encompasses some of these other groups. In the Netherlands, for instance, care not only encompasses child welfare, but also mental health and youth justice placements; this not only gives some explanation as to why the proportion of children and young people in care in this country is almost double that of England, but also will impact on any assessment of outcomes. Research on care leavers has traditionally focused on young people emerging from child welfare provision, but if valid international comparisons are to be made, then it might be necessary to include other young people placed away from home under different circumstances.

Variations in the proportions of children and young people in public care and the length of care episodes may also be indicative of differences in the thresholds for entry. Not all the countries illustrated collect data concerning the percentage of children placed in care, and it is not always possible to distinguish between snapshot data (the numbers in care on any day) and longitudinal data (the numbers admitted over a given period).

Nevertheless, where data are clear and available, they reveal substantial differences between jurisdictions. In Spain about one in 250 (0.4%) children and young people are in public care, in Sweden one in 111 (0.9%) and in Romania one in 66 (1.5%). There are also extensive variations within countries: in two different cantons in Switzerland the rate varies between one in 72 (Neuenburg/Neuchâtel) and one in 833 (Obwalden). In almost all the countries illustrated, children and young people from disadvantaged groups (Roma children in Hungary, and Aboriginal children in Australia, for instance) are over-represented in the care system.

Countries with lower proportions of children in public care may have a lower incidence of the types of need that precipitate young people into the system; on the other hand, they may be operating a higher threshold. Those with higher proportions of children in care may have a higher profile of need, but they may also be operating lower thresholds. For instance, Hungary's relatively high proportion of children in care (1%) may to some extent reflect findings that up to a third of children are admitted primarily for economic rather than child protection reasons, in spite of policies designed to discourage this (see Chapter 6).

In some countries with low numbers in care, strong kinship networks or extensive support services may ensure that children's needs are adequately met within the community, thus providing alternative solutions to separation. Spain, for instance, with its low proportion of children in care (0.4%), is a society in which the balance of responsibility leans towards the wider family, and so children are more likely to be looked after by relatives rather than the state. It is noteworthy that the vast majority of formal foster placements made in Spain are also with kin (see Chapter 13). On the other hand, the low proportion of children in care in Norway (0.6%) may reflect the substantial provision of universal family support services in this country where the state is regarded as having extensive responsibilities for the well-being of children. In the UK, however, where there is much ambivalence concerning the appropriate balance of responsibilities, there is evidence that relatively low numbers of children in care (0.5%) have not always been accompanied by strong family support systems or extensive state-sponsored provision in the community, and it seems clear that policies aimed at reducing the care population, often for economic reasons, have resulted in some children only being admitted after prolonged exposure to damaging circumstances at home (Skuse and Ward 2003). Here, the profile of need displayed by the care population may be considerably more concentrated than that shown in a population where lower thresholds are operating (see Ward, Holmes and Soper 2008).

Moreover each population is by no means homogeneous. A recent study of a cohort of 648 children and young people who stayed for at least a year in the care of six English local authorities found that, at entry, 19 per cent had physical or learning disabilities, at least 50 per cent had emotional or behavioural difficulties, 17 per cent had been convicted of criminal offences and between 20 and 30 per cent showed no evidence of additional support needs (see Darker, Ward and Caulfield in press; Sempik, Darker and Ward 2006; Ward, Hardy and Munro forthcoming). The difficulties that some care leavers encounter in making the transition to adulthood will reflect their experiences prior to entry as well as during and immediately after the care episode, a factor which needs to be taken into account in any research on outcomes.

If the purpose of making international comparisons is to explore how outcomes for care leavers differ, we also need to decide what is the necessary minimum length at which a care episode can be expected to produce an impact on the young person's future life chances. Lengthy care episodes are only common in a few of the countries illustrated (note particularly Romania, Hungary and Israel). How can their impact be compared with, for instance, care in Australia, where over half of all episodes last for less than a year, or Sweden, where even for those children who are committed to care on a mandatory order, the median length of stay is less than 17 months?

One of the difficulties in making comparisons is that in some countries care is seen as having a specific purpose in its own right, while in others it is part of a continuum of services, all aimed at supporting vulnerable children and their families, although often with the subsidiary objective of reducing expenditure in either the short or the long term. In countries such as Hungary and Romania, until relatively recently care has had a strong ideological and educative purpose; in Israel, where over 18 per cent of ultra-orthodox children are educated in out-of-home arrangements, a similar trend can be discerned. The same was true in 19th-century Britain, where the voluntary societies played a major role in separating children from their families in order to ensure that they received a Christian upbringing (Ward forthcoming). Where care has a strong ideological or religious purpose, children and young people are likely to enter at an earlier age and stay for longer periods. However, where care is seen as part of a continuum of services, admissions are likely to occur only after many other options have been tried. The objective here is to preserve family relationships and prevent the need for children to come into care, so children are likely to enter later, and stay for shorter periods.

Differences in thresholds at entry, length of stay and the reasons why children and young people enter care mean that the profile of a care population will vary from one country (and indeed from one child welfare agency) to another. Moreover there will also be changes over time, as some children leave and others enter the system. Extensive differences in such profiles make international comparisons particularly problematic.

Who is a care leaver?

While the task of determining what we mean by public care, and which children should be included, is far from simple, that of deciding who should be deemed a care leaver is also problematic. In some countries such as the Netherlands, Hungary and Switzerland, for instance, the term refers to all children who exit the care system, whether they are young children placed for adoption, older children returning to parents after varying lengths of time in care or young adults who have been brought up in care, but have now aged out of the system.

However, in the context of monitoring the transition to adulthood, the term 'care leaver' is usually taken to refer to a young person who has reached an age at which the state is withdrawing 'parental' support to allow him or her to move towards independence. It is important to have a clear definition of who can be deemed a 'care leaver' in this context because, as we have indicated, these young people face particular difficulties in making the transition to adulthood. As the next part of this chapter demonstrates, following evidence that care leavers show poor coping indicators, some countries have developed legislation and policy aimed at ensuring that such support cannot be withdrawn prematurely or precipitately, without taking sufficient account of the young person's continuing needs. However, deciding which young people might be eligible for such support is by no means simple. Should it be offered to all young people in care when they reach a certain age, for instance school-leaving age? But would it be justifiable to include young people who enter care just a few days before they reach that age? Should it be offered to young people who have spent several years in care, but then return to their families once they have reached an age at which they are no longer supervised by the state? But would it be justifiable for the state to offer support to these young people when it might more properly be the responsibility of their families to provide it? On the other hand, we know that many young people who return to their families after lengthy periods in care only stay with them for a short time (Skuse and Ward 2003), so is it justifiable to deny them support if the placement breaks down? Once again, differences in what is perceived as the appropriate balance of responsibilities between the state, the family and the individual will influence how these questions are answered.

Legislation to support care leavers

The definition of who can be deemed a 'care leaver' is determined by observations concerning young people's history and circumstances, and also by decisions made concerning eligibility for support. The Regulations and Guidance that accompany the legislation introduced to ensure that care leavers receive adequate support from the state in England, Wales and Northern Ireland include a legal definition of a care leaver, specifying that the following young people are eligible:

> Children aged 16 and 17 who have been looked after for at least 13 weeks since the age of 14 and are still looked after. (Department of Health 2000, p.8)

Young people who meet the criteria but return home having spent a period in care aged 16 or 17 may receive support as 'relevant children' if the placement breaks down (Children (Leaving Care) Act 2000; Children (Leaving Care) Act, Northern Ireland 2002).

Under this legislation the state therefore acknowledges some continuing responsibilities for all young people who have been in care for a specific period at a specific age; even where such responsibilities have been taken on by parents or other family members – or the young people themselves – the state may resume them if these arrangements fail.

While England, Wales and Northern Ireland may be alone in offering a legal definition of a care leaver, about half of the countries illustrated in this book have developed or are in the process of developing legislation and policies aimed at ensuring that these young people receive adequate support during the period of transition. In Norway, for instance, legislation introduced as early as 1954 included regulations for the provision of after care for young care leavers; in the US, federal funding to prepare care leavers for independent living has been made available since 1986; and in Hungary support for care leavers was introduced by the Child Protection Law of 1997.

Such legislation has been introduced in response to the evidence showing the adverse consequences both for young people and for society as a whole of failing to prepare care leavers for independent adulthood and of withdrawing 'parental support' at too early a stage. This evidence is further discussed in Chapter 21. The services provided under such legislation include two elements, one educative and one supportive, and cover formal education and life skills training, as well as the continuing provision of accommodation and financial and emotional support for an extended period, usually into the early twenties.

The balance between the two types of services again reflects the ways in which responsibilities for negotiating the transition are seen to be divided between the individual, the state and the family. In the US, where much social policy emphasises the importance of individuals taking responsibility for themselves, the 1985 legislation focused on life skills training and education and employment assistance. States were not initially allowed to use federal funding for accommodation or financial support for care leavers as that would encourage an unhealthy dependence, although this was overturned by later legislation, introduced in 1999. In

Hungary, on the other hand, the strong ideological basis of care provision under the communist regime led to greater emphasis on continuing support from the state than on the development of skills for independence. On the surface it appears that care leavers in Hungary receive extensive statutory support: they may remain in their care home until the age of 24, or, if they leave, they are entitled to a substantial lump sum for the purchase of accommodation and a year of after care. However, in practice, the provision does not meet the needs of care leavers, who may be institutionalised following years of residential care and who do not receive adequate preparation for independence and employment (see Chapter 6).

In both the US and Hungary, provision for care leavers is offered by the state in order to provide support in preparation for independence. However, in both countries such provision is permissive rather than obligatory and depends on the young person's *needs*. In the US in particular there is a low take-up of services with wide differences between states. In contrast, services aimed at supporting care leavers in Norway have been shaped by concepts of young people's *rights* and *empowerment*. The original legislation, implemented in 1954, provided for after care until the young person reached the age of 23. However, following criticisms from the media and some right-wing politicians that the state was over-intrusive and that young people were not being given adequate opportunities to manage their own independence, this was repealed in 1992. Care leavers were left to manage on their own, without what was seen as interference from carers and professionals. When, six years later, provision for leaving care was reintroduced, the views of care leavers played an important part in the development of the new legislation, which allows for the continuation of services 'when the child approves'.

The legislative and policy frameworks for the provision of after care appear to reflect different combinations of three elements: financial and emotional support, preparation for independence through skills training and education, and the weight given to service users' views. Once again, the balance of responsibilities, and particularly the extent to which self-reliance is valued, will influence the prominence given to each of these elements, all of which are likely to be factors in the successful transition to adulthood.

Delivery of services for care leavers

Policies to support care leavers through the transition to independence include a wide variety of services, many of them imaginative and innovative, that are likely to benefit young people in any country. In France, for instance, young adults may receive a personal budget which can include a grant to complete studies, gain a driver's licence or purchase equipment necessary for job training. In Romania, care leavers are entitled to receive significant financial support to either buy or rent accommodation for three years, and there are incentives to encourage employers to offer them work. In Illinois, there are wage subsidies for care leavers aged under 21. In countries such as Switzerland and the Netherlands, young people who have entered care through a youth justice route may remain in placement for several years longer than those who enter through a child welfare route, though it is unclear how far this is intended as a supportive rather than a punitive measure.

However, while the legislative and policy frameworks provide the theoretical basis for offering quite wide-ranging support, young people's practical experience of service delivery may be very different from what is envisaged. First, much of the legislation is permissive rather than compulsory, *allowing* agencies to spend government funding on the provision of services, but not *requiring* them to do so. Second, care leavers often have to apply for the support available, and may be rejected if funds are limited or they are not considered to be sufficiently in need of help. These factors may lead to a poor take-up of available services. Moreover, they may encourage patchy and sporadic provision. This is likely to be exacerbated in federalist countries such as the US and Canada, where there may be wide variations between states and provinces in the implementation of policy and the delivery of services, and indeed where each state may introduce its own idiosyncratic variations.

Lack of available resources to deliver policy objectives is a common feature in child welfare in many countries, but particularly evident in developing states, such as Hungary and Romania. In some rural areas of these countries basic services such as health care and education may not be available. Under these circumstances it is not surprising that the implementation of policies to support care leavers is problematic: the financial support available to help care leavers buy accommodation in Romania and Hungary, for instance, is insufficient to cover the costs, particularly in those areas where they are most likely to find employment. Innovative policies may also challenge a culture where children in care may be stigmatised and resented for their dependency on the state; in both Romania and Hungary there are hints that an ill-trained and dissatisfied workforce may obstruct the implementation of policies to support care leavers.

Care leavers and related policy areas

Legislation and policy intended to support care leavers can only be adequately assessed within a wider framework of interlocking policy areas, all of which may influence the transitions to adulthood of vulnerable young people. Education, social security, health, housing and, in some countries, youth justice policy will all reflect the extent to which the state substitutes for or complements the family in supporting young people as they move towards independence, and therefore will impact on the transitions to adulthood of care leavers. A striking example, for instance, is provided by Israel, where compulsory military service has a substantial impact on the experience of care leavers, offering those who are selected opportunities for personal advancement as well as secure income and housing for a period, while confirming the low status and social exclusion of those who are rejected.

In those countries with a strong ideology of independence and a residual welfare state, there may be no free universal provision in areas such as health care or higher education, or free provision may cease once a young person reaches the age of majority and is expected to enter the labour market. In the US, for instance, young, unemployed childless adults are not entitled to income support or to health care. Care leavers who cannot find adequate employment may also find themselves without access to health care – a key issue given the high proportion of young people in care with mental health problems – as well as without an income. Leaving care policy in the US is therefore aimed at addressing these issues as well as those that are universally specific to care leavers, such as the loss of accommodation and emotional support following a move out of a care placement and the withdrawal of support from child welfare services.

In several countries the retraction of the welfare state – or its absence – has a particular impact on unemployed adults without children, a large number of whom will be young people in their late teens and early twenties. While children may be regarded as having a right to support from the state to safeguard them from harm and promote their satisfactory development, once adulthood is reached young people are expected to support themselves through employment. In several of the countries illustrated the retraction of the market for unskilled labour has been met with an increased expectation that parents will continue to offer support to young people as they complete an extended education and establish themselves in employment. Those young people who leave school at the earliest opportunity with few skills or qualifications, as do many care leavers, are at a particular disadvantage. They are unlikely to earn enough to support themselves, nor, in many countries, do they receive full income support until well into their twenties. In some countries they can only access certain forms of support such as social housing (England) and income support (US) when they become parents themselves. In France, for instance, care leavers and other young adults without adequate family support networks who meet certain criteria may receive practical, financial and emotional support from child welfare agencies until they are 21; but then there is a four-year gap before they are eligible for income support at the age of 25. In the UK, recent policy developments to support care leavers through the transition to independence have aimed to reduce some of these anomalies by integrating the delivery of services from, for instance, housing, education and social services and social security. This is also the theory behind the concept of chain care, described in Chapter 10.

While leaving care legislation and policy may serve to overcome some of the difficulties faced specifically by care leavers, it is possible that this group of young people may equally benefit from policies aimed at improving the well-being of much wider groups – for instance all those at risk of social exclusion, or indeed all young people of their age facing similar, though not necessarily such problematic, transitions. In this respect it may be valuable to explore policies introduced by countries such as the Netherlands and Norway, where much responsibility for supporting young people is invested in the state. The Netherlands, for instance, has an extensive range of policies aimed at supporting vulnerable young people at risk of unemployment. Care leavers may benefit from such provision, even if they are not specified as the target group. They may also benefit from strong universal services. There is some evidence, for instance, that educational outcomes for care leavers in Germany could be more positive than those found in some other countries (see Bürger 1990). It may be that the German education system, which is compulsory until 18, provides greater support for vulnerable young people than that found in some other countries – although Bürger's data were collected some time ago, this remains an issue worth exploring.

Conclusion

The different ways that different societies balance the responsibilities of the individual, the state and the family are reflected in the development of child welfare legislation and policy and may prove a fruitful way of exploring the support offered to (or withdrawn from) care leavers as they make the transition to adulthood. There is obviously much to be learnt from international comparisons about how these young people can be better supported during this period. However, the first step in making such comparisons would be to reach an agreement as to which populations would be regarded as being placed in public care, and who should be termed a care leaver.

The 16 illustrative chapters offer many indications of the type of comparisons that could eventually be made. This chapter has attempted to draw together some of the issues that would warrant further exploration. There is much to be learnt at an individual level concerning how specific after care packages are experienced, what is valued and what is not, and how individual care leavers perceive their own involvement in decisions that may have a major impact on their future. At a national level, comparisons could be made about how the different ways responsibilities are balanced influence both the development of legislation and policy and service delivery. A more comprehensive comparison than can be given in this chapter of differences in child welfare legislation and policy – and their impact on the experiences of the young people concerned – would be particularly valuable. At a global level, as Chapter 18 suggests, the differential impact of the UNCRC could be explored, and perhaps evaluated against the development of leaving care provision in the US – one of two countries that has not signed up to this treaty. However, the purpose of this book, and indeed any subsequent studies, is to explore how the experience of care leavers can be improved: identifying whether different policies produce better experiences and better outcomes should be the primary consideration which drives more comprehensive international comparisons.

References

Alcock, P. (2001) 'The Comparative Context.' In P. Alcock and G. Craig (eds) *International Social Policy*. Basingstoke: Palgrave Macmillan.

Becker, S. and Dearden, C. (2000) *Growing up Caring: Vulnerability and Transition to Adulthood – Young Carers' Experiences*. London: National Youth Agency.

Biehal, N. and Wade, J. (1996) 'Looking back, looking forward: Care leavers, families and change.' *Children and Youth Services Review 18*, 4/5, 425–446.

Bullock, R., Courtney, M.E., Parker, R., Sinclair, I. and Thoburn, J. (2006) 'Can the corporate state parent?' *Adoption and Fostering 30*, 4, 6–19.

Bürger, U. (1990) *Heimerziehungg und Soziale Teilnahmechancen*. Centaurus: Pfaffenweiler.

Bynner, J., Elias, P., McKnight, A., Pan, H. and Pierre, G. (2002) *Young People's Changing Routes to Independence*. York: York Publishing Services.

Children Act (1989). London: HMSO.

Children (Leaving Care) Act (2000). London: HMSO.

Children (Leaving Care) Act, Northern Ireland (2002). London: HMSO.

Darker, I., Ward, H. and Caulfield, L. (in press) 'An analysis of offending by young people looked after by local authorities.' *Youth Justice*.

Department of Health (2000) *Children (Leaving Care) Act 2000: Regulations and Guidance*. London: Department of Health.

HM Treasury (2006) *International Comparisons in Policy Making Toolkit*. Accessed 24/09/07 at www.policyhub.gov.uk/better_policy_making/icpm_toolkit/index.asp

Jones, G. and Bell, R. (2000) *Balancing Acts: Youth, Parenting and Public Policy*. York: York Publishing Services in association with Joseph Rowntree Foundation.

Knapp, M., Scott, S. and Davies, J. (1999) 'The cost of anti-social behaviour in younger children.' *Clinical Child Psychology and Psychiatry 4*, 457–473.

Kufeldt, K. and Stein, M. (2005) 'The Voice of Young People: Reflections on the Care Experience and the Process of Leaving Care.' In J. Scott and H. Ward (eds) *Safeguarding and Promoting the Well-being of Children, Families and Communities*. London: Jessica Kingsley Publishers.

Morrow, V. and Richards, M. (1996) *Transitions to Adulthood: A Family Matter?* York: York Publishing Services.

Pinkerton, J. (2006) 'Developing a global approach to the theory and practice of young people leaving state care.' *Child and Family Social Work 11*, 191–198.

Pinkerton, J. and Macrae, R. (1999) *Meeting the Challenge? Young People Leaving State Care in Northern Ireland.* Aldershot: Ashgate.

Raman, S., Inder, B. and Forbes, C. (2005) *Investing for Success: The Economics of Supporting Young People Leaving Care.* Melbourne: Centre for Excellence in Child and Family Welfare.

Romeo, R., Byford, S. and Knapp, M. (2005) 'Economic evaluations of child and adolescent mental health interventions: a systematic review.' *Journal of Child Psychology and Psychiatry 46*, 9, 919–930.

Sempik, J., Darker, I. and Ward, H. (2006) *Emotional and Behavioural Difficulties of Children and Young People at Entry into Care. Report to Department for Education and Skills.* Loughborough: Centre for Child and Family Research, Loughborough University.

Skuse, T. and Ward, H. (2003) *Listening to Children's Views of Care and Accommodation. Report to Department for Education and Skills.* Loughborough: Centre for Child and Family Research, Loughborough University.

Stein, M. (2004) *What Works for Young People Leaving Care?* Barkingside: Barnardo's.

Thoburn, J. (2007) *Globalisation and Child Welfare: Some Lessons from a Cross-National Study of Children in Out-of-Home Care, Social Work Monographs.* Norwich: University of East Anglia.

Thomas, P. (2003) 'Charter Implications for Proactive Child Welfare Services.' In K. Kufeldt and B. McKenzie (eds) *Child Welfare: Connecting Research, Policy and Practice.* Waterloo, Ontario: Wilfrid Laurier University Press.

UNCRC (2002) *Concluding Observation: United Kingdom of Great Britian and Northern Ireland.* CRC/c/15/Add.188, 9 October.

United Nations (1990) *Millennium Development Goals.* Accessed 06/03/08 at www.un.org/millenniumgoals

United Nations (2002) *A World Fit for Children.* Accessed 06/03/08 at www.unicef.org/specialsession/wffc/index.html

Vogel, J. (2002) 'European welfare regimes and the transition to adulthood: A comparative and longitudinal perspective.' *Social Indicators Research 59*, 275–299.

Ward, H. (forthcoming) *Separating Families: How the Origins of Current Child Welfare Policy and Practice Can be Traced to the Nineteenth-century Child Rescue Movement.* London: Jessica Kingsley Publishers.

Ward, H., Hardy, A. and Munro, E.R. (forthcoming) *'Serial Parenting': Moves within the Care System, their Reasons and their Consequences.* Loughborough: Centre for Child and Family Research, Loughborough University.

Ward, H., Holmes, L. and Soper, J. (2008) *The Costs and Consequences of Placing Children in Care.* London: Jessica Kingsley Publishers.

Chapter 20

Use of Secondary Data to Understand the Experiences of Care Leavers

Cross-National Comparisons

Mark E. Courtney

Introduction

Studies of care leavers[1] generally rely on data collected directly from youth for research purposes. However, other sources of information can shed important light on the experiences of care leavers. For the purposes of this chapter I distinguish between data that were generated specifically to study the experiences of youth leaving care, which I will refer to as *primary data*, and other data that can be used to understand the experiences of youth leaving care but that were not originally generated for that purpose, which I refer to as *secondary data*. I discuss below three categories of secondary data on care leavers: administrative records on their care experiences; government records pertaining to other aspects of their lives; and research data collected on population-based samples of young adults, some of whom were care leavers. I also organize the information provided in the country-specific chapters of this volume to provide an overview of how secondary data have been used around the world to understand the lives of care leavers. The information synthesized in this chapter was generated in response to the following questions that were posed to the contributors:

- Does your country or an important jurisdictional subunit of your country have reliable administrative data on the care experiences of care leavers? What are the characteristics of these data (e.g. time period covered; range of variables available for analysis; reliability and validity of the data)?

- Does your country or an important jurisdictional subunit of your country have reliable administrative data on outcomes of importance for care leavers (e.g. earnings, crime, health)? What kinds of outcomes do these data cover, over what period, and what are the reliability and validity of the data?

- Are there population-based studies of young adults in your country that identify care leavers?

- What are the legal and ethical issues affecting the use of secondary data to study care leavers in your country with respect to all three of the potential data sources described above?

- What studies of care leavers have been conducted in your country using secondary data?

As the discussion below will make clear, secondary data on care leavers are scarce or non-existent in many countries and even where they exist they have generally not been put to much use.

My description is intended to stimulate discussion rather than to explore all of the issues that are relevant to using secondary data to study care leavers. I have not tried to provide an exhaustive list of potential sources of secondary data or the potential uses of such data. Nor have I tried to examine all of the advantages and disadvantages of the various types of data I describe. While I use examples from the countries represented in this volume to illustrate the ways in which secondary data have been used, I make no claim regarding how representative these examples are of the situation in other countries.

Table 20.1 provides a simple categorization of the availability and use of secondary data in understanding the experiences of care leavers in the countries represented in this volume. In general, I used fairly generous criteria for deciding to include a country as having a given type of data and for its use in research. Those criteria are described below as they pertain to each distinct type of secondary data.

Table 20.1: Availability and use of secondary data for understanding the experiences of care leavers

Country	Data on care experiences		Government data used for research	Data from population-based studies	
	Nation	Subunit		Available	Used for research
Australia		X			
Canada		X		X	
France		X			X
Germany	X				
Hungary					
Ireland		X			
Israel	X				
Jordan	X				
The Netherlands	X				
Norway	X		X		
Romania	X				
Spain		X			
Sweden		X	X		X
Switzerland		X			
United Kingdom	X				X
United States	X		X		X

Administrative records on care experiences

Many though not all governments maintain databases on the characteristics and care experiences of young people in out-of-home care. The nature of the data contained in these databases varies considerably between jurisdictions. One of the major sources of variation in data quality stems from whether the architects of a given data system sought solely to generate information for basic management purposes ("management information") or whether they went beyond that to generate information that could be used for case-level decision-making purposes ("clinical information"). Systems established solely to meet the needs of program administrators or policymakers often contain only the data necessary to keep track of how many young people are in care at any point in time and to describe them in very basic demographic terms. In contrast, clinical information systems may collect a wide range of data on children's families, their experiences before entering care, their current functioning, services they receive while in care, and selected outcomes at discharge from care. To be included in Table 20.1 as having data on care leavers' experiences in care, a country merely had to have data at either the national or subunit level that describes the basic demographic characteristics of youth in care (i.e. "management information" data as opposed to "clinical information"). If a country has data at the national level then that box is checked, if only at the subunit level then that box is checked, and, if neither, then neither box is checked. Eight of the countries have some form of national data that uniquely identifies youth in care, another seven have data on at least some subunits, and one country has no such data available.

Although administrative data on care experiences generally do not provide any insight into how young people fare after they leave care, such data can serve important roles in research on care leavers. First, administrative data are often used to identify a population of recent or potential care leavers for study. In fact, it can be difficult if not impossible to identify a representative group of care leavers in the absence of reasonably good administrative data on the out-of-home care population in a particular jurisdiction. For example, the sample for the ongoing Midwest Study of the Adult Functioning of Former Foster Youth, conducted in the US, was drawn from the administrative databases of the three participating US states (Courtney and Dworsky 2006). The care of the 732 young people involved in the study was supervised by hundreds of separate public and private child welfare agencies within the three states. In the absence of reliable data from a centralized database in each state it would have been virtually impossible to draw the random sample of young people participating in the study.

Second, administrative data can be invaluable in characterizing the experiences of care leavers while they were in care, before they entered care, and, in some cases, at the point of exit. Even fairly basic data on young people's care histories can be used to examine the maltreatment histories of the young people prior to their entering care, the types of settings they lived in while in care, and the level of placement instability they experienced. Assessment data, when available, can be particularly useful background information. For example, the quality control data system used to monitor residential care in Israel has been used to assess the psychosocial and educational functioning of children and youth who reside in various children's institutions (Chapter 8). Available child welfare administrative data in Germany show that almost a third of the young adults exiting care neither attend a school nor undertake vocational training when assistance ends (Chapter 5). Administrative data can be particularly important to research on care leavers when self-report data on phenomena of interest can have poor reliability due to problems with recall or social desirability (e.g. details of placement or maltreatment histories). Administrative data are of relatively low marginal cost in comparison to collecting similar information via primary data collection methods.

What is striking from a review of Table 20.1 is how many countries represented in our volume do not have basic data on the care careers of youth about to leave care for the transition to adulthood. As noted above, in the absence of administrative records on care experiences, it is likely impossible for countries to use other kinds of government records to examine adult outcomes for care leavers.

Government records

Governments collect data on young people for the purposes of administering programs in which young people are involved. Under certain circumstances, these data can be used to examine the experiences of care leavers both before and after they leave care. Some examples of the types of information found in government administrative data include:

- diagnostic data on health and mental health problems and data on the utilization of health and mental/behavioral health services

- utilization of public assistance programs (e.g. cash or in-kind subsidies for food, housing, or other basic necessities)

- incarceration and other forms of involvement with criminal justice programs

- enrollment and performance in educational institutions

- earnings and income

- births and deaths.

Presumably most countries have some kind of government data on adults that could be used to understand the experiences of care leavers. Table 20.1 notes those countries where such data have actually been used for research on care leavers. Based on the reports of the authors of our country-specific chapters, only three of the countries represented here have seen this kind of research conducted.

Assuming that administrative data on these or other outcomes exist in a given jurisdiction, two primary issues govern whether they can be used to study the experiences of care leavers: the ability to distinguish care leavers from other individuals represented in the government data using unique identifiers or other methods (e.g. probabilistic matching) and whether linking data on care leavers to the outcomes available in administrative data is legal and ethical in a given country or other relevant jurisdictional unit. Administrative data are only useful to study care leavers when they include unique identifiers that are shared with data on care leavers (e.g. national identification numbers) or include enough information (e.g. name, gender, date of birth) to allow for probabilistic matching to data on care leavers.

The data on care leavers could come either from a database on out-of-home care or from primary data collected from care leavers themselves. Some countries undoubtedly have records on care leavers' care experiences, but no unique identifier that would make it possible to link such records to other government or private sector data.

In addition, legal and ethical standards regarding protecting privacy when using government data for research purposes must be met and these standards vary from country to country and even within countries. In some countries, notably Sweden and Norway among those represented here, the adult population is well covered in government records and there is a long tradition of using such records to conduct research on income, work, education, health, social welfare services, etc., with well-developed methods of protecting personal privacy. In many cases, however, administrative data on important outcomes for care leavers exist but cannot be used because of legal obstacles or ethical concerns. For example, in the United Kingdom and Australia, concerns about privacy have tended to limit or preclude research use of general administrative records that might facilitate analysis of adult outcomes of care leavers (see Chapters 2 and 16). In the US, based on similar concerns, human subjects institutional review boards will generally not allow the linking of survey data collected from individuals for research purposes to government administrative records without written consent from the individual survey participants.

Population-based research data on young adult populations

Studies need not be focused specifically on care leavers in order to generate important data on their experiences. Population-based studies of young people can provide important insights into how care leavers are faring and can facilitate comparison of care leavers to their peers. Two primary criteria determine the utility of secondary research data for studying care leavers. First, the population-based sample must be large enough to include a subgroup of care leavers that is large enough to warrant the interest of researchers studying care leavers. This criterion can be difficult to meet given that care leavers generally represent a very small percentage of all young people in a given country. For example, only 35 young people in foster care were included in the 1994–95 cycle of the Canadian National Longitudinal Survey of Children and Youth and all were dropped from subsequent cycles (Chapter 3). Thus, only population-based datasets with very large samples are likely to be useful for studying care leavers. Second, it must be possible to distinguish care leavers from the other young people in a study sample. This implies that, in order for a popula-tion-based study to be useful to researchers studying care leavers, the creators of the population-based study must have asked questions that allow researchers to clearly identify care leavers. Given the relatively small percentage of youth who ever experience out-of-home care, let alone leave care during the transition to adulthood, it is unlikely that researchers con-ducting population-based studies will of their own accord collect the kind of detailed information necessary to make their data useful to researchers studying care leavers (e.g. when the young person entered care; their care experiences; when they left care). Nevertheless, five countries represented in this volume have seen research conducted on care leavers based on data collected on broader populations. In addition, there is the expectation that an existing longitudinal study of the young adult population will help shed light on young adult outcomes for care leavers in Canada (Chapter 3).

Summary and future directions

Secondary data can be a powerful torch with which to shed light on the transition to adulthood for care leavers. It can provide information, at rela-tively low marginal cost in comparison to primary data collection strate-gies, pertaining to crucial adult outcomes (e.g. education, employment, health, family formation, crime, reliance of public benefit programs). It can be used to generate meaningful comparison groups to which care leavers' outcomes can be compared. Table 20.1, however, provides a rather sobering picture of the ability of researchers around the world to use sec-ondary data to understand the experiences of care leavers. In spite of the great potential of secondary data, only the US has basic data at a national level on the care experiences of care leavers, has government data that has been used to track adult outcomes of care leavers, and has seen research on care leavers conducted using population-based studies; even in the US researchers have barely scratched the surface of the potential of secondary data to help describe the transition to adulthood for care leavers. While all but one of the countries has some data on the care experiences of care leavers for at least some subunits of the country, in less than one-fifth of the countries government data has been used to track adult outcomes and in less than one-quarter of the countries population-based studies have included and reported on outcomes for care leavers.

The reasons for this situation are many. There is no question that economic development, and the concomitant development of social welfare institutions, has not progressed enough in some countries to warrant the investment required to maintain the data systems and national longitudinal research infrastructure necessary to generate reliable secondary data on care leavers. However, their level of economic and social development cannot be used to explain the limited use of secondary data in most of the countries represented in this volume. Decentralization of responsibility for provision of child welfare services, and, in some cases, other social services, certainly plays a large role in some countries. Concern about the privacy of care leavers also plays a role in some cases, though the tone of some of the chapters suggests that this concern is at least sometimes a veiled attempt by child welfare and other social welfare bureaucracies to avoid being held accountable for the outcomes experienced by those they serve. Last, it seems likely that to some extent the poor information infrastructure surrounding care leavers is a function of their limited political capital; care leavers are a group that can easily be ignored by the powers that be.

Progress will be slow in coming. Research using secondary data requires the development of data systems, which can take many years. Fortunately there are a number of countries that have experience developing such systems, making it possible for those who have not to avoid reinventing the wheel. Linking data between child welfare data systems can be a complex undertaking, particularly when different social institutions use distinct identifiers. Once again, though, there are trailblazers from whom others can learn. For countries that are not averse to using universal national identifiers, Sweden provides a model of how to use national government data to track adult outcomes. Researchers in the US, based both in government and academia, now have extensive experience using probabilistic methods to link data on individuals across social institutions that use varying identifying information, while maintaining individual privacy. Finally, survey researchers in many countries are conducting population-based studies that could be tracking adult outcomes for care leavers, if they only knew which questions to ask to identify them.

Note

1. I use the term "care leavers," commonly used in the UK and some other English-speaking countries, to describe young people who leave out-of-home care because they have reached the age at which they are allowed to do so of their own accord or because the care system is no longer obligated to provide them with care and supervision. However, the usage of this term is far from universal. In the US, for example, this would be referred to as "emancipation" or "aging out of care."

Reference

Courtney, M.E. and Dworsky, A. (2006) 'Early outcomes for young adults transitioning from out-of-home care in the U.S.A.' *Child and Family Social Work 11*, 209–219.

Chapter 21

Transitions from Care to Adulthood

Messages from Research for Policy and Practice

Mike Stein

The international seminar programme which gave birth to this publication was in response to the growing evidence of the social exclusion of young people leaving care and the desire to share our experiences of different ways to promote positive outcomes and more successful transitions to adulthood for this highly vulnerable group of young people. Following a discussion of the research context, drawing on the thematic chapters, this concluding chapter will review the research evidence from the 16 countries,[1] beginning with the starting point for our Brussels seminar, social exclusion. The chapter will then draw upon these findings to explore the different stages of young people's journeys through care and the policy and practice implications arising from them. This will include their experiences of care; their transitions from care; and their lives after care. The chapter will conclude by identifying the future challenges of comparative work in this field.

Research in context

Young people's transitions from care to adulthood in different countries, including the legal and policy framework, the type and range of services they receive, and the collection of data, are shaped by a set of complex processes. There are no simple transferable international solutions. There are differences, for example, between countries in the care population: who comes into care, the use of different types of care placements, who stops in care and who leaves care, as well as the purpose of care itself – whether the aim is family rehabilitation, or not. Differences in legal and policy frameworks may reflect different views about how countries see the balance between individuals, the family, the role of the welfare state and the labour market, which in turn may be underpinned by differences in countries' welfare regimes, as well as the opportunities and risks associated with economic, social, legal and global influences.

For young people leaving care and moving to adulthood, these diverse and complex influences may become embodied in the role of the 'corporate parent'. The evidence from the international chapters suggest that in practice this role will depend on a number of factors, including: the balance between universal services for all young people and specialist services for care leavers; legislation that is framed as a 'duty' or as 'permissive'; how services are accessed by young people – whether as a 'right' or 'discretionary'; levels of funding for services; inspection and quality control mechanisms; and training and workforce planning.

Just as a young person's journey to adulthood in these different countries needs to be seen in this wider context, so does the research, and the messages for policy and practice, discussed below.

Social exclusion

In European social policy discourse, social exclusion has come to mean both material disadvantage and marginalisation. Whereas the former is usually associated with low income and relative poverty, the latter refers to the way groups may be excluded, omitted or stigmatised by the majority, due to characteristics such as gender, age, ethnicity, appearance or behaviour. Also, these two meanings are often linked, merging causes and outcomes, such as unemployment and social isolation.

In this context, international research in this volume has shown the high risk of social exclusion for young people leaving care, although the evidence base is variable. Sweden and the US, two very contrasting countries, have large data sets, or sizable research studies, that include normative or comparative samples. In Sweden, for example, analysis of registers of former care leavers, compared with cohorts of young people from adverse circumstances but with no experiences of out-of-home care, shows the care leavers sample to have higher risks of mortality, mental health problems, suicide attempts, poor educational attainments and teenage pregnancies. The portfolio of care leavers' research from the US also highlights the many difficulties faced by care leavers during their transition to adulthood, in comparison to their peers, including: unemployment, poverty, mental health problems, social isolation, homelessness, instability and involvement in crime.

In Australia, Canada and most of the European countries, the studies are, in the main, smaller scale and qualitative. The findings from longitudinal studies of small samples of care leavers, and case analysis, from several of these countries, although differing in length of follow-up period, and the use made of primary or secondary normative data, is generally consistent with the larger quantitative studies discussed above in showing the difficult transitions and poor outcomes for many care leavers.

There is also evidence from European studies that specific groups of care leavers have a higher risk of social exclusion. In the Netherlands this includes young males, immigrant young people and early care leavers. In Switzerland, although outcomes are generally better in French-speaking areas than in German-speaking ones, outcomes for young women in both areas are better than for young men. In Ireland young people who left care later have better outcomes. In the UK, black and minority ethnic young people, including those of mixed heritage, may experience identity problems derived from a lack of knowledge, or contact with family and community, as well as the impact of racism and discrimination. Unaccompanied refugee and asylum-seeking young people in England may be excluded from services, or receive poorer services than other looked after young people, especially in respect of support from leaving care teams. There is also evidence from England that young disabled people may experience inadequate planning and poor consultation, and their transitions from care may be abrupt or delayed by restricted housing and employment options and poor support aftercare.

Research from the UK shows that young women who have been in care are more likely to become teenage parents than other young women and many have short-term difficulties in finding suitable accommodation, as well as accessing personal and financial support. French research shows that, for some young people, parenthood can be a positive experience, a partner providing significant support. However, there is evidence, longer-term, that teenage parenthood is associated with reduced employment opportunities, dependency on benefits, social housing, as well as poorer physical and mental health (Hobcraft and Kiernan 1999).

Australian research, carried out by economists and social work researchers, comparing samples of young people with 'positive' and 'poor' outcomes, has shown the very high economic costs of the socially excluded group, associated with high service use, including loss of earnings and being involved with health and mental health, police, criminal justice and housing.

Organising research evidence within a social exclusion framework contributes to a greater awareness of the reduced life chances of young people leaving care, their potential links with other excluded groups, their costs, as well as providing a focus for international policy and practice interventions. However, this represents only one part of the picture. Many of the studies referred to also identify what contributes to positive outcomes – what we can learn from young people who succeed 'against the odds'.

Young people's experiences of care

Providing stability and care placements

Research findings from Australia, France and the UK show that young people who experience stable placements providing good quality care are more likely to have positive outcomes than those who have experienced further movement and disruption during their time in care. Stability helps young people in two respects. First of all, by providing young people with a warm and redeeming relationship with a carer – a compensatory secure attachment which may in itself reduce the likelihood of placement breakdown. Second, and not necessarily dependent on the first, stability may provide continuity of care in young people's lives, which may give them security and contribute to positive educational and career outcomes. In promoting positive outcomes, providing stability and continuity may be as important for some young people as secure attachment, depending on their age on entry to care and their history, including the quality of their family relationships and links (Stein 2004).

Conversely, as French and Spanish studies show, instability is associated with poor outcomes. For too many young people, their experiences of care, far from helping them overcome the damaging emotional legacy of family problems, had rendered them unable to form the very relationships they needed so much. A consistent finding of studies of care leavers in the UK since the 1980s has been the 30–40 per cent of young people who experience four-plus moves and within this group the 6–10 per cent who have a very large number of moves – as many as ten or more (Stein 2005). There is also evidence from Ireland that a 'deep dissatisfaction with the idea of being in care' combined with instability can contribute to later homelessness.

Research from France and the UK has shown that foster care placements generally have better outcomes than children's homes. They are more likely to provide longer-term placements, stability and meet young people's emotional and educational needs. However, evidence from Switzerland shows that smaller children's homes with positive cultures can also assist social integration. Research into the effects of a socio-pedagogical approach in residential care in Germany, evaluating seven criteria (school and vocational training; criminal behaviour; social relationships; life management; personality development; family background; and social problems), showed that assistance had been successful in 57 per cent of all cases, and in 16 per cent a 'positive balance had been drawn'. The 'follow-up' showed that the achievements were maintained four to five years after the end of the residential placement.

Research findings from Spain into the circumstances of young people leaving residential care also highlights positive outcomes on a similar wide range of indicators. But there is evidence of great variation in the quality of residential homes. In Jordan, for example, the only descriptive study of their residential care homes (provided by non-government organisations) showed that just under 90 per cent did not provide care plans, psychological services, academic support or preparation for leaving care. In Hungary and Romania there is evidence that the main characteristics of classic institutionalisation impact on young people.

Identity – 'a sense of belonging and connectedness'

Identity formation is an ongoing challenge for all young people, as society has become more complex in terms of industrial change, more consumerist in its ideals and less certain in class, gender, geographical and ethnic identities. In what has been described as today's 'risk society', identity formation is a dynamic and reflexive process, less given and pre-determined (Beck 1992; Giddens 1991).

German research has highlighted the significance of care leavers being able 'to connect biographically developed patterns of actions and coping'. In a similar vein, Australian research has identified the importance of 'a sense of belonging and connectedness' in contributing to positive outcomes for young people living independently.

Helping care leavers develop a positive identity will be linked, first of all, to the quality of care and attachments experienced by looked after young people; second, to their knowledge and understanding of their family background and personal history; third, to their experience of how other people perceive and respond to them; and finally, to how they see themselves, and the opportunities they have to influence and shape their own biography (Stein 2005). Research into young people leaving care has shown that the main barrier to helping them achieve a secure sense of identity, in addition to instability, is the failure of those entrusted with their care to help them understand *why* their parents had abused or neglected them or were unable to care for them and how this had influenced subsequent events – to understand their feelings of rejection and resentment (Biehal *et al.* 1995).

Family relationships are often a major dilemma for many of these young people. They need and want to have a sense of family, not surprising given the centrality of 'the family' in ideology, policy and practice. There is also evidence from Australia, Romania, the UK and the US that positive family links can be of great assistance to these young people. Yet many of these young people have been damaged by their family experiences, and they also need to be able to commit themselves to their carers and then move on to new relationships (Sinclair *et al.* 2005). As the French research suggests, a deeper and more profound story is often required by these young people, through skilled professional help, to assist them to make sense of their past, including their fractured family relationships, so they can psychologically 'move on' and look to the future.

Education

One of the most consistent findings across the 16 countries is the low educational attainment of care leavers, often representing a continuation of underachievement at school. However, as research from the US has shown, success in high school education can contribute to better adult outcomes.

Studies from France and the UK suggest that successful educational outcomes are more closely associated with placement stability and being looked after longer, more often although not exclusively achieved in foster care placements, being female, combined with a supportive and encouraging environment for study. Without such stability and encouragement, post-16 employment, education and training outcomes are also likely to be very poor. Generally, UK studies found that young people who left care earlier, at 16 or 17, had more unsettled careers and challenging behaviours. They were also more likely to be unemployed and have very poor outcomes.

UK research has shown that young people who go on to higher education are more likely to have had a stable care experience, continuity in their schooling which may compensate for placement movement, been encouraged by their birth parents, even though they were unable to care for them, and have been greatly assisted by their foster carers in their schooling.

Preparation

Preparation for leaving care may also provide young people with opportunities for planning, problem solving and the learning of new competencies. The development of these programmes across the 16 countries is patchy, and there have been few evaluations.

In the Netherlands, examples of preparation programmes for young people leaving residential homes include *Exit Training* and *Work-Wise*. The main focus of the former was skills training on practical issues, social skills and creating social networks. An evaluation at the end of training and six months later showed that three-quarters of young people had fulfilled four of the five key targets. The *Work-Wise* programme also had a high degree of success in preparing young people for education, training, work experience, housing, social networks and leisure time activities.

In the UK, preparation programmes include three main dimensions: the development of self-care skills – personal hygiene, diet and health, including sexual health; practical skills – budgeting, shopping, cooking and cleaning; and interpersonal skills – managing a range of formal and informal relationships. Leaving care services can assist young people successfully with life skills and there is evidence from Scottish research of a significant association between preparation before leaving care and 'coping' after care (Dixon and Stein 2005). Leaving care services can also help young people to some extent in furthering social networks, developing relationships and building self-esteem, although these dimensions are also closely connected with young people having positive, supportive informal relationships with family members or friends, or former foster carers (Biehal *et al.* 1995).

Young people's transitions from care

Two main patterns of transition from care emerge from the international experiences described within this book: accelerated and compressed; and extended and abrupt.

First, and most common, in Europe, Australia, Canada and the US, many young people leaving care are expected to undertake their journey to adulthood, from restricted to full citizenship, far younger and in far less time than their peers. For these young people, leaving care is often a final event. There is no option to return in times of difficulty. Also, they often have to cope with major status changes in their lives at the time of leaving care: leaving foster care or their children's home and setting up a new home, often in a different area, and for some young people starting a family as well; leaving school and finding their way into further education, training or employment, or coping with unemployment. In short, their journey to adulthood is both accelerated and compressed.

Second, it is the experience of the former communist countries that young people may stay in institutional care until their mid-twenties, but feel unprepared for coping with adult life. In Romania, for example, research has highlighted the isolation of residential care, its 'all providing' and 'one plan fits all' approach, the lack of preparation and the expectation of 'instant adulthood', findings also echoed by the limited research and knowledge of care leavers in Hungary.

The challenges posed by transition are identified by research carried out in Israel which found that better relationships between young people and group home parents, while living in care, were associated with *more* difficult transitions to independent living, and the longer young people stayed in care, the tougher they saw their transition to independent living.

The international evidence discussed above suggests that transitions which are accelerated and compressed, or extended and abrupt, generally fail to equip young people adequately for their journey to adulthood.

Drawing on the 'focal model of adolescence', developed by Coleman, it is evident that many young people leaving care are denied the psychological opportunity and space to focus, or to deal with these important issues over time. The empirical testing of this model shows that having the opportunity to deal with interpersonal issues, spread over time, is how most young people cope successfully with the challenges of transition. Conversely, those young people who have to face a number of interpersonal issues at the same time are likely to experience significant problems of adjustment (Coleman and Hendry 1999).

Ethnographic research also highlights the significance of transition for young people during their journey to adulthood. The process of social transition has traditionally included three distinct, but related, stages: leaving or disengagement; transition itself; and integration into a new or different social state. In post (or late) modern societies, providing more opportunities but also more risks, this process has become more extended and less structured, although the 'activities' associated with the three stages still remain. But for many young people leaving care there is the expectation of instant adulthood. They often miss out on the critical prep-aration stage, transition itself, that gives young people an opportunity to 'space out', and provides a time for freedom, exploration, reflection, risk taking and identity search (Stein 2006).

For a majority of young people today this is gained through the expe-rience of further and, especially, higher education but, as the research dis-cussed in this publication shows, many care leavers, as a consequence of their pre-care and care experiences, are unable to take advantage of these educational opportunities. Also, in the context of extended transitions, the family plays an increasing role in providing financial, practical and emo-tional support. But for many care leavers their family relationships at this important time may be missing or problematic rather than supportive.

As the international experiences described in this book have shown, transition planning is challenging. Young people need psychological space, in order to cope with changes over time, including recognition of the different stages of transition, especially the significance of the middle stage, transition itself. This should be reflected in the organisation and quality of care placements, and the culture and expectations of leaving care services.

Young people's lives after care

The findings of the survey of international leaving care research, policy and practice, completed in preparation for our 2003 Brussels seminar, revealed the wide variation in both outcomes research and the collection of outcome data by governments. The available evidence is presented in this volume's international chapters. Drawing on this data in this chapter has, so far, highlighted the social exclusion of care leavers, as well as the implications for improving the outcomes for young people living in care and during their transitions from care. What about the lives of young people after they have left care?

In exploring this question at our Belfast and Budapest seminars, drawing on UK research findings carried out between 1980 and 2006, I suggested that care leavers may fall broadly into three outcome groups, those 'moving on' from care, those 'surviving' and those who are 'strugglers'. (The latter group I have identified in earlier literature as 'victims', but the majority 'international view', at the Belfast seminar, was to call these 'strugglers' – a less deterministic and more optimistic description.) There was broad agreement that identifying these three groups provides a helpful way of connecting the international research findings, discussed above, to young people's lives, including the implications for improving outcomes, or promoting their resilience (Gilligan 2001; Stein 2006).

However, there are important qualifications. First, most of the outcome research data discussed in the international chapters refers to the period of transition, or early adulthood, usually when young people are aged 16–20 years of age. This is a difficult time for most young people, so perhaps it is unsurprising that outcomes are poorer for more vulnerable groups of young people, and that they will require additional services. Research findings from France showed that movement and psychosocial difficulties occurred most frequently after the first years of leaving care and then lessened. More positive longer-term outcomes could be helped by a partner, as well as having had a stable placement and therapeutic assistance. Research from Spain also found a significant correlation between age and the level of social integration: young people aged 16–21 years were more likely to be marginalised, and young adults aged 25–29 showed much greater social integration. Norwegian research found that about two-thirds of 30-year-olds who had received help from a treatment project for young people with behavioural problems were coping reasonably well.

Second, as ethnographic research using life course theory to explore the transitions of young people leaving care reminds us, there are many complexities in evaluating outcomes. These include: the need to recognise the different starting points of young people, given the diversity of their family backgrounds and care experiences; the dynamic nature of 'outcomes' for young people – they often change between 'official' measurement periods; the separation of outcome areas – for example, education, health and well-being – from each other, even though they are often closely inter-connected; and the normative assumptions held by agencies about young people, whose lives have not been easy, achieving independence by 18 years of age.

It is within the context of these limitations that these three outcome groups are discussed, drawing on the findings from the body of international research work.

Moving on

The first group, those young people 'moving on' successfully, are likely to have had stability and continuity in their lives, including 'felt security', or a secure attachment relationship; made sense of their family relationships, so they could psychologically move on from them; have a positive identity; and have achieved some educational success before leaving care. Their preparation had been gradual, they had left care later and their moving on was likely to have been planned. Participating in further or higher education, being settled in accommodation, having a job they liked or being a parent themselves played a significant part in 'feeling normal'.

The 'moving on' group welcomed the challenge of living independently and gaining more control over their lives. They saw this as improving their confidence and self-esteem. In general, their resilience had been enhanced by their experiences both in and after care. They had been able to make good use of the help they had been offered, often maintaining contact and support from former carers, or family members with whom they had positive links. They were able to become less dependent on formal leaving care services, although could avail themselves of their assistance, if they needed help.

Survivors

The second group, the 'survivors', had experienced more instability, movement and disruption while living in care than the 'moving on' group. They were also likely to leave care younger, with few or no qualifications, and often following a breakdown in foster care or a sudden exit from their children's home. They were likely to experience further movement and problems after leaving care, including periods of homelessness, low-paid casual or short-term, unfulfilling work and unemployment. They were also likely to experience problems in their personal and professional relationships through patterns of detachment or dependency. Many in this group saw themselves as 'more tough', as having done things 'off my own back' and as 'survivors' since leaving care. They believed that the many problems they had faced, and often were still coping with, had made them more grown-up and self-reliant – although their view of themselves as independent was often contradicted by the reality of high degrees of agency dependency for assistance with accommodation, money and personal problems.

The available research evidence in this volume shows that what made the difference to their lives was the personal and professional support they received after leaving care. Specialist leaving care workers and key workers could assist these young people. Also, mentoring, including mentoring by ex-care young people (or peer mentoring), may assist young people during their journey to independence, and offer them a different type of relationship from professional support or troubled family relationships. Helping young people in finding and maintaining their accommodation can be critical to their mental health and well-being. Families may also help, but returning to them may prove very problematic for some young people. Overall, some combination of personal and professional support networks could help them overcome their very poor starting points at the time of leaving care.

Strugglers

The third group of care leavers was the most disadvantaged. They had the most damaging pre-care family experiences and, in the main, care was unable to compensate them, or to help them overcome their past difficulties. Their lives in care were likely to include many further placement moves, the largest number of moves in the different research studies cited above, and the associated disruption to their lives, especially in relation to their personal relationships and education. They were also likely to have a cluster of difficulties while in care that often began earlier, including emotional and behavioural difficulties, problems at school and getting into trouble. They were the least likely to have a redeeming relationship with a family member or carer, and were likely to leave care younger, following a placement breakdown. At the time of leaving care their life chances were very poor indeed. After leaving care they were likely to be unemployed, become homeless and have great difficulties in maintaining their accommodation. They were also highly likely to be lonely, isolated and have mental health problems, often being defined by projects as young people with very complex needs. Aftercare support was unlikely to be able to help them overcome their very poor starting points and they also lacked or alienated personal support. But it was important to these young people that somebody was there for them.

Improving outcomes

The international research findings discussed in this book have shown that young people leaving care, as a group, are likely to have a difficult journey to adulthood. For most, their journey may be shorter and more severe, or, for some, longer, more protected and more abrupt, than the journey undertaken by most young people who have not been in care. The evidence suggests that, although, as a group, these young people have a high risk of social exclusion, there are differences in their outcomes, between those who successfully 'move on', those who 'survive' and those who 'struggle', and that these different pathways are associated with the quality of care they receive, the nature of their transitions from care, and the support they receive after they leave care. It is these areas that are the focus of the key policy and practice recommendations aimed at improving outcomes, identified in the international chapters.

Improving the quality of care

This will mean providing better quality care to compensate young people for their damaging pre-care experiences, through stability and continuity, 'felt security in care', a positive sense of identity, assistance to overcome educational deficits and holistic preparation. Also, as French research shows, the screening for mental health problems and the provision of therapeutic services for young people who need them may help prevent later problems. Foster care, small children's homes with a positive culture and residential care providing psychological interventions or socio-pedagogy, to children and young people, may achieve positive outcomes. Large institutional settings seem very ill-equipped to meet the social, emotional and educational needs of young people.

Transitions from care

Young people leaving care should be provided with opportunities for more gradual transitions from care – less accelerated and compressed, or extended and abrupt – more akin to normative transitions within their cultures. This will include giving young people 'psychological space' and recognising the different stages of transition, common to 'emerging adulthood'. As German research shows, early independence is an 'excessive demand' on young people, often to meet the criteria 'from the perspective of the youth officer, not when it was right from the perspective of the young person'. Opportunities for gradual transitions are best provided by placements, where young people are settled and their carers are able to support them into adulthood, or if that is not possible, transitional or 'half-way' supportive arrangements.

Support after care

There is an international consensus that young people leaving care, who are often estranged from their families, should be supported during their journey, well into adulthood – from 21 to 25 – not just at the time of leaving care. As Australian research shows there are considerable 'costs' in poor outcomes, both to young people themselves and public services. There are different ways of providing support services.

In the UK specialist leaving care schemes have developed to respond to the core needs of care leavers for assistance with accommodation, finance, education and careers, personal support networks and health and well-being. Each young person leaving care has a personal adviser who is responsible for carrying out a needs assessment and a pathway plan. An important part of the work of specialist teams is the development of inter-agency links, to ensure an integrated approach to assisting young people with a range of different needs including education, health and well-being.

Outcome studies evaluating specialist leaving care services have shown that they can make a positive contribution to specific outcomes for care leavers. They work well in assisting young people in finding and settling in accommodation and in helping young people out of homelessness (Biehal *et al.* 1995). Research carried out in England provides evidence of the association between stability in accommodation after young people leave care and positive outcomes in terms of an enhanced sense of well-being, to some extent independent of young people's past care careers (Wade and Dixon 2006).

Leaving care services can also assist young people successfully with life skills and there is evidence from Scottish research of a significant association between preparation before leaving care and 'coping' after care (Dixon and Stein 2005). Leaving care services can also help young people to some extent in furthering social networks, developing relationships and building self-esteem, although these dimensions are also closely connected with young people having positive, supportive informal relationships with family members or friends, or former foster carers.

Secondary data and research

There is also a consensus about the need for more use to be made of secondary data to understand the experiences of young people leaving care. As Courtney suggests, it can provide information on a range of key adult outcomes, including education, health and well-being, social integration and use of public services, as well as allowing for comparisons to be made with the outcomes for other groups of young people. However, as Chapter 20 shows, in spite of its great potential, very little use is made of secondary data by the 16 countries. This may be as a consequence of the decentralisation of services, attitudes to the privacy of care leavers, and the 'limited political capital' of care leavers as a group. However, the development of secondary data systems in those countries that do not have them could be greatly progressed by learning from those who do, including the use of 'universal national identifiers', and probabilistic methods to link data across institutions that use identifying information which varies, while maintaining individual privacy.

Carrying out more cohort studies, based on large representative samples, would also provide a more sophisticated understanding of 'risk' and 'protective' factors over time. There is also a need for more evaluative research on the effect of specific interventions, using experimental and quasi-experimental designs – as the Romanian authors suggest, 'a culture of outcomes evaluation would promote best practice examples, leading to improved work with young people'. More ethnographic research would also add to qualitative knowledge.

Comparative work and young people leaving care: next steps

The contributions contained within this volume represent the beginnings of comparative work in the field of young people's transitions from care to adulthood. This includes a descriptive account of their welfare regimes, legal and policy frameworks, use of secondary data and research findings.

In terms of Pinkerton's conceptual framework for cross-country comparison, most of this material falls within the mezzo or national context. There is a need for more work in this domain within the existing countries on each of the four main themes, as identified in the thematic chapters. As is evident from the international and thematic chapters, there is great variation between countries in the existing material, especially in the availability and use of secondary data and primary research. Also, at this initial stage of our comparative exploration, most of the contributions are from Europe and North America, and their welfare regimes are viewed through Esping-Andersen's eurocentric lens, derived from a traditional 'production' view of welfare. A wider representation will enhance our network and understanding.

The volume also contains some material at the micro or local domain, through the brief case examples of young people leaving care, and by the findings from some of the research studies which describe local services. However, there is scope for more work at this level, especially exploring the connections between young people's transitions, services and locality. In respect of the global or macro level, there is reference in some of the international chapters to the impact of the United Nations Convention on the Rights of the Child (UNCRC) upon national legal and policy frameworks. However, this just touches the surface. We have not begun as yet to describe and analyse global processes and their impact on young people leaving care.

As detailed above, this volume, through its international and thematic chapters, has provided an initial exploration of the field, and identified the gaps and opportunities. The three-domain approach provides a conceptual model for organising future comparative work and the challenge for our international network will be to identify the foci. This volume has also shown that a parochial understanding of young people's transitions to adulthood is no longer an option. If we are committed to improving the outcomes for this highly vulnerable group of young people, we need to understand the impact of local, national and global processes upon their lives, and what we can learn from each other, through cross-national exploration.

Note

1. Throughout this concluding chapter, reference to the country (for example, 'in Australia studies show…') draws upon research cited in the country chapter.

References

Beck, U. (1992) *Risk Society: Towards a New Modernity*. London: Sage.

Biehal, N., Clayden, J., Stein, M. and Wade, J. (1995) *Moving On: Young People and Leaving Care Schemes*. London: HMSO.

Coleman, J.C. and Hendry, L. (1999) *The Nature of Adolescence*. London: Routledge.

Dixon, J. and Stein, M. (2005) *Leaving Care, Through Care and Aftercare in Scotland*. London: Jessica Kingsley Publishers.

Giddens, A. (1991) *Modernity and Self-identity: Self and Society in the Late Modern Age*. Cambridge: Polity Press.

Gilligan, R. (2001) *Promoting Resilience: A Resource Guide on Working with Children in the Care System*. London: BAAF.

Hobcraft, J. and Kiernan, K. (1999) *Childhood Poverty, Early Motherhood and Adult Social Exclusion. Case Paper 28*. London: London School of Economics.

Sinclair, I., Baker, C., Wilson, K., and Gibbs, I. (2005) *Foster Children: Where They Go and How They Get On*. London: Jessica Kingsley Publishers.

Stein, M. (2004) *What Works for Young People Leaving Care?* Barkingside: Barnardo's.

Stein, M. (2005) *Resilience and Young People Leaving Care*. York: Joseph Rowntree Foundation. Accessed 14/03/06 at www.jrf.org.uk/bookshop/eBooks/185935369X.pdf

Stein, M. (2006) 'Young people aging out of care: The poverty of theory.' *Children and Youth Services Review 28*, 4, 422–435.

Wade, J. and Dixon, J. (2006) 'Making a home, finding a job: Investigating the early housing and employment outcomes for young people leaving care.' *Child and Family Social Work 11*, 3, 199–208.

M Stein 2006:

YP Ageing out of care:
The Poverty of theory'
Ch + Youth Services review
28, 4, 422-435

3 domain approach,
impact of ~~local~~
local
national
+ global processes upon.
YP cl's lives.

Glossary

Accommodated children (UK): In England and Wales, this term refers to children placed away from home on a voluntary basis (under section 20 of the Children Act 1989). Parents still retain parental responsibility.

Acogimiento familiar (Spain): Foster care – placement of looked after children in a family home.

Adoption and Foster Care Analysis and Reporting System (AFCARS) (US): Children's Bureau, US Department of Health and Human Services AFCARS collects case-level information on all children in foster care for whom State child welfare agencies have responsibility of placement, care or supervision and on children who are adopted under the auspices of the State's public child welfare agency.

Aftercare services (UK): The term used in Scotland to describe support for young people who have moved on from care.

Aged out of care (US): The term used to describe young people who were in care but who have reached the age of majority, so the State is no longer obligated to provide them with care or supervision.

Aide sociale à l'enfance (France): Child welfare services, depending on local authority.

Allocations Jeune Majeur (France): Allowances and/or support from the child welfare services to young people who come of age between 18 and 21 years of age.

Anstalt für Nacherziehung (Switzerland): Correctional education setting – a type of residential home, created in 1971 for juvenile delinquents with specific educational needs.

Assisted young people (Romania): Young people still in residential care who benefit from support either on the placement centre's premises (e.g. separate accommodation within the centres) or in the community (e.g. boarding schools, rented accommodation); the term is used in the field but not in official documents.

Bagrut (Israel): Matriculation tests.

Barneverntjenesten (Norway): The name of the local authorities in the Norwegian chapter called Child Welfare Services.

Bufetat (Norway): A municipal authority organised in five regions under a central leadership.

Bureau Jeugdzorg (BJz) (The Netherlands): Youth Care Agency.

Care and protection orders (Australia): Legal processes involving the care and protection of children including administrative arrangements or care applications to the Court.

Centros de menores (Spain): Children's homes – residential child care facilities in general.

Children (Leaving Care) Act 2000 (English legislation referenced in the UK and Jordanian chapters): The rationale of this Act is to promote the welfare and improve the life chances of youth in and leaving care. 'Its main aims are: to delay young people's discharge from care until they are prepared and ready to leave; to improve the assessment, preparation and planning for leaving care; to provide better personal support for young people after leaving care; and to improve the financial arrangement for care leavers' (Department of Health 2001, p.5).

Conseil Général (France): Local authority, independent from the State since the decentralisation. Each is autonomous in administrative and budgetary matters. There exist 99 administrative and geographic jurisdictions of local authorities. Continental France includes 95 grouped into 22 regions.

Diótörés Alapítvány (Hungary): 'Nutcracking Foundation'. Established in 1997, this Hungarian foundation is a non-profit organisation that supports youngsters' re-socialisation through special training, receiving some state funding for its activities. See www.diotores.hu/index_1.html

Emancipation (to independent living) (US): The term used in the US to describe young people who leave out-of-home care because the courts have determined that they are able to live independently before reaching the age of majority.

Erziehungshilfen (Germany): Rearing support for children with problems: a generic term embracing all the services supporting families. These include residential and non-residential forms such as child guidance, social group work and family support, as well as residential and foster care.

Ettervern (Norway): Aftercare – this is the most common Norwegian concept to identify work with young people as they leave care. Storø (2001) has argued that this concept is not very useful.

Exit Training (ET) (The Netherlands): Aims to minimise residential youths' chances of becoming homeless and living on the fringes of society. The main focus of this skills training programme is on practical and material issues, personal competences (social skills) and creating a network (see Spanjaard 2006).

Family and Childhood Directorate (Jordan): Within the Ministry of Social Development (MOSD) the Directorate is further divided into three sub-units dealing with children from birth to age 18: unit for youth in conflict with the law, childhood unit dealing with children from broken homes, unknown parentage and orphans, and the family protection unit dealing with abuse and neglect.

Fellesorganisasjonen for barnevernpedagoger, sosionomer og vernepleiere (FO) (Norway): The Norwegian Union of Social Educators and Social Workers.

Framework for the Assessment of Children in Need and Their Families (originated in England; referred to in the Jordanian chapter): The Framework for the Assessment of Children in Need and Their Families (often referred to simply as the Assessment Framework) provides guidance to local authorities and other agencies on the assessment of children in need under the Children Act 1989. It describes a systematic approach to information gathering across three domains of a child's life: the child's developmental needs, parenting capacity, and family and environmental factors. (See Department of Health, Department for Education and Employment and Home Office 2000.)

Kanton (Switzerland): Canton – a province or local authority as part of the confederation. There are 26 cantons. Each of them has its own constitution.

Lakásotthon (Hungary): Group homes accommodating no more than 12 children. Most were established after 1997 replacing former big residential homes.

Landsforeningen for barnevernbarn (LFB) (Norway): The national organisation for children and young people either in care or receiving other types of assistance from Child Welfare Services.

Looked after child (UK): This term includes children in care subject to a court order (e.g. a care order, in which case parental responsibility is shared by the parent and the local authority) and those accommodated (see above) by a local authority. Children become looked after if, for example, their parents are temporarily unable to care for them, or they have been abused or neglected.

Looking After Children records (originated in England; since implemented in a number of countries and referred to in the Australian, Hungarian and Jordanian chapters): Developed in England, Looking After Children is an approach to assessing the development of children in public care. The forms include: essential information records, care and placement plans, reviews and assessment and action records. The seven developmental dimensions covered are: health, education, family and social relationships, social presentation, identity, emotional and behavioural development and self-care skills. (See Department of Health 1995; Ward 1995.)

Norsk Fosterhjemsforening (NFF) (Norway): The Norwegian Foster Care Association.

Orr Shalom (Israel): A large network of group homes in Israel.

Otthonteremtési támogatás (Hungary): Home setting-up support – care leavers are entitled to this to be able to buy/rent a home.

Out-of-home care (Australia): The provision of alternative accommodation to children and young people who are unable to live with their parents, both on court order or in voluntary care. Children and young people may be in out-of-home care on court orders that transfer parental responsibility to the Minister (equivalent of 'looked after children') or on a voluntary basis ('accommodated children').

Out-of-home care (US): Children enter out-of-home care when a court determines that they should be removed from their home in order to protect them from abuse or neglect. In the US this may involve placement in non-relative foster home care, foster home care with relatives, or various forms of group care.

Overgangen til en selvstendig tilværelse (Norway): Transition to independent living. Storø (2005) suggests that this is a better concept than *ettervern* (see above) and this seems to come more in use even if it means using many words to describe the phenomenon.

Pathway plan (UK): Once an eligible young person in public care reaches age 16, the local authority should allocate them a personal adviser (this may be a social worker) to draw up a pathway plan, based on an assessment of their needs. Plans must outline the services and practical and emotional support the young person requires to move to independence. Typically plans include arrangements for education, training, finance, meeting health needs and living arrangements.

Permanency plan (US): Plan of care directed towards ensuring a safe, stable and permanent home for a child as soon as possible (e.g. rehabilitation to birth family, adoption or guardianship).

Placement Centres (Romania): Former school and preschool *children's homes* and *leagane* ('cradles') for 0–3-year-olds, now no longer age segregated, and targeted for closure and replacement with family-type homes and social flats.

Protection judiciaire de la jeunesse (France): Judicial Juvenile Protection.

Quality Protects Initiative (UK): A programme launched by the Government in 1998 as part of its wider strategy to tackle social exclusion. Quality Protects aimed to deliver effective protection, better quality care and improved life chances to children in public care.

Semi-rentier state (Jordan): Oil-producing countries (e.g. Saudi Arabia) were classified as rentier states. In short, 'income derived from externally generated rents are available due to the gap between cost of production and the price of commodity. Financial resources generated are directly acquired by externally produced rents rather than through domestic means like taxation' (Piro 1998, p.11).

Stortinget (Norway): Norwegian Parliament.

Therapieheim (Switzerland): Therapeutic home – a type of residential home, created in 1971 for juvenile delinquents with specific therapeutic needs.

Throughcare (UK): The term used in Scotland to describe support to prepare young people for leaving care.

Tutela (Spain): Guardianship – responsibility for the custody of children taken on by the Autonomous Community Government.

Védelembe vétel (Hungary): Registered as in need of special protection – those children registered after voluntary local services have failed.

Vormundschaftsbehörde (Switzerland): Guardianship authority – control of local social services, elected by the public, in some regions non-professionals.

Work-Wise (WW) (The Netherlands): Comprises a number of integrated activities in the areas of assessment, education and training, work experience and housing. Attention also focuses on debt reduction, restoring relationships, social skills, creating social networks and leisure time activities (see Klomp 2005).

'Zo zo zo beleid' policy (The Netherlands): Youth care has to be given *as* lightly as possible, *as* close to home as possible and for *as* short a time as possible (see Knorth 2005).

References

Children Act (1989). London: HMSO.

Department of Health (1995) *Looking After Children: Good Parenting, Good Outcomes.* London: HMSO.

Department of Health (2001) *Children (Leaving Care) Act 2000: Regulations and Guidance.* London: The Stationery Office.

Department of Health, Department for Education and Employment and Home Office (2000) *Framework for the Assessment of Children in Need and Their Families.* London: The Stationery Office.

Klomp, M. (2005) 'Arbeidstoeleiding.' ['Steering to the Labour Market.'] In J. Hermanns, C. van Nijnatten, F. Verheij and M. Reuling (eds) *Handboek Jeugdzorg. Deel 2: Methodieken en Programma's.* Houten: Bohn Stafleu van Loghum.

Knorth, E.J. (2005) 'Wat maakt het verschil? Over intensieve orthopedagogische zorg voor jeugdigen met probleemgedrag.' ['What makes the difference? Intensive care and treatment for children and adolescents with serious problem behaviour.'] *Kind en Adolescent 26,* 4, 334–351.

Piro, T. (1998) *The Political Economy of Market Reform in Jordan.* New York: Rowman and Littlefield.

Spanjaard, H.J.M. (2006) *Handleiding bij De Vertrek Training: Intensief Ambulante Hulp Gericht op Competentievergroting en Netwerkversterking. [Manual of Exit Training: An Intensive Training Directed at Enhancement of Competencies and Network Support.]* Amsterdam: Uitgeverij SWP.

Storø, J. (2001) *På Begge Sider av Atten: Om Ungdom, Barnevern og Ettervern.* Oslo: Universitetsforlaget.

Storø, J. (2005) *Å gå over brennende bruer. En kvalitativ studie av barnevernungdommers overgang til en selvstendig tilværelse.* Oslo: Høgskolen i Oslo.

Ward, H. (ed.) (1995) *Looking After Children: Research in Practice.* London: HMSO.

The Contributors

Roxana Anghel is a doctoral research student in the Institute of Health and Social Care, Anglia Ruskin University, Cambridge, England.

Rami Benbenishty is Gordon Brown Professor of Social Work in the School of Social Work and Social Welfare, Hebrew University of Jerusalem, Israel.

Judy Cashmore is a visiting associate professor at the Social Policy Research Centre, University of New South Wales, Sydney, Australia.

Mark E. Courtney is Executive Director, Partners for Our Children, and Ballmer Chair in Child Well-Being, School of Social Work, University of Washington, United States.

Jorge F. del Valle is a professor in the Faculty of Psychology, University of Oviedo, Spain.

Gabriela Dima is a doctoral research student at Queen's University, Belfast, Northern Ireland.

Annick-Camille Dumaret is based at the Centre de Recherche Médecine, Sciences, Santé et Société (CERMES) and Institut National de la Santé et de la Recherche Médicale (INSERM), Paris, France.

Robert J. Flynn is Director of the Centre for Research on Community Services and Principal Scientist in the Institute of Population Health at the University of Ottawa, Canada.

Thomas Gabriel is Head of Research on Socialpedagogy at the Pädagogisches Institut, University of Zurich, Switzerland.

Robbie Gilligan is Head of the School of Social Work and Social Policy and Associate Director of the Children's Research Centre at Trinity College, Dublin, Ireland.

Mária Herczog is a senior researcher at the National Institute of Criminology, Budapest, Hungary.

Ingrid Höjer is a senior lecturer and researcher in the Department of Social Work at the University of Göteborg, Sweden.

Rawan W. Ibrahim is a doctoral research student in the School of Social Work and Psychosocial Sciences at the University of East Anglia, England.

Erik J. Knorth is a professor at the University of Groningen in the Department of Special Education and Child Care, The Netherlands.

Jana Knot-Dickscheit is an assistant professor at the University of Groningen in the Department of Special Education and Child Care, The Netherlands.

Stefan Köngeter is a research associate at the University of Hildesheim, Germany.

Philip Mendes is a senior lecturer in the Department of Social Work, Monash University, Australia.

Emily R. Munro is a research fellow at the Centre for Child and Family Research, Loughborough University, England.

John Pinkerton is a professor at the School of Social Work, Queen's University, Belfast, Northern Ireland.

Wolfgang Schröer is a professor at the University of Hildesheim, Germany.

Mike Stein is a research professor at the Social Policy Research Unit, York University, England.

Renate Stohler is a research associate at the Pädagogisches Institut, University of Zurich, Switzerland.

Jan Storø is an assistant professor at Oslo College University, Norway.

Johan Strijker is an assistant professor at the University of Groningen in the Department of Special Education and Child Care, The Netherlands.

David Vincent is Research Coordinator at the Centre for Research on Community Services, University of Ottawa, Canada.

Jim Wade is a senior research fellow at the Social Policy Research Unit, York University, England.

Harriet Ward is Director for the Centre for Child and Family Research and Professor in the Department of Social Sciences at Loughborough University, England.

Maren Zeller is a research associate at the University of Hildesheim, Germany.

Subject Index